of **PSYCHOLOGICAL ASSESSMENT** Series

Everything you need to know to administer, score, and interpret the major psychological tests.

KT-569-718

**I'd like to order the following
ESSENTIALS OF PSYCHOLOGICAL ASSESSMENT:**

All titles are $34.95* each

- ❏ WAIS®-III Assessment / 0471-28295-2
- ❏ WISC-III® and WPPSI-R® Assessment / 0471-34501-6
- ❏ WJ III® Cognitive Abilities Assessment / 0471-34466-4
- ❏ Cross-Battery Assessment / 0471-38264-7
- ❏ Cognitive Assessment with KAIT & Other Kaufman Measures / 0471-38317-1
- ❏ Nonverbal Assessment / 0471-38318-X
- ❏ PAI® Assessment / 0471-08463-8
- ❏ CAS Assessment / 0471-29015-7
- ❏ MMPI-2™ Assessment / 0471-34533-4
- ❏ Myers-Briggs Type Indicator® Assessment / 0471-33239-9
- ❏ Rorschach® Assessment / 0471-33146-5
- ❏ Millon™ Inventories Assessment, Second Edition / 0471-21891-X
- ❏ TAT and Other Storytelling Techniques / 0471-39469-6
- ❏ MMPI-A™ Assessment / 0471-39815-2
- ❏ NEPSY® Assessment / 0471-32690-9
- ❏ Neuropsychological Assessment / 0471-40522-1
- ❏ WJ III® Tests of Achievement Assessment / 0471-33059-0
- ❏ Individual Achievement Assessment / 0471-32432-9
- ❏ WMS®-III Assessment / 0471-38080-6
- ❏ Behavioral Assessment / 0471-35367-1
- ❏ Forensic Assessment / 0471-33186-4
- ❏ Bayley Scales of Infant Development—II Assessment / 0471-32651-8
- ❏ Career Interest Assessment / 0471-35365-5
- ❏ WPPSI™ Assessment / 0471-28895-0
- ❏ 16PF® Assessment / 0471-23424-9
- ❏ Assessment Report Writing / 0471-39487-4

Please complete the order form on the back

TO ORDER BY PHONE, CALL TOLL FREE 1-877-762-2974
To order online: www.wiley.com/essentials
To order by mail refer to order form on next page

Essentials

of **PSYCHOLOGICAL ASSESSMENT** Series

Order Form

Please send this order form with your payment (credit card or check) to:

John Wiley & Sons, Inc.
Attn: J. Knott
111 River Street
Hoboken, NJ 07030

Name _____

Affiliation _____

Address _____

City/State/Zip _____

Phone _____

E-mail _____

❑ Please add me to your e-mailing list

Quantity of Book(s) ordered _____ x $34.95* each

Shipping charges:	Surface	2-Day	1-Day	
First Item	$5.00	$10.50	$17.50	
Each additional item	$3.00	$3.00	$4.00	**Total $_____**

For orders greater than 15 items, please contact Customer Care at 1-877-762-2974.

Payment Method: ❑ Check ❑ Credit Card (*All orders subject to credit approval*)
                        ❑ MasterCard ❑ Visa ❑ American Express

Card Number _____ Exp. Date_____

Signature _____

* Prices subject to change.

TO ORDER BY PHONE, CALL TOLL FREE 1-877-762-2974
To order online: www.wiley.com/essentials

Ⓦ**WILEY**

Essentials of Assessment Report Writing

Essentials of Psychological Assessment Series
Series Editors, Alan S. Kaufman and Nadeen L. Kaufman

Essentials

of Assessment

Report Writing

Elizabeth O. Lichtenberger

Nancy Mather

Nadeen L. Kaufman

Alan S. Kaufman

John Wiley & Sons, Inc.

Published by John Wiley & Sons, Inc., Hoboken, New Jersey.
Published simultaneously in Canada.

Library of Congress Cataloging-in-Publication Data:

Essentials of assessment report writing / Elizabeth O. Lichtenberger . . . [et al.].
        p. cm. — (Essentials of psychological assessment series)
     Includes bibliographical references and index.
     ISBN 0-471-39487-4 (pbk.)
        1. Psychodiagnostics. 2. Report writing. 3. Clinical psychology—Authorship.
I. Lichtenberger, Elizabeth O. II. Series.

RC469.E875 2004
616.89'0075—dc22

                                                                2003066066

Printed in the United States of America

10 9 8 7 6 5 4 3

To Julie . . .
Your passion for books and writing
inspires me to keep writing.
Your love of being a grandmother
inspires me to be a good mother.
Thank you for providing
such loving inspiration.

E. O. L.

To Michael for listening and loving. . .
To Ben and Dan and the joy and purpose you bring to my life . . .
To the late Dr. Samuel Kirk, who taught me the importance of linking
assessment results to practical interventions.

N. M.

To Mom and Dad—Hannah and Seymour Bengels—
who have the courage to make it look easy to grow old.
We love you both and appreciate your lifelong support of us as professionals
and as your children.

N. L. K. and A. S. K.

CONTENTS

SERIES PREFACE

I n the *Essentials of Psychological Assessment* series, we have attempted to provide the reader with books that will deliver key practical information in the most efficient and accessible style. The series features instruments in a variety of domains, such as cognition, personality, education, and neuropsychology. For the experienced clinician, books in the series will offer a concise yet thorough way to master utilization of the continuously evolving supply of new and revised instruments, as well as a convenient method for keeping up-to-date on the tried-and-true measures. The novice will find here a prioritized assembly of all the information and techniques that must be at one's fingertips to begin the complicated process of individual psychological diagnosis.

Wherever feasible, visual shortcuts to highlight key points are utilized alongside systematic, step-by-step guidelines. Chapters are focused and succinct. Topics are targeted for an easy understanding of the essentials of administration, scoring, interpretation, and clinical application. Theory and research are continually woven into the fabric of each book but always to enhance clinical inference, never to sidetrack or overwhelm. We have long been advocates of what has been called intelligent testing—the notion that a profile of test scores is meaningless unless it is brought to life by the clinical observations and astute detective work of knowledgeable examiners. Test profiles must be used to make a difference in the child's or adult's life, or why bother to test? We want this series to help our readers become the best intelligent testers they can be.

In *Essentials of Assessment Report Writing,* the authors provide readers with succinct, straightforward methods for writing case reports from beginning to end. Assessment reports are written in a variety of settings, and this book is designed to help a broad spectrum of clinicians, including school psychologists, clinical psychologists, neuropsychologists, forensic psychologists, diagnosticians, and speech/language pathologists. The basic guidelines and writing principles highlighted here will guide readers through writing each of the critical components of a report: reason for referral and background information, appearance and behavioral observations, test results and interpretation, summary and diagnostic impressions, and recommendations.

Alan S. Kaufman, PhD, and Nadeen L. Kaufman, EdD, Series Editors
Yale University School of Medicine

Essentials of Assessment
Report Writing

One

INTRODUCTION AND OVERVIEW

Comprehensive written reports are the summation and culmination of most psychological and psycho-educational evaluations. These reports summarize the data from test administration, integrate relevant qualitative information, and directly address the posed concerns. Because these documents inform decision making and remain for years in academic, as well as medical and psychological records, they must be well written. When well written, assessment reports can enhance treatment, guide and inform instruction, and provide critical information to the referral source and others. The findings and observations are presented clearly so that they are understandable to parents, teachers, clients, and other professionals. In contrast, when poorly written, assessment reports may be incomprehensible to parents and teachers and the recommendations impossible or unrealistic to implement (Salend & Salend, 1985). Because the results from a report can affect decisions and influence decision making for years beyond the initial evaluation, the creation of assessment reports requires special attention and care.

The purpose of this book is to review the essential elements and structure of well-written psychological and psycho-educational reports. This book is designed for novice report writers, students and interns in training, and professionals who are required to read and understand reports prepared by others. The book is also intended for professionals in the field who desire to improve their skills in preparing and writing assessment reports. As Salend and Salend (1985) asked: "What if professionals were given a letter grade on the educational assessment reports they write? Would you get an 'A' or an 'F' or merely an average 'C?' Yet we all recognize the importance of these reports which contain data used to formulate IEP goals and subsequent programming" (p. 277).

This text is designed to cover all aspects of preparing a written report as well as to provide illustrative samples of clear, informative reports. This first chapter provides an overview of the purposes of report writing as well as a brief discussion of the major sections of a report. The second chapter reviews many technical aspects of writing.

Each subsequent chapter focuses on the creation of a specific part of a report: the reason for referral and background information (Chapter 3), discussion of appearance and behavioral observations (Chapter 4), test results and interpretation (Chapter 5), summary and diagnostic impressions (Chapter 6), and recommendations (Chapter 8). The seventh chapter discusses personality assessment. The ninth chapter presents special issues related to reports, including feedback, follow-up, and the use of computer-generated reports. The tenth and final chapter presents several sample case reports. An Appendix at the end of the book provides information about tests cited throughout the text.

Assessment reports are written for a variety of audiences (e.g., parents, teachers, clients, physicians, attorneys) as well as to answer a variety of referral concerns (e.g., psychological, linguistic, behavioral, or academic). Reports are also written by a variety of professionals (e.g., school psychologists, clinical psychologists, neuropsychologists, diagnosticians, educational evaluators, and speech and language therapists). Although the roles of these professionals differ, they all prepare written assessment reports. Thus, the skills required to both understand and write clear, informative assessment reports are critical for a wide range of professionals in fields of psychology and education.

PURPOSES OF ASSESSMENT REPORTS

As we have noted, the general purposes of an assessment report are varied. Ownby (1997) suggested the following four desired outcomes:

1. Answering the referral questions as explicitly as possible
2. Providing the referral source with additional information when it is relevant
3. Creating a record of the assessment for future use
4. Recommending a specific course of action

Similarly, Sattler (2001) specified the following four purposes:

1. To provide accurate assessment-related information (e.g., developmental, medical, and educational history) as well as current interpersonal skills, intellectual and cognitive abilities, motor skills, and personality to the referral source and other concerned parties
2. To serve as a source of clinical hypotheses and appropriate interventions
3. To provide meaningful baseline information for evaluating progress after interventions have been implemented or time has passed
4. To serve as a legal document

Kaufman and Lichtenberger (2002) outlined several principles of *intelligent testing*. The report writer's main roles are to (1) generate hypotheses about the person being assessed, (2) support or refute those hypotheses with qualitative information and test data, and (3) propose recommendations related to the initial referral. Regardless of the types of questions posed by the referral

> # DON'T FORGET
> ....
> ### Objectives of Psychological Reports
> - answer the referral questions
> - describe the person
> - organize the data
> - recommend interventions

source, as Ownby, Sattler, and Kaufman and Lichtenberger suggest, the central objectives of assessment reports are to answer questions, describe the individual and his or her situation, interpret and integrate qualitative and quantitative data, and then recommend appropriate treatment, therapies, or interventions (see Don't Forget).

In a school setting, reports are the cornerstone for determining appropriate adjustments, supports, and accommodations; recommending behavioral interventions and instructional strategies; and considering eligibility and need for services. These types of reports inform the decision-making process by making a direct connection between the obtained assessment results and the most relevant types of interventions.

Although the general purposes of written reports are similar across specialty areas, some differences exist in the types of evaluation as well as the recipients. The focus in some evaluations is on the educational needs of an individual, whereas in others the focus is on behavioral or psychological concerns. For example, speech language therapists are most concerned with disorders in spoken and written language and a person's general ability to communicate to others using speech and gestures. In some instances, a report is written for another professional (e.g., a neuropsychologist to a physician, a clinical psychologist to a psychiatrist, a school psychologist to a teacher, or a forensic psychologist to an attorney; Figure 1.1). In other instances, a report is prepared for the parents of a child in school or directly for the individual. Regardless of the recipient of the report, always assume that parents or the examinee will read it. Therefore, the language in the report must be readily understandable.

School psychologists, speech and language therapists, diagnosticians, and educational evaluators most often assess children who are not functioning well in aspects of school due to cognitive, academic, developmental, linguistic, or emotional concerns. These assessments usually focus on determining an individual's

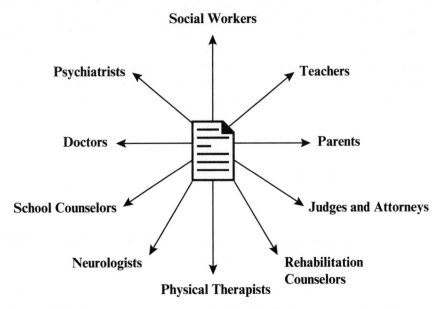

Figure 1.1 Assessment reports may be shared with many types of people.

strengths and weaknesses, as well as specific educational needs. The results then inform the development of an educational program as well as the selection of methodologies. Evaluations are also conducted to identify gifted and talented children who would benefit from enrichment and accelerated curricula.

The roles of clinical psychologists and neuropsychologists are diverse, as are the reports they prepare. These professionals may work in hospitals, university counseling centers, community clinics, or private practices. Clinical psychologists commonly share their reports with psychiatrists, psychiatric nurses, psychiatric social workers, and other medical personnel. Most often they are concerned with the assessment and treatment of disorders in behavior, whereas neuropsychologists are more concerned with neurological functioning and how various abilities relate to learning and behavior. Because evaluators work in different settings and write reports for various professionals and purposes, the formats and language of these reports will vary. In addition, reports will vary based upon the types of tests selected as well as the theoretical orientations of evaluators.

In this book, our primary focus is upon the use and interpretation of psychological and educational tests in clinical and educational settings. We present tests and reports that illustrate samples from the domains of neuropsychology, clinical psychology, school psychology, and education. Although some details in formats of a report may vary, the majority of aspects of the reports are standard across domains.

One significant commonality of all assessment reports relates to content: The writer must focus upon the individual and the problem being assessed. The central goal of all reports is improved outcomes for the person being evaluated. Another common aspect of all assessment reports relates to writing style: The author must create the separate sections of the report but provide integration so that the report forms a cohesive whole. These two topics are discussed next.

FOCUS ON THE PERSON AND THE PROBLEM

Regardless of the type of report written, the focus is upon the person being evaluated and the problem or problems of concern. Because testing data are gathered during an assessment, some evaluators spend too much time writing about the obtained test scores rather than about what these scores mean. Novice report writers often find it challenging to maintain focus on the individual. Because the sheer amount of data can be overwhelming, it seems easier to describe the tests and obtained scores than to interpret what these results imply or mean (Figure 1.2). Unfortunately, when scores become the focal point of a report, the person being assessed seems to disappear in the array of numbers. Keep in mind that the referral source is not interested in the scores per se but in what these scores mean in regard to an individual's intellectual or academic functioning. Although data are often discussed within a report, present the results in such a way that the reader does not lose sight of the individual. Explain how the person responded to specific tasks, rather than simply reporting and discussing a profile of test scores (Kaufman & Lichtenberger, 2002).

O'Neill (1995) noted that some reports provide little interpretation beyond the test scores, whereas others are based on a complex process of problem solving. She describes three diverse levels of clinical interpretation: (1) the concrete level, (2) the mechanical level, and (3) the individualized level. Reports written at the concrete level do not draw conclusions beyond scores. The emphasis is placed on describing the various obtained scores. Reports written at the mechanical level focus upon the differences among subtests and factor scores. Conclusions are drawn, but they are based only upon the differences among the obtained scores. Reports written at the individualized level draw conclusions that are based upon an integration of background information, behavior, and scores. They are explanatory and include qualitative information. O'Neill explains that these reports look at the scores through the person rather than looking at the person through the scores. The most useful reports are written at the individualized level.

Figure 1.2 Even though the amount of data may seem overwhelming, remember to write about the person and what the scores mean rather than just describing the tests and scores.

COHESION AND ORGANIZATION OF THE REPORT

A typical report includes the sections listed in Rapid Reference 1.1. Although these sections are presented separately, to communicate effectively you should organize the assessment report so that it is integrated and forms a cohesive whole. Consider information in the background section when writing the test behaviors section. Integrate both background information and test behaviors with the test results and interpretation. Base the diagnostic impressions and recommendations on the referral question, background information, and observations, as well as the test results. This process of integration does not mean that the specific sections of the report lose their unique identities, but rather that one section relates to another.

To help with integration and organization, one rule of thumb is that findings from an *earlier* section of the report may be integrated when writing a *later* section, but not vice versa. A second rule of thumb is to attempt to answer the referral questions, even if the answers are tentative or speculative. It is preferable to write

≡ *Rapid Reference 1.1*

Components of Typical Reports

- title or heading
- identifying information
- reason for referral
- background information
- tests administered

- behavioral observations
- test results and interpretation
- summary and diagnostic impressions
- recommendations
- psychometric summary of scores

Note. Some reports also contain an appendix that includes any additional handouts or readings that the evaluator wishes to share to help implement the recommendations, such as an informational sheet on pharmaceutical treatment of Attention-Deficit/Hyperactivity Disorder (ADHD) or a specific technique to use for spelling instruction.

CAUTION

Rules of Thumb

Rule of Thumb	Example
Do not integrate findings from a later section into an earlier section of the report.	Do not describe test results in the section on test behaviors.
Never ignore referral questions.	It is better to write "The results are inconclusive" or "Cannot be determined" than to ignore the referral questions.

that the results are inconclusive than to ignore the questions. The reader will then be assured that the concerns were not overlooked but presented difficult challenges that are yet to be resolved. The accompanying Caution reviews these rules of thumb. The next section provides a brief discussion of how the various sections of a report relate to and build upon each other.

Reason for Referral

The reason for referral determines the focus of an evaluation and provides the rationale for the assessment. Write all other sections of the report with the referral question or questions in mind. The reason for referral also helps determine the types of assessment tools that will be selected to complete the evaluation. A referral regarding behavior may involve the use of checklists, rating scales, and classroom and playground observations; a referral regarding academic concerns may involve specific standardized measures of intelligence and achievement (e.g., a reading or math test) as well as informal classroom assessments and a review of recent homework papers.

Background Information

The background section serves the important function of placing the assessment results within a pertinent context that highlights personal history. This history is often summarized chronologically. This section may include developmental history, medical history, educational history, family constellation, employment history (if relevant), and the results of previous evaluations. In many cases, an evaluator can write this section before the evaluation is conducted, basing it on a careful review of available records and notes taken during interviews. After the evaluation, additional findings may be added based upon other factual information (such as hobbies, interests, attitudes toward school or work) that are discovered during the course of the evaluation. In general, describe past history that may be relevant to present situations (e.g., frequent school absences, motorcycle accident resulting in head injury). Do not include current test behaviors or test results in this section.

Behavioral Observations

The Behavioral Observations section covers pertinent observations related to establishing rapport as well as behaviors during the assessment, such as levels of attention, motivation, persistence, and frustration. This section is devoted primarily to behaviors observed during the testing session. If the individual was observed in another setting (e.g., in a classroom, in the waiting room, on the playground, at home), then those observations may also be included in this section. When nontest behaviors are incorporated into this section, state the specific context of the observation (e.g., classroom), describe the behaviors observed in the real-life context (e.g., cooperative), and explain whether these behaviors were consistent with those observed during testing. You may also compare behaviors observed in past assessments to the ones observed in the present assessment.

Consider the referral question and information from the background section when describing observed behaviors during testing. For example, Ben, a fourth-grade student, was referred to the school psychologist for poor attention. Ben's limited attention was described as a notable and pervasive problem. Similarly, both Ben's mother and teacher described him as inattentive. When describing test behaviors, note Ben's level of inattentiveness with specific examples observed during the testing session (e.g., Ben continually had to be redirected to tasks). In general, review the concern (inattention) and determine if the present behaviors are consistent or inconsistent with this concern. If consistent, note specific examples of inattention; if inconsistent, note the differences between the behaviors reported and those that were actually observed. As another illustration, if a teacher describes a child as unmotivated (background) but the child is seen as motivated during the evaluation (test behavior), discuss the differing perceptions. When you encounter contradictory perceptions, generate hypotheses that will be supported or rejected later.

Whereas previously mentioned background information can be discussed in the behaviors section, do *not* bring test results or performance on specific individual tests or subtests into the Behaviors section. These test results will be presented systematically and organized carefully in the Test Results and Interpretation section.

Test Results and Interpretation

In the Test Results and Interpretation section, some of Ben's test scores would probably relate to level of attentiveness, such as performance on tests requiring listening, memory, or speed. For example, on timed tests, Ben looked up frequently and had to be prompted to keep working. Ben also had trouble on tests that required following lengthy oral directions and would often request repetitions. You would then want to integrate these findings with the other observed behaviors, such as the report by the school psychologist, which noted that the obtained low test scores seemed to reflect Ben's inattention rather than his ability to perform speeded tasks per se. As another example, if low scores on English language tests are related to a child's being raised in a monolingual Spanish-speaking family (background), reiterate this information in the test interpretation section.

Diagnostic Impressions and Recommendations

Further integration occurs when writing the Diagnostic Impressions and Recommendations sections. Relate the diagnostic impressions, as well as the recommendations, directly to the referral question(s). For example, if the referral questions were about how to improve a child's basic reading and writing skills, focus the recommendations upon the instructional methods that would be most appropriate given the child's background, age, and prior interventions, as well as the severity of the problem. A written summary is optional. If a summary is written, highlight the most crucial background information, behaviors, and test results.

✎ TEST YOURSELF ✎

1. **The main purpose of an assessment report is to**
   - (a) summarize the test data.
   - (b) convince the person that he or she needs psychological or educational services.
   - (c) answer the referral question.
   - (d) describe current behaviors.

2. **Assessment reports are mainly used to communicate between professionals within the fields of psychology and education.** True or False?

3. **Reports are most useful when they are written at the _____ level.**
   - (a) concrete
   - (b) mechanical
   - (c) individualized
   - (d) abstract

4. **The test scores are the most valuable pieces of information gained from an assessment and should therefore be the main focus of all reports.** True or False?

5. **A well-written report will always include a summary of findings at the end.** True or False?

6. **A well-integrated and organized report will**
   - (a) integrate findings presented early in the report (such as behavioral observations) with later findings (such as test results), but not vice versa.
   - (b) preview relevant findings from test results in an earlier section of the report (such as behavioral observations) when relevant.
   - (c) keep the various sections of the report distinct (i.e., background, behavioral observations, test results) and never integrate findings until the summary section.

7. **It is acceptable to write tentative or speculative answers to referral questions if the assessment results are inconclusive.** True or False?

Answers: 1. c; 2. False; 3. c; 4. False; 5. False; 6. a; 7. True.

Two

TECHNICAL ASPECTS OF WRITING

When you are first attempting to write assessment reports, the technical aspects of writing can be challenging. Even experienced report writers often find themselves mired in grammatical considerations, such as maintaining consistent verb tense and checking the accuracy of subject-verb agreement. Managing the subtle nuances of English grammar and style requires careful attention to detail. Errors in grammar, punctuation, and spelling detract from the quality of a report, and an assessment report riddled with errors loses credibility. If these technical aspects of your writing are not perfect, people reading your report will not only doubt your writing abilities but will also question your clinical and diagnostic skills.

In this chapter, we review the most common stylistic and grammatical problems found in assessment reports. We discuss the basic principles of writing that are most relevant for preparing grammatically correct, error-free reports. Some of the rules that we present are followed by examples to illustrate how to apply these writing principles and how to detect and correct common mistakes.

As you read through the following suggestions for report writing, you may note that sometimes the writing in this book violates the rules that we recommend. For example, we tell you not to use contractions when writing reports so that the writing will be more formal in tone. We don't, however, adhere to this rule, because the style of writing in this book is more casual and conversational in tone.

REPORT FRAMEWORK

Although the styles of reports will vary according to the person, the setting, the severity of the problem, and the types of decisions to be made, some elements are common across all reports. As we noted in Chapter 1 in Rapid Reference 1.1, reports follow an outline that includes standard sections. Although some sections of a report may be longer or shorter depending on the nature of the referral question, the complexity of the evaluation, and the writing style of the evaluator, the general sections provide the structure for organization.

COMPONENTS OF WRITING STYLE

All written reports should communicate assessment results clearly and effectively. When writing is clear and organized, the ideas are presented in a logical sequence, smooth transitions exist between topics, and paragraphs and sentences are easy to understand.

Logical Organization

Organize a report logically on all levels: globally (so that the report forms a cohesive whole), within sections, and within paragraphs. To maintain the global organization of a report, keep the content relevant to a particular section within that section. As we suggested in Chapter 1, do not describe test behaviors in the section on background information, and do not put instructional recommendations in the section on test interpretation. Within each section of a report, organize the information by topic. For example, organize the background information into discrete paragraphs on developmental history, medical history, educational history, socioeconomic environment, and/or current family situation. Similarly, organize the behavioral observations into discrete paragraphs on topics such as level of rapport, level of attention, attitude, and tolerance for frustration. Some sections may require only one paragraph, whereas others may contain enough information for several. In the subsequent chapters of this book, we will provide specific suggestions on how to organize topics within the various sections.

Smooth Transitions

One factor that contributes to good writing is ensuring that the text has unity. Good writers often accomplish unity through the use of cohesive ties (the words that help connect ideas and clarify the relationships among ideas). Cohesive ties help achieve continuity in writing by linking ideas across time, by cause and effect, by addition, or by contrast (Bates, 2000). The Don't Forget box provides a list of words that are commonly used to signal transitions. Samples of poor and good transitions are illustrated in Rapid Reference 2.1.

A common error we see in reports is that the writer assumes that the indentation of a paragraph signals a transition. Regardless of indentation, an abrupt shift in topic makes writing seem disjointed.

≡Rapid Reference 2.1

Examples of How to Improve Transitions

Poor Transition	Better Transition
Michael was quite anxious. He had excessive motor activity and rapid speech. He maintained his focus and concentration.	Michael was quite anxious, which was evident from his excessive motor activity and rapid speech. *However, despite this anxiety,* he maintained his focus and concentration.
Lauren had well-developed language skills. Her motor skills were above the level of most children her age.	Lauren had well-developed language skills. *Similarly,* her motor skills were above the level of most children her age.
Jonathan had an unremarkable medical history. He had no major injuries or illnesses requiring hospitalization. He was treated for depression via psycho therapy at age 16. He was then treated again at age 21.	Jonathan had an unremarkable medical history. He had no major injuries or illnesses requiring hospitalization. *However,* he was treated for depression via psychotherapy once at age 16 and again at age 21.

DON'T FORGET

Transition Words

Time Links	Cause-Effect Links	Addition Links	Contrast Links
• then	• therefore	• in addition	• however
• next	• consequently	• moreover	• but
• after	• as a result	• furthermore	• conversely
• while		• similarly	• nevertheless
• since			• although
			• whereas

Concise Wording

Some writers believe that lengthy, complex sentences and the use of sophisticated vocabulary will help clarify meaning. In general, simple words and concise sentences are more effective for communicating the key findings. To keep writing concise, consider the principles outlined in the following sections.

Avoid Redundancies and Circumlocutions

Reports can become cumbersome and lengthy when wording is repetitive or when sentences contain unnecessary information. Redundancy occurs when a writer tries to make a strong point by stating and restating it. As a rule, a simply stated fact makes a stronger point. Some evaluators also try to talk around points that are uncomfortable for them to discuss. For example: "He has excess weight around his midriff area given what is typical for a child his age." Better: "He is currently overweight." Rapid Reference 2.2 provides examples of redundancies and circumlocutions.

Sentence Length

Although it is often helpful to combine related points into a single sentence, lengthy sentences can be difficult to follow. Likewise, an overabundance of short, choppy sentences disrupts the flow of the writing. A balance of short and long sentences helps to maintain the reader's interest. Similarly, making sure that sentences don't frequently repeat the same word will help keep readers focused upon the content.

One way to reduce the number of short, choppy sentences is to combine sen-

≡ Rapid Reference 2.2

Repairing Redundancies and Circumlocutions

Example Problem	Example Solution
She had a generally poor mood and was feeling unsettled.	She was depressed.
The client complained of anxiety and nervousness.	The client complained of anxiety.
The student indicated that he is doing poorly.	The student indicated that he is doing poorly in his math class.
He appeared motivated and was willing to try his best on each and every one of the tasks that were placed before him.	He was motivated and willing to try all tasks.
She was melancholy and had an aura of sadness about her.	She was despondent.
Although he denied drinking and smoking, he appeared to have a somewhat unusual aroma about him, as the scent of peppermint schnapps and cigarettes gently lingered in the air of the room for what seemed like hours after he left.	He smelled of peppermint schnapps and cigarettes in the examination room, which made his alcohol and nicotine use apparent.

tences that are parallel in content. For example: "She takes Prozac for depression. Zantac is taken for ulcers. Her doctor prescribes Valium on occasion for anxiety." Better: "She takes Prozac for depression, Zantac for ulcers, and, on occasion, Valium for anxiety."

Another way to reduce unnecessary words is to restructure a series of sentences to eliminate the repetition of the same word phrase or idea. For example: "Mrs. Smith reported that her daughter has difficulty falling asleep. She also said that her daughter has difficulty remaining asleep." Better: "Mrs. Smith said her daughter has difficulty falling asleep and remaining asleep." Too many phrases, however, can make a sentence unwieldy: "She indicated that she ate too much that night before bed, which resulted in her feeling guilty due to the fact that she was not adhering to her low-fat diet." A more succinct sentence would be "She indicated that she ate too much that night and felt guilty because she did not adhere to her low-fat diet." The Don't Forget box provides further examples of various types of short, choppy sentences and unnecessarily long sentences. Examples illustrate how to remedy the problem. The Caution lists some commonly used phrases that contain unnecessary words and suggests ways to eliminate them.

DON'T FORGET

Improving Sentence Length

Goal	Example Problem	Example Solution
Combine sentences that are parallel in content	Her first hospitalization that year was for depression. The second time she was admitted to the hospital was for anorexia. Finally, she was hospitalized for a suicide attempt.	She was hospitalized on three occasions one year: for depression, anorexia, and attempted suicide.
Avoid repeating the same word, subject, or phrase	Her psychologist tried cognitive-behavioral therapy to improve the problem. He felt the therapy was not successful. His report indicated that she did not participate in homework assignments.	Her psychologist tried cognitive-behavioral therapy, but it was not successful in resolving the problem because she did not complete the homework assignments.
Avoid numerous prepositional phrases in one sentence	Since she had low self-confidence, her personal belief was that she was the root cause of all of her own problems.	Because of her low self-confidence, she believed that she was the cause of her problems.

CAUTION

··

Make Every Word Count

Phrase with Needless Words	Simple Substitute
the question as to whether	whether
whether or not	whether
he is a man who	he
call your attention to the fact that	remind you
due to the fact that	because
in order to	to
for the purposes of	to *or* so *or* for
in the event that	if
in an effort to	to
by means of	with
in connection with	with
for the length of time that	while
with the result that	so
is supportive of	supports
of great benefit	beneficial
in such a state that	so *or* such that
pertains to the problem of	concerns
at this point in time	now
am in agreement with	agree
insofar as	so
with reference to	regarding
many in number	many
round in shape	round
audible to the ear	audible
second time in my life	second time
quickly with haste	quickly
there were several members of the family who said	several family members said
they were both alike	they were alike
four different teachers said	four teachers said
absolutely essential	essential
one and the same	the same

in close proximity	in proximity *or* close time
period of time	
the reason is	because
summarize briefly	summarize
Although it cannot be definitely established, it is quite probable that the patient, in all likelihood, is suffering some degree of aphasia.	The patient appears to have some degree of aphasia.

Source: Adapted from Bates (2000) and Sattler (2001).

Paragraph Length

Also pay attention to the length of your paragraphs. Long paragraphs are often difficult to understand because the reader loses sight of the main point. As a simple rule, if a paragraph is longer than one double-spaced manuscript page, then it is probably too long (American Psychological Association [APA], 2001). Sattler (2001) states that a paragraph that is longer than a quarter of a page "strains the reader's attention span and impairs the reader's ability to recognize the unifying themes and ideas" (p. 711).

Paragraph Organization

Generally, a well-written paragraph has a concisely written topic sentence that explains what will follow in the next few sentences. Subsequent sentences refer to and explain that point. The last sentence of the paragraph may summarize the main point or provide a transition into the next paragraph. When a paragraph contains too many different ideas, reorganize the information into more than one paragraph.

Clear and Accurate Writing

All statements in a report need to be clear and accurate. Try to avoid ambiguous, abstract, vague, and technical terms. In addition to the discussion that follows, the next Don't Forget (p. 21) provides a summary of obstacles to clear and accurate writing.

Clarify Statements

Carefully select words so that every word conveys exactly what you intended. Try to avoid unnecessary words, such as *very*. For example, instead of writing, "She is a *very* good student," write "She maintained a grade point average of 3.5." Using a word incorrectly can also impede the clarity of a sentence. The English language has many pairs of words that are easily confused. Consider the misuse of the verb *affect* in this sentence: "The new medication had a favorable *affect* on Susan." The correct wording would be "The new medication had a favorable *effect* on Susan" or "The new medication seemed to *affect* Susan favorably."

Another technique to improve clarity in writing is to express statements in a positive manner. For example, "Karen did not pay attention to the directions on four of the six tasks presented" is more clearly stated as "Karen paid attention to the directions on two of the six tasks presented." Another factor that can affect clarity is *overstating*. For example, "Jennifer is absolutely brilliant!" Better: "Jennifer obtained a score in the Very Superior category on the Wechsler Adult Intelligence Scale–Third Edition (WAIS-III)."

Clarify or Remove Ambiguous Terms

The fields of psychology and education have a host of terms to describe a person's performance and behavior. Depending upon the orientation, different terms can be used to describe the same problem. For example, a school psychologist may describe a reading problem as a "learning disability"; a clinical psychologist may describe the reading problem as a "Specific Reading Disorder"; a neuropsychologist may label the condition "dyslexia"; and a speech/language pathologist may refer to the problem as a "learning disability" or, more precisely, a "reading disability." When a more technical term is commonly used in a profession, clarify the exact meaning of the term.

In addition to differences in terminology across disciplines, descriptive words can have different interpretations. Choose the most accurate words to describe the individual. For example, a person may be described as quiet or withdrawn. These words can result in different images. Although both words refer to someone who does not say much, a quiet person is notably different from a person who is withdrawn. Similarly, a child may be described as working carefully or working slowly. Although either style may result in low scores on timed tests, the reason for the low scores differs.

As with selecting words to describe behaviors, select words describing performance carefully. For example, do not use "cognitive ability" when "nonverbal ability" is what is really meant. If a person is *weak* in a particular ability, do not state that the person "lacks" the ability.

Make sure that what you write communicates what you want to say. When you are uncertain if what you have written will be clear, a good rule is to simplify the language and clarify any terminology that may not be readily understood. In some instances, ambiguous terms may be clarified by describing behaviors. For example, the statement "Monica appears inattentive and distractible" is vague. Words such as "appears" and "seems" convey your hesitancy, and thus the statement loses power. This statement can be clarified by a direct statement ("Monica was inattentive and distractible") followed by specific examples: "In the classroom Monica was able to attend to specific tasks for 2 or 3 minutes. She switched rapidly from one activity to the next and was easily distracted by noises both inside and outside the classroom." Other techniques for writing clear, accurate descriptions on behavior are explained in more detail in Chapter 4.

Minimize the Use of Technical Terms

Simple language is always better than complex, technical jargon (Kamphaus, 1993). It is better to say that the child has extreme difficulty forming letters when writing than to say that the child is suffering from severe dysgraphia. Reports that use an overabundance of technical terms or esoteric words have been described as instances of "exhibitionism" (Tallent, 1993). To write without the use of technical terms requires clear thinking (Tallent, 1993). Furthermore, parents and others (e.g., classroom teachers) who are not trained in the subject matter will not only not understand the jargon but also may be intimidated or too embarrassed to ask for an explanation. At one team meeting, a speech language therapist described Errol as "dysfluent," whereupon the parent responded that he also had a problem with stuttering (i.e., dysfluency). Misunderstandings such as this one can be avoided by not using complex, technical words. It is sometimes difficult to determine whether a word is too complex (i.e., unclear to the average reader). In general, avoid an elaborate word when a simple one will suffice (Tallent, 1993). An assessment report is not the place to display an extensive, effusive, copious vocabulary (Kamphaus, 1993).

Avoid Colloquialisms

Many words that are part of our everyday informal speech have inexact or multiple meanings. These terms are referred to as *colloquialisms*. Examples of such terms include *write-up* for *report; feel* for *think* or *believe; lots, a great deal,* or *quite a few* for *a specific number;* and *made a fuss about* for *became angry*. Because these terms can be easily misunderstood, avoid using them in your reports.

The exception to this rule is when you are directly quoting what a person has said. In these cases, indicate that what you have written is a direct quotation. As with colloquialisms, avoid foreign language phrases that many readers may not know or fully understand (e.g., *c'est la vie,* meaning *that's life* in French, or *la dolce vita,* meaning *the sweet life* in Italian).

Define Acronyms and Avoid Abbreviations

Writers use acronyms to save space or simplify their writing. Even if an acronym is widely known in an educational or clinical setting (e.g., ADHD for Attention-Deficit/Hyperactivity Disorder) write it out the first time it occurs in the report.

Acronyms are widely used for test names. The first time a test name is used, write out the complete name, followed by the acronym. For example, write "The Wechsler Intelligence Scale for Children–Fourth Edition (WISC-IV) and the Kaufman Test of Educational Achievement–Second Edition (K-TEA-II) Comprehensive Form were administered." When you refer to the tests later in the report, use of the acronym is acceptable because it has already been defined.

Sometimes report writers who are not highly familiar with an instrument invent their own acronyms for a test rather than using the one specified by the test developers. For example, the acronym used in the manual for the Woodcock-Johnson III Tests of Achievement is WJ III ACH. Do not create your own acronym (e.g., WJ 3-A).

Also make sure to indicate what edition of the test was used and to note how that edition is abbreviated (i.e., with Arabic or Roman numerals—ITPA-3 or ITPA-III). Do not say the Wechsler Intelligence Scale for Children (WISC) was administered when the test administered was the WISC-IV, not the original version. As a general guideline, always use the same acronym that is used in the test manual or on the test protocol.

As with test names, write out all acronyms for special programs. Do not write "Roberta is currently enrolled in the school's GATE program." Instead, write "Roberta is currently enrolled in the school's Gifted and Talented Education program." If you plan to use the acronym later within your report, include it in the sentence—for example, "Gifted and Talented Education (GATE) program." Also, avoid all abbreviations (e.g., bldg., misc., psych., %ile) when writing reports.

Avoid Passive Voice

Whenever possible, write in the active, not passive, voice. In the active voice, the subject of the sentence performs the action (subject-verb-object order); in the passive voice, the subject receives the action and appears earlier in the sentence than the person or thing that causes the action. "The psychiatrist recommended hospitalization" is active, whereas "Hospitalization was recommended by the psychiatrist" is passive. Excessive use of the passive voice makes writing clumsy, dull, and unclear to the reader (Gardner, 1983). The passive voice may even "alienate the experienced reader, or at very least make it hard for him to concentrate . . . and undercut the writer's authority" (Gardner, 1983, p. 99). The active voice is more direct and vivid. Making the "actor" the subject of the sentence helps bring the sentence to life.

To change a sentence from passive to active voice take what was formerly the *direct object,* or *complement* of the *transitive* verb, and transform that word into the subject of the sentence (e.g., "Mary was hit by Bill" becomes "Bill hit Mary"). Rapid Reference 2.3 provides several examples of how to change sentences from passive to active voice.

DON'T FORGET

Writing with Clarity and Accuracy

Roadblock to Clear Writing	Example	Solution
Qualifiers	• Lakeisha was *pretty* articulate. • Juan was *a little* shy. • *a very* unusual approach	• Lakeisha articulated her response clearly. • Juan's shyness was evident when he hid behind his mother's legs. • an unusual approach
Misuse of words	• Elizabeth was *anxious* to meet the examiner. • The WISC-IV *is composed of* 14 subtests. • The child *laid* down on the floor. • The family discord has had a negative *affect* on the child.	• Elizabeth was *eager* to meet the examiner. • The WISC-IV has 14 subtests. • The child *lay* down on the floor. • The family discord has had a negative *effect* on the child.
Stating in negative terms	• Philippe *did not provide* succinct answers. • Heidi's response to the personal questions was not positive.	• Philippe's answers were wordy. • Heidi became tearful and withdrawn during the interview, indicating her level of discomfort with the personal questions being asked.
Overstatement	• Sloan was *paralyzed* with anxiety. • Isabelle's *lack of* drawing skill caused her to fail.	• Sloan's desire to answer questions correctly prevented him from responding quickly. • Isabelle obtained scores in the Below Average range on several visual-motor tasks.
Ambiguous terms	• Juanita lacked emotional control. • Ian was overly sensitive to criticism about his errors in spelling.	• Juanita's emotions fluctuated rapidly between sadness and happiness. • Ian cried when his teacher suggested that he correct his spelling errors.

(continued)

Technical terms	• No basal was established, so the test was discontinued. • Monica's unconscious passive-aggressive tendencies to her mother's requests have contributed to a poor relationship with her mother.	• She completed only a few of the simplest items on the test, so an accurate measure of her cognitive abilities was not attained. • Monica's inconsistent responses to her mother's requests have contributed to their poor relationship.
Fancy language	• Keesha's *loquacious* nature was evident in the lengthy *disquisition* she gave when asked to define a simple word. • Julia's *idiosyncratic interpersonal presentation* was problematic within her *family system*.	• Keesha provided a lengthy definition of a simple word. • Julia's parents and brother complained about her nose ring and tattoos.
Colloquialisms	• Xander and his father had a *blowout* in the waiting room about who was responsible for payment. • Dimitre was *sort of* confused and didn't know what day it was.	• Xander and his father argued in the waiting room about who was responsible for payment. • Dimitre could not recall what day it was.
Abbreviations, acronyms, and contractions	• CBT • ADHD • K-BIT-2 • DAS • Don't • Can't	• Cognitive Behavioral Therapy • Attention-Deficit/Hyperactivity Disorder • Kaufman Brief Intelligence Test–Second Edition • Differential Ability Scales • Do not • Cannot

══ Rapid Reference 2.3

Common Grammatical Problems

Goal	Problem	Solution
Avoid sentence fragments	• Although she participated in the classroom activity during the classroom observation. She did not interact often with her peers, though she said it was enjoyable.	• During the classroom observation, she participated in the class activity but had minimal peer interaction. Her lack of peer interaction was in contrast to the fact that she said she enjoyed interacting with her peers.
	• He was not frustrated by the task. In spite of the fact that he could not finish before the time ran out.	• Even though he could not complete the task before the time ran out, he was not frustrated.
Use action verbs rather than nouns; avoid passive voice	• The documentation of her behavioral problems at school was completed by her teacher.	• Her teacher documented her behavioral problems at school.
	• Confrontation was his parents' suggested course of action.	• His parents wanted to confront him.
	• His realization was that his drinking was "out of control."	• He realized that his drinking was "out of control."
Make sure the verb of a sentence agrees with the subject	• All of the injuries acquired in the car accident was affecting his ability to concentrate.	• All of the injuries acquired in the car accident were affecting his ability to concentrate.
	• Her fidgeting, inattention, and talkativeness was disruptive.	• Her fidgeting, inattention, and talkativeness were disruptive.
Make the participial phrase at the beginning of a sentence refer to the subject	• When attempting to complete the puzzle, the pieces did not fit together.	• While attempting to complete the puzzle, he could not fit the pieces together.
	• Administering a test of emotional functioning, the client revealed suicidal thoughts.	• Responding to questions on a test of emotional functioning, the client said that he had thought of killing himself.

(continued)

Goal	Problem	Solution
Avoid unnecessary shifts in number, tense, subject, voice, or point of view	• He earned good grades in elementary school but they deteriorate to failing marks by high school. • Sue took many medications, but Valium was her "drug of choice" in recent years.	• He earned good grades in elementary school that deteriorated to failing marks by high school. • Sue took many medications but preferred Valium as her "drug of choice" in recent years.
Do not end sentences with a preposition	• The dark blue pen is the only one that she would write with. • He could not articulate what he was afraid of.	• She would only write with the dark blue pen. • He could not articulate the things he feared most.
Avoid indefinite "this"	• During the assessment, Joanie was sad one moment and happy the next. This supported her parents' statements about her unpredictable moods.	• During the assessment, Joanie was sad one moment and happy the next. These rapid mood shifts supported her parents' statements about her unpredictable moods.
Avoid misplaced modifiers	• At age five, his mother said the fear of the dark began. • Susan's difficulty hearing caused a miscommunication between the doctor and her patient.	• His mother said that when her son turned five, he began to fear the dark. • Because of her difficulty hearing, Susan misunderstood the doctor's instructions.

Source: Adapted from Bates (2000) and Sattler (2001).

GRAMMAR

Although a review of the grammatical rules of the English language is beyond the scope of this book, certain types of grammatical errors are problematic in many assessment reports. For a more extensive discussion of grammar and usage, consult comprehensive references on the topics (e.g., Bates, 2000; Lovinger, 2000; Sabin, 2001). The *Publication Manual of the American Psychological Association* (APA, 2001) also provides examples of problems of grammar and usage that occur frequently in manuscripts submitted to APA journals. Many of the examples cited in the APA *Publication Manual* apply to written reports as well. Rapid Reference 2.3 lists examples of typical grammatical problems in reports and provides suggestions of how to correct them.

PUNCTUATION

Punctuation involves the correct use of commas, periods, quotation marks, colons, and semicolons. Punctuation cues the reader to when one idea has ended and a new one has begun. It also helps clarify pauses and inflections. As with errors in grammar, errors in punctuation can confuse and distract the reader.

One commonly recurring error in reports is the positioning of punctuation marks with respect to quotation marks. Students and practicing clinicians alike have trouble recalling whether to put punctuation before or after the closing quo-

DON'T FORGET

Rules of Thumb Regarding Punctuation and Quotation Marks

Rule	Example
• A period or comma is always placed before the closing quotation mark, even when the quotation marks enclose only a single word.	• Susan said that she was "tired of his antics." • He had trouble pronouncing words beginning with the /l/ phoneme, such as "little," "long," and "left."
• A colon or semicolon is placed after the closing quotation mark.	• Saki's pediatrician stated that "she would likely benefit from medication"; he prescribed a trial medication regimen.
• A question mark is placed after the closing quotation mark, unless it is part of the quoted material.	• Tatiana's father wondered, "Why doesn't she work harder?" • Do you feel "out-of-it"?

tation mark. Some even place punctuation inside the quotation marks half the time and outside the other half. Unlike in British English, the quotation marks in American English are placed after the punctuation mark when it is a period or comma. The Don't Forget box lists some rules regarding the use of punctuation and quotation marks.

Another common error involves use of the hyphen. Rules for hyphenation are complex; the *Publication Manual of the American Psychological Association* (APA, 2001) devotes several pages to these rules. In assessment reports, one of the most commonly hyphenated words is a person's age. When an age is a noun (the 10-year-old) or a compound adjective (a 10-year-old girl), it is hyphenated. Another commonly hyphenated type of word is ethnicity. The rule is to hyphenate an adjective-and-noun compound when it precedes the term it modifies. Thus, "a middle-class woman" is hyphenated, but "She is middle class" is not. Similarly, a "fourth-grade student" is hyphenated, but "She is currently in fourth grade" is not.

The correct use of hyphens is also confusing when two or more compound modifiers have a common base and the base is omitted in all but the last modifier (e.g., long- and short-term memory; 5-, 15-, and 30-minute delays).

Although using contractions is technically not an error, in formal writing (such as report writing), it is better to write out the words. It is preferable to write "She would profit from speech-language therapy" rather than "She'd profit. . . ."

Another common error involves use of the word *its* and the contraction *it's*. Remember that *it's* stands for *it is* and does not modify a noun (e.g., *its* contents).

CAPITALIZATION

Certain conventions also apply to capitalization. Capitalize the title of a subtest but not the skill it is measuring (capitalize WISC-IV Arithmetic subtest, but not "her arithmetic abilities"). Routinely capitalize classifications that describe a person's test scores (e.g., Below Average, Superior, etc.), but do not capitalize classifications that describe performance or behavior (e.g., Antonio's teacher described his math performance as below average). The next Don't Forget box provides examples of rules of capitalization.

OTHER DETAILS OF WRITING

Other factors that influence the impact of your report include verb tense, page numbering, line spacing, and signature.

DON'T FORGET

When to Capitalize

Rule	Example
• The first word in a complete sentence	• The patient was lethargic all day.
• The first word after a colon that begins a complete sentence	• Two recommendations for decreasing lethargy follow: Eat more fruits and vegetables and exercise daily.
• Major words in titles and headings	• Summary and Diagnostic Impressions
• Proper nouns and trade names	• Prozac, Kleenex, Xerox
• Titles of tests	• Kaufman Assessment Battery for Children–Second Edition
• Titles of subtests	• Vocabulary, Symbol Search, Arithmetic, Letter-Word Identification
• Names of descriptive categories	• Average, Superior, Well Below Average

Verb Tense

Deciding what verb tense to use can also cause difficulty in report writing. Most reports are written in past and present tense. These general rules can help with consistency of verb tense (also consult Rapid Reference 2.4):

- Use past tense to describe a person's history.
- Use past tense to describe test behaviors.
- Use present tense to describe enduring traits such as ethnicity, gender, and physical characteristics.
- Use present tense to discuss a person's test performance and current circumstances, such as grade level or occupation.

Page Numbering

No matter who receives a report (e.g., a supervisor, professor, agency, teacher, colleague, or parent), number the pages on either the bottom center or the top right corner of the page. Numbering ensures that if a page is missing or if pages are out of order, the problem can be identified and resolved quickly and easily.

≡ Rapid Reference 2.4

Past and Present Tense

Incorrect	Correct
Incorrect Use of Present Tense	**Correct Use of Past Tense**
• His mother reports that he is "short-tempered."	• His mother reported that he is "short-tempered."
• Sam is nervous, as he is biting his fingernails and rapidly swinging his foot under the table.	• Sam was nervous; he bit his fingernails and rapidly swung his foot under the table.
Incorrect Use of Past Tense	**Correct Use of Present Tense**
• Joe was a 25-year-old student of average height and weight.	• Joe is a 25-year-old student of average height and weight.
• Amber was functioning in the Above Average range of cognitive ability.	• Amber is currently functioning in the Above Average range of cognitive ability.

Spacing

Line spacing in a report varies according to circumstance. If you are in training and giving a report to a supervisor or professor, then double-space the report to allow for corrections and comments. If you are in practice, single-spacing is preferable.

Signature and Credentials

After the body of the report, but before a summary of scores, most evaluators include their signatures. The signature provides proof of the report's authenticity. Include the credentials of the author of the report under the name (e.g., Licensed Psychologist, Speech-Language Pathologist). If you are a student in an internship or practicum, write your name and title (e.g., Practicum Student, Intern, Trainee, Doctoral Candidate) and the name and credentials of your supervisor.

BEFORE AND AFTER WRITING

The following sections provide suggestions to follow before and after you write your report.

Use an Outline Before Writing

Using an outline to write a case report is different from using an outline to write something with less structured form, such as a short story. Chances are that your supervisor, place of employment, or instructor will provide guidance in the global form of your report. Thus, each report you prepare is likely to follow a similar template of headings (e.g., Reason for Referral, Background Information, Behavioral Observations, Test Results and Interpretation, Summary, and Recommendations).

To create an outline, review your referral questions and your observations, and determine the main interpretative points. Once you have decided exactly what information you want to address, you are ready to make an outline. For example, in the test interpretation section of the report, you may have two main points to communicate: strong visual-spatial abilities but a low level of vocabulary and acquired knowledge. These two points may then have ancillary points below them. Creating an outline of main points under each heading helps ensure that you will include all pertinent data.

Read Your Rough Draft and Edit and Revise It After Writing

Whether you read over your report the same day it is finished or within the next few days, pay careful attention to the content, as well as mechanical errors. Some people also find it useful to wait a day or a week before editing, to permit viewing their work more objectively. Sometimes when you read what you wrote immediately after writing it, you only see what you *intended* to communicate, not what is actually down in type. Rereading what you have written will help you see where revisions are necessary to communicate more clearly. You can also identify places where your writing needs to be more streamlined and concise, or, in some instances, more detailed. As you are editing and revising your report, evaluate whether it can be easily understood. As a guideline, the language in your report should not be more complex than that used in a daily newspaper.

Careful proofreading will help you eliminate spelling errors, grammatical errors, omitted words, and typos. Spelling and grammar checks on computers can help you locate errors and awkward sentence constructions, but be sure to check that the computer's advice is what you intended. If English is not your first language, you may want to have other colleagues review your rough drafts to help you increase your English proficiency. For whatever reasons, if you have difficulty editing your own reports and noticing and correcting errors, you may want to find a colleague who would be willing to proofread your report for you. If someone else will be reading your report, remember to remove all identifying information to preserve confidentiality. With experience you will find what works best for you in terms of revising and editing your reports.

🐟 TEST YOURSELF 🐟

1. **Which sentence is written in passive voice?**
   - (a) The teacher told Jason to return to his chair immediately.
   - (b) The psychologist noted that the client was waiting patiently.
   - (c) Andrea's reaction stunned her parent.
   - (d) The child was observed by the psychologist.

2. **One of the best ways to transition to a new topic when writing is simply to indent and start a new paragraph.** True or False?

3. **Which is true about writing?**
   - (a) When in doubt, always write more rather than fewer words to make your point.
   - (b) Stating and restating is the best way to clearly articulate a point.
   - (c) Complicated, lengthy sentences maintain readers' interest the best.
   - (d) If a paragraph cannot be summarized in a topic sentence because it has too many different ideas, then you should reorganize it into more than one paragraph.

4. **Which is correct?**
   - (a) a 10-year-old girl
   - (b) a 10-year old girl
   - (c) a 10 year old girl
   - (d) a 10-year-old-girl

5. **Which of these sentences did not use proper verb tense?**
   - (a) Adrien was an African American male with a slender build and short, curly black hair.
   - (b) Emily twisted her hair when taking tests of verbal ability.
   - (c) Because Rodney excelled in his job, he advanced to the level of senior manager.
   - (d) Jasmine's level of intelligence is in the Above Average range.

6. **Which of these sentences has incorrect subject-verb agreement?**
   - (a) The vase of flowers was on the teacher's desk.
   - (b) The members of the multidisciplinary team were all present.
   - (c) The consulting psychologist and Esther's family were happy with the improvement in emotional functioning.
   - (d) The box of pencils were well within his reach.

Answers: 1. d; 2. False; 3. d; 4. a; 5. a; 6. d

Three

REFERRAL AND BACKGROUND INFORMATION

This chapter discusses the initial part of the assessment report: the identifying information, the referral questions, and background information.

TITLE AND IDENTIFYING INFORMATION

Most reports begin with a title that is followed by important identifying information. The title of the report is typically centered across the top of the first page (e.g., "Psychological Evaluation," "Neuropsychological Evaluation," "Psychoeducational Assessment," or "Speech and Language Evaluation"). At times, a disclaimer is included to protect the individual's privacy, such as "for confidential use only." Under the title, standard identifying information is recorded, typically including

- name of examinee
- date of birth
- chronological age
- grade (if testing a student) or occupation (if relevant)

- date(s) of testing
- date of report
- examiner's name
- supervisor's name (if relevant)

Depending on the setting and the purpose of the evaluation, other information may be included, such as parents' names, teacher's name, or the name of the school.

REASON FOR REFERRAL

The next heading, Reason for Referral, sets the stage for the rest of the report. The reason for referral is your reason for testing. This section is usually no more than one or two paragraphs long, and its central purpose is to express concisely and clearly the questions and concerns of the person or people requesting the evaluation (the referral source). The referral section includes the names and positions (e.g., third-grade teacher) of the referral source as well as the specific reasons for referral. If specific questions have not been posed, then contact the referral source to clarify the nature and scope of the concerns. The following illustrates the reason for referral for Jonas, a fourth-grade student:

> The multidisciplinary team at his school referred Jonas for his three-year review of special education services. For the past three years, he has been receiving occupational therapy and learning disability services in a resource setting. In addition, both his fourth-grade teacher, Ms. Mantell, and his parents have expressed concern about his overall motor development, particularly his poor handwriting, and want to know ways to help Jonas.

For some evaluations, the referral question is not about problems. For example, a student may be referred to help determine eligibility for certain types of special programs, such as placement in a program for gifted and talented students. Or an adolescent may be referred with the purpose of providing ideas for vocational planning. Also, some school districts mandate periodic testing to ensure that a student's services are appropriate or still needed. In general, however, unless you work at a specialized clinic or hospital, most referrals stem from concerns regarding a client's academic, linguistic, cognitive, behavioral, or social development.

Rapid Reference 3.1 presents several examples of questions that can help you formulate the referral section, and Rapid Reference 3.2 provides illustrations of

DON'T FORGET
....

Important Information to Gather About the Referral Question

- When did the child's problems start?
- How old was she when the problems were noted?
- How old was she when her parents first became concerned?
- If person is a child, do the parents agree about the problem? Do others who regularly see the child agree (e.g., grandparents, babysitters, teachers)?
- How long have these concerns been present?
- If concerns have existed for a while, why are the parents coming in now?
- How frequent is the problem?
- What is its duration?
- How intense is it?
- Ask: "What are some specific *examples* of the problem?"
- Ask: "What do you hope to gain from this evaluation?"

Sample Referral Questions

Psychoeducational/school psychology assessment:

- Does Juanita have a reading disability? If so, what methods of instruction would be most effective?
- Is Graham socially and intellectually ready to begin kindergarten?
- Does Gavin have a diagnosable disability that warrants having extra time to take the SAT or other standardized tests?
- Should Haley be retained in second grade?
- Would Jenna benefit from participating in the school's gifted and talented program?
- Do Sixto's behavioral problems at home and at school warrant a diagnosis (and, therefore, treatment) of Attention-Deficit/Hyperactivity Disorder?
- Is Delia at risk for engaging in violent behavior at school?
- What modifications need to be made to accommodate Lydia when she returns to school after surgery?
- Is Ana (a 15-year-old) at risk for dropping out of school?
- Does Nicole (a kindergarten child) have a school phobia?

Vocational/developmental disabilities assessment:

- Is Caroline capable of living independently?
- Will Alan, who has developmental disabilities, be able to transition to a group home or a supervised apartment setting rather than remaining at home?
- Which areas of vocational study will Mr. Jackson be able to benefit from given his interests and abilities?

Neuropsychological functioning:

- Is the memory impairment Elinor experiences indicative of early dementia such as Alzheimer's-Type Dementia?
- Have Charles's years of alcohol abuse caused any impairment in cognitive functioning?
- What are the neuropsychological effects of Bryan's head injury?
- Are attention or memory problems impacting Andrea's school performance?
- Has Lily's high exposure to lead affected her cognitive abilities?

Assessment of emotional functioning:

- Is Charlene suicidal?
- Is Noel suffering from a mood or anxiety disorder?
- Does Michael appear to have Post-Traumatic Stress Disorder (PTSD)?

Forensic assessment:

- What will be the best custody arrangement for Todd?
- Did Elmer meet the legal definition for insanity when he committed the murder?
- Is Esther competent to stand trial?

≡ *Rapid Reference 3.2*

Sample Reason for Referral Sections

- His foster parents, Jim and Arlene Mueller, and the teachers at Project First Step, a special needs preschool program, referred Tariq. Tariq's foster parents are pursuing adoption and wanted information on cognitive development as relative to his age-peers. The Muellers also wondered if Tariq has Fetal Alcohol Syndrome.

- Her mother, Ms. Jaffe, a kindergarten teacher, referred Anna, a 4-year-old preschool student. Ms. Jaffe expressed concerns in regard to Anna's social, emotional, and linguistic development. She described Anna as not showing much interest in people but showing considerable interest in the wheels on toy cars. She also noted that Anna rarely makes eye contact, engages in imaginative play, or talks. She wondered if Anna would benefit from occupational therapy, speech therapy, family counseling, or some type of social skills training.

- Rebecca was referred for an evaluation by her social worker at the Department of Economic Security, Amelia Forrester. Ms. Forrester reported that Rebecca's preschool teacher felt she was immature and slow in developing pre-academic skills. Ms. Forrester requested a brief assessment to help establish appropriate pre-academic educational goals for Rebecca.

- Her father, Pierre Whitman, referred Maria. Mr. Whitman wondered if Maria has a learning disability that is impeding her math development. Specifically, he noted that Maria appears to be far behind her classmates in math despite several years of tutoring. In contrast, she has had little difficulty learning other school-related subjects.

- Michael was referred for evaluation to see if learning disabilities, in addition to his psychiatric diagnoses, are contributing factors in his difficulty learning and retaining academic skills. Additionally, the results of this evaluation are expected to provide information to aid in determining effective instructional techniques, as well as the best educational placement for Michael in his next Individualized Educational Plan meeting.

- Amy Reid was seen for a neuropsychological evaluation at the request of her parents, Michael and Nancy Reid, who were concerned about her lack of progress in school. Mrs. Reid stated, "Amy cannot read, does not know her numbers, and takes lots of time to recall the letters." Amy's parents requested the evaluation to help determine the cause of her learning difficulties and to determine appropriate instructional strategies.

- His itinerant teacher of the Hearing Impaired, Pat Adler, referred Tony to this clinic. Ms. Adler expressed concerns regarding his ongoing difficulties in written language, which is affecting his success in middle school. She requested more information about the reasons for these difficulties as well as specific recommendations for intervention.

- Although he is an intellectually capable student, Paul currently is failing several classes at Westchester Preparatory Academy. His father and stepmother requested this evaluation. Teachers from Westminster Preparatory reported that Paul's father and stepmother are concerned about his weak academic performance and question whether there is a "processing deficit" of some kind. Paul's stepmother specifically mentioned the possibility of a weakness in memory. Paul's cognitive profile, general adjustment, and academic skills will be investigated as *one* source of information for educational planning in conjunction with teacher and parent observations, educational history, and present levels of academic performance.

- The purpose of the present evaluation was to determine Jen's eligibility for a gifted and talented education program and, depending on the outcome, to consider ways to adapt and enrich the curriculum to challenge her.

- His grandmother, Mrs. Gwen Stevens, referred Tyler to this academic tutoring center for an evaluation. Mrs. Stevens was concerned about Tyler's poor school grades and lack of motivation. Tyler has just failed most of his seventh-grade classes, and retention has been recommended. Mrs. Stevens wanted an estimate of how far behind Tyler was in school, an opinion regarding whether he should be referred for a comprehensive evaluation in his school, and an opinion regarding the advantages and disadvantages of his repeating seventh grade.

- Tania Martin, his sixth-grade teacher, referred Gregory for evaluation due to his poor attention in class and extreme difficulty getting along with peers. She further noted that he talks nonstop during class and often interrupts conversations to say something completely unrelated. Ms. Martin wondered if Attention-Deficit/Hyperactivity Disorder is the cause of Gregory's behavioral and social difficulties.

- Donald is currently incarcerated in a maximum-security setting for juvenile offenders. Eleanor Earle, his case manager, referred him for an evaluation. Results from the assessment will be used to develop goals and objectives for his new Individualized Education Program as part of the Kilmore County Jail's Education Assessment program.

- Noelle, a sophomore in pre-medicine, referred herself for an evaluation because of difficulties with spelling. Many of her teachers over the years have suggested that she be tested, but she never pursued an evaluation. Recently, a college English professor spoke to her about her many mistakes in writing and strongly recommended that she contact the University Learning Disabilities clinic for dyslexia testing. Noelle would like a better understanding of why she has such difficulty spelling, as well as suggestions for how she can improve her skill.

- Gavin was referred by his parents for an evaluation because of concerns regarding his present performance in law school. Although he understands the concepts of the presented material, he finds that he often does not have enough time to complete examinations. Consequently, he is unable to demonstrate his mastery of the information. He also finds that he spends an inordinate amount of time completing assigned readings. The purposes of the present evaluation were to determine Gavin's present levels of performance, consider eligibility and need for services, and propose appropriate accommodations.

how the "Reason for Referral" section may appear when written in a report. The Don't Forget box lists types of questions to ask the referral source that can help clarify the purpose of the evaluation and the nature of the problem. In the report, in addition to stating the referral questions succinctly and directly, you may also include in this section a short summary of the specific behaviors or symptoms that led to the referral. You may provide examples and brief anecdotes to illustrate the reasons for concern.

There are many ways to collect information from a referral source. You may have contact primarily over the phone, in person, or from a written form. Figures 3.1 and 3.2 provide samples of forms for collecting information about the referral questions. The type of referral information requested on a written form will vary according to the setting. For example, a medical setting such as a hospital will probably request more information about specific medically related issues, whereas a form used in a school setting will request information that pertains mainly to academic issues and behavior. If you choose to use written forms for gathering referral information, tailor them to make them most useful for your specific situation.

BACKGROUND INFORMATION

Sources for information for the background section include the person, a parent, a teacher, a boss, a supervisor, a physician, a therapist, or other specialists. You may also obtain information from anyone who has regular contact with the person, such as a coach, babysitter, primary day care provider, or nurse. In addition, it is good practice to gather information from previously written records, such as psychological and educational evaluations, medical records, and academic records based upon the nature of the referral. As an example, Jonas was referred for an evaluation in regard to concerns about motor development. His relevant background information is presented in Rapid Reference 3.3.

As illustrated in Rapid Reference 3.3, the background section contains information that is pertinent to test interpretation or to issues related to the referral concern. Often you will collect more information than you will actually report. Do not include information that is personal in nature and not pertinent to the evaluation itself (Kamphaus & Frick, 1996). For example, Ted was referred for an evaluation because concerns were noted in regard to his math computational skills. During the course of the evaluation, you learned that Ted's mother is recovering from bulimia. Because this finding does not appear to be related to the

**MEDICAL PROFESSIONAL'S REQUEST FOR
PSYCHOLOGICAL EVALUATION**

To: _____

Name of patient: _____

Date of birth: _____ Age: _____

Diagnosis (if one has been made): _____

Medical problems: _____

_____

_____

_____

Reason for referral: _____

_____

_____

_____

Behaviors or symptoms that led to this referral: _____

_____

_____

_____

Special Testing Concerns:

Y / N   Limitation of movement that might interfere with testing

Y / N   Hearing Loss (specify severity and if corrected _____
_____)

Y / N   Poor Vision (specify severity and if corrected _____
_____)

Y / N   Speech impediment

Y / N   English is second language (how English proficient is client? _____
_____)

Y / N   Poor understanding of language

Y / N   Poor cooperation

Y / N   Medication

         Name _____ Dose _____

         Side effects _____

         _____

Figure 3.1 Sample Referral Request used by Personnel in a Medical Setting

Source: Adapted from Tallent (1993).

Note. Although an initial request may be made from a physician with such a written form, you must follow up the written request by gathering more detailed information from the referral source.

Student's name _____ Date of referral _____

Referring person _____

Age _____ Grade _____ Grades repeated _____

Communication Problems	Never	Sometimes	Often
Expressive language (problems in grammar, limited vocabulary)	❏	❏	❏
Receptive language (difficulty with comprehension, not following directions)	❏	❏	❏

Classroom Behavior	Never	Sometimes	Often
Overly energetic, talks out, out of seat	❏	❏	❏
Very quiet, uncommunicative	❏	❏	❏
Acting out (aggressive, hostile, rebellious, destructive, cries easily)	❏	❏	❏
Inattentive (short attention span, poor on-task behavior)	❏	❏	❏
Doesn't appear to notice what is happening in the immediate environment	❏	❏	❏
Poor peer relationships (few friends, rejected, ignored/abused by peers)	❏	❏	❏

Academic Problems	Never	Sometimes	Often
Reading (poor word attack, comprehension)	❏	❏	❏
Writing (illegible, reverses letters, doesn't write)	❏	❏	❏
Spelling (cannot spell phonetically, omits or adds letters)	❏	❏	❏
Mathematics (poor computation, concepts, application)	❏	❏	❏
Social sciences, science (doesn't handle concepts, doesn't understand relationships, poor understanding of cause and effect)	❏	❏	❏

Physical Problems	Never	Sometimes	Often
Gross motor coordination (poor eye-hand, manual dexterity)	❏	❏	❏
Visual (cannot see blackboard, squints, rubs eyes, holds book too close)	❏	❏	❏
Hearing (unable to discriminate sounds, asks to have instructions repeated, turns ear to speaker, often has earaches)	❏	❏	❏
Health (example: epilepsy, respiratory problems, etc.)	❏	❏	❏

Treatment Currently Received	No	Yes	Frequency
Speech therapy	❏	❏	_____
Physical therapy	❏	❏	_____
Psychological therapy	❏	❏	_____
Occupational therapy	❏	❏	_____
Medications (if yes, list type)	❏	❏	_____

Other problems: _____

How have you tried to solve the problem? _____

Signature and position of referring person: _____

Figure 3.2 Sample Referral Form Used by Schools

Source: Adapted from Kamphaus and Frick (1996).

referral concern, you would not mention it. *As a general rule, only include information that relates to the interpretation of the person's scores or test behaviors or is relevant to the referral questions.*

To collect information from sources other than the person, you must have a signed release of information form. If the person is a child, then the parents should sign this form. Permission forms are necessary to obtain written information (previous reports or medical records) and even to collect information over the telephone.

When collecting information from various sources, be sure to protect the confidentiality of the person. Confidentiality refers to the ethical obligation never to reveal information obtained through a professional relationship without consent. The Ethical Standards of the American Psychological Association (APA, 2002) provide guidelines related to the issues of confidentiality, privacy, and disclosure. Specifically, these APA guidelines note that a psychologist must protect the *confidentiality* of the information obtained during the evaluation. In graduate training, the supervisor has responsibility for assuring that all trainees maintain confidentiality. The only exceptions to confidentiality are (1) when the person (or guardian) gives consent to release the information; (2) when the examiner is working with other professionals within a school, clinic, or agency; or (3) when failure to release information would violate the law.

For example, you may suspect during an evaluation that a child is being physically abused by a family member. To protect the child, you would want to have these allegations confirmed or rejected by others with specialized expertise in abuse issues to ensure adequate safety for the child. Familiarize yourself with your state laws for guidance about confidentiality and the reasons for breaking confidentiality that are considered to be justified.

How to Collect Background Information

Once the initial contact with the person or parents has been made, the process of collecting data begins. Usually face-to-face interviews are better than interviews over the telephone because you are able to see subtle nonverbal cues that may be relevant to the case. If parents are divorced or separated, you may be able to see only one of them in person. Attempt, however, to interview both parents (and stepparents), even if contact can only be made by telephone.

Several styles of interviews are appropriate for gathering background information; what works best for one examiner may not work well for another. You may obtain background information through unstructured, semistructured, or

Sample of Background Information from Child's Report

Jonas is an only child who currently resides with his parents, Dr. Arthur Haggerty, a dentist, and Dr. Margaret Rawson, a college professor. Both parents work full time. The Rawsons adopted Jonas at birth. His biological mother was 14 years old and reported that she smoked cigarettes throughout the pregnancy. Although little is known about prenatal care, concerns have been raised about possible drug and/or alcohol use during pregnancy.

Dr. Haggerty reported that Jonas attended preschool for two years and then entered Ashton Cove Elementary School for kindergarten. Based upon both parental and teacher concerns regarding motor development, he was referred for an occupational therapy evaluation in first grade. Results from the Peabody Developmental Motor Scale indicated delays of up to 17 months in fine-motor development and up to 26 months in gross-motor development. He demonstrated weakness in his flexor muscles, particularly abdominals and hip flexors; toe walking; and weaknesses in visual-motor planning. Jonas was unable to hop on one foot without losing his balance. On the Gardner Test of Visual-Perceptual Skills (nonmotor), Jonas obtained average scores on measures of visual discrimination and visual-spatial relations, and a below average score in visual memory. Recommendations were made for occupational therapy with the goals of improving fine- and gross-motor skills, visual-perceptual motor planning, and muscle weaknesses. In addition, Jonas began to receive resource support for reading, writing, and math.

Dr. Rawson reported that although Jonas has tried to participate in team sports (both soccer and baseball), the experiences were not positive. During baseball games, Jonas would often sit down in the outfield. On the soccer field, Jonas tried to stay away from the ball. His mother reported that on several occasions, when she picked Jonas up from practice, he would be crying. Presently, Jonas is enrolled in a karate program that he attends once a week. Because of problems with balance, he has been unable to advance to the next belt level.

Now that Jonas is in fourth grade, delays are still apparent in his gross-motor development. At the age of 9, Jonas is unable to ride a bike or tie his shoes with ease. He walks with an awkward gait and often trips. Because of continued toe walking, Jonas is currently wearing casts on both legs to stretch his heel cords and position his feet flat on the ground. When the casts are removed, Jonas is scheduled for physical therapy to help strengthen his legs. Recent results from a brain magnetic resonance imaging (MRI) indicated subtle cortical dysplasia involving the cerebellar hemispheres (the area of the brain involving motor development and balance). These findings are supported by clinical observations.

For the past three years, Jonas has received special education services in a resource setting under the category of Specific Learning Disability. He has also received half-hour weekly Occupational Therapy services. He currently uses an Alpha Smart, a small computer with a screen and a keyboard, in his classroom to assist with lengthy writing assignments. Jonas reports that he wants to quit his karate class and that his favorite activities are playing with his Game Boy, watching television, and eating candy.

Despite his difficulties, Jonas's parents note that he is creative and articulate and has a good sense of humor. When asked to write what he likes to do on the weekends, Jonas wrote, "Watch TV, play Nintendo, and fall down the stairs."

structured interviews. No specific guidelines exist in regard to how long an interview should take, but the following general recommendations can help orchestrate the process.

Structure of an Interview

The length of an interview depends on how talkative the person is and how structured an interview you conduct. Some examiners prefer to gather information from a questionnaire completed before the interview and then spend less time on the actual one-on-one interview. The completed questionnaire can be brought to the interview and the person's or parent's responses can be used as a starting point for asking follow-up questions. You may want to review the questionnaire prior to the interview so you have time to think about specific topics that you want to discuss. The process of completing a questionnaire may help prepare the person or parent for the types of questions you will be asking.

Even if a questionnaire is completed ahead of time, many people reveal additional details when they speak with you. In addition, a frequent complaint that parents have (especially in custody evaluations) is that they did not have enough time to "tell their story" (Ackerman, 1995). Thus, sufficient face-to-face time helps to ensure that the people you are working with feel validated, understood, and pleased with the assessment process. To further ensure satisfaction, make sure that the referral persons are happy with how you have perceived and interpreted their referral questions. Always check to confirm that you understand exactly what is being asked of you so that you are clear about the purposes of the evaluation.

Some clinicians prefer a loosely structured interview that moves freely from one topic to another; others prefer to ask questions one by one from a highly detailed questionnaire. Several structured interviews are available for gathering developmental histories. Sample history forms include the Structured Developmental History of the Behavior Assessment System for Children (BASC; Reynolds & Kamphaus, 1992) and the Checklist for Referral and Background Information form of the Kaufman WISC-III Integrated Interpretive System (K-WIIS; Kaufman, Kaufman, Dougherty, & Tuttle, 1994). (See Figures 3.3 and 3.4 for excerpts from these forms.)

Some examiners prefer to gather information on personal history from birth to the present. Others prefer to focus the interview on areas that are specifically relevant to the referral question, while including only introductory questions about development or other areas (Ackerman, 1995). You may use what is known as a branching procedure to pursue topics that are of particular relevance

DEVELOPMENTAL MILESTONES AND EARLY CHILDHOOD

1. How would you describe the child's temperament during early childhood?

_____ 1. Do not know

_____ 2. Calm

_____ 3. Hyperactive

_____ 4. Sociable

_____ 5. Withdrawn

_____ 6. Happy

_____ 7. Unhappy

_____ 8. Alert

_____ 9. Sleepy

_____ 10. Affectionate

_____ 11. Frequent crying

_____ 12. Difficult

_____ 13. Irritable

_____ 14. Hypersensitive

_____ 15. Angry

_____ 16. Fearful

_____ 17. Curious

_____ 18. Playful

_____ 19. Other (please specify)_____

2. When did the child develop physical skills such as sitting, crawling, and walking?

_____ 1. Do not know

_____ 2. Earlier than most children

_____ 3. At about the same time as most children

_____ 4. Later than most children

_____ 5. Other (please specify)_____

3. How would you describe the child's language development (e.g., first words, talking in sentences, vocabulary, etc.) during early childhood?

_____ 1. Do not know

_____ 2. Advanced in comparison with other children

_____ 3. Average in comparison with other children

_____ 4. Slow in comparison with other children

_____ 5. Tended to express needs nonverbally

_____ 6. Other (please specify)_____

4. How would you describe the child's motor development and skill acquisition (e.g., toilet training, running, jumping, throwing a ball, catching, etc.) during early childhood?

_____ 1. Do not know

_____ 2. Advanced in comparison with other children

_____ 3. Average in comparison with other children

_____ 4. Slow in comparison with other children

_____ 5. Other (please specify)_____

5. How would you describe the child's social development (e.g., development of friendships, relationships with peers, relationships with adults) during early childhood?

_____ 1. Do not know

_____ 2. Advanced in comparison with other children

_____ 3. Average in comparison with other children

_____ 4. Slow in comparison with other children

_____ 5. Other (please specify)_____

6. How would you describe the child's cognitive development (e.g., counting, knowledge of alphabet, doing puzzles, understanding concepts, etc.) during early childhood?

_____ 1. Do not know

_____ 2. Advanced in comparison with other children

_____ 3. Average in comparison with other children

_____ 4. Slow in comparison with other children

_____ 5. Other (please specify)_____

SCHOOLING

1. Which one of the following preschool programs has the child attended?

_____ 1. Do not know

_____ 2. None

_____ 3. Infant day care

_____ 4. Preschool

_____ 5. Kindergarten

_____ 6. Head Start

_____ 7. Other (please specify)_____

2. What is the child's current grade in school?

_____ 1. Do not know

_____ 2. Kindergarten

_____ 3. 1st

_____ 4. 2nd

_____ 5. 3rd

_____ 6. 4th

_____ 7. 5th

_____ 8. 6th

_____ 9. 7th

_____ 10. 8th

Figure 3.3 Excerpts of K-WIIS Checklist for Referral and Background Information

Source: Adapted from Kaufman, Kaufman, Dougherty, and Tuttle (1994).

Medical History

Childhood Illnesses/Injuries

Please check the illnesses this child has had an indicate age (year/month)

❏ Measles _____   ❏ Rheumatic fever _____
❏ German measles _____   ❏ Diphtheria _____
❏ Mumps _____   ❏ Meningitis _____
❏ Chicken pox _____   ❏ Encephalitis _____
❏ Tuberculosis _____   ❏ Anemia _____
❏ Whooping cough _____   ❏ Fever above 104° _____
❏ Scarlet fever _____
❏ Head injury: Describe _____
❏ Coma or loss of consciousness: Describe _____
❏ Sustained high fever: Describe _____

Please describe other serious illnesses or operations:

Illness/Operation	Age

Has this child ever been on long-term medication (more than 6 months)?   No   Yes
      If yes, when? _____ What kind? _____

Adaptive Skills

Please indicate whether this child has the following skills.

Dresses self.. No Yes   Bathes self............................. No Yes
Buys gifts or presents for others............... No Yes   Helps with household chores..... No Yes
Knows how to get help or find home if lost.. No Yes   Has good table manners........... No Yes
Says "please" and "thank you".................. No Yes   Tells time accurately............... No Yes
Does this child receive an allowance?....... No Yes
      If yes, how does he/she spend it? _____

Educational History

Preschool
Does or did this child attend preschool?........No Yes   At what age? _____
      Amount of time per day _____   Days per week _____
      Any problems with preschool? ....No Yes   If yes, describe _____

Does or did this child attend kindergarten?.....No Yes   At what age? _____
      Amount of time per day _____   Days per week _____
      Any problems with kindergarten? ......No Yes   If yes, describe _____

Figure 3.4 Excerpts of BASC Structured Developmental History

Source: Adapted from Reynolds and Kamphaus (1992).

to the referral question. When interviewing someone (the person, parents, or teachers), you may find it helpful to change your line of questioning if something of particular relevance is revealed. For example, if you find out that the child missed 30 days of school because of a hospital stay after a head injury, branch off into a line of questioning about the head injury. This branching procedure keeps flexibility in an interview and allows you to pursue relevant topics in more depth.

Content of the Background Section

Like the structure of the interview, the content of the information collected for the background section of the report will vary from case to case. Certain general topics, however, are often addressed. Rapid References 3.4 through 3.7 provide a detailed outline of information that may be collected during an interview with a person or with parents. If the informant is a medical doctor, the questions would revolve around the medical history. If the informant is a teacher, then the information would revolve around academic history and present classroom performance.

Organize the background section in a logical progression from topic to topic. The lists of topics in Rapid References 3.4 through 3.7 provide a useful way to structure the report itself. Typically, you will have separate paragraphs on early development, school history, medical history, and so on. Try to keep the content of each paragraph on one distinct topic. If you have little to say about a topic (e.g., Jose's medical history was unremarkable, with no major illnesses or injuries), then integrate that information with another related topic, such as results from vision or hearing screenings.

The following example, adapted from Mather and Jaffe (2002), illustrates a sample paragraph that focuses on ocular albinism and the conditions affecting a child's vision:

> Gregory Blackhawk is a 7-year-old second-grade boy who has been diagnosed with ocular albinism, the result of which is impaired acuity and moderate horizontal nystagmus. Results of a functional vision evaluation last year completed by Dr. Martin, an ophthalmologist, indicated near acuity approximating 20/160 and distance acuity of 20/100. In addition, he has astigmatism, mild myopia in the right eye, and a left eye muscle imbalance. Gregory has binocular vision at a distance of up to two feet; at greater distances, he uses only his right eye. He also has the pigmentation of albinism, with pale skin, light blond hair, and blue eyes.

≡Rapid Reference 3.4

Sample Topics for Developmental History of Children

Mother's pregnancy

- Was the mother under a physician's care?
- Any problems or complications?
- Any prescribed medications or nonprescription drugs taken?
- Alcohol consumed? Amount?
- Cigarettes smoked? Amount?
- Illegal drugs such as marijuana used? Amount?
- Weeks of gestation (37–40 weeks is considered full-term)?
- prematurity (fewer than 37 weeks gestation)?

Delivery

- Type of delivery?
- Any fetal distress during delivery?
- Anything that caused disruption of oxygen?

After birth

- Weight and length at birth?
- APGAR scores? 5 min. and 10 min. scores are not predictive, but low (below 7) are suggestive of potential fetal distress.
- Any special care or medical tests needed?
- How long were mother and child in the hospital?
- Was the baby's schedule predictable? (helps to determine temperament)
  —eating
  —sleeping
  —frequency and intensity of crying

Developmental milestones

- sitting
- crawling
- walking
- first words
- short phrases
- toilet training

You will often want to organize parts of this section in chronological order, progressing from the earliest incidents up to the present situation. Rapid Reference 3.8 provides an example of a boy's educational history.

Recency of Information

A review of history can help you determine how long a problem has existed. When adults state why they are coming in for an assessment, they usually list the

≡Rapid Reference 3.5

Sample Topics for Educational and Occupational History

Acquire Information About All Levels of Schooling That Apply:

- day care and preschool (for children)
- kindergarten and grade school (for children/adolescents)
- high school (for adults/adolescents)
- college (for adults)
- technical/vocational training (for adults)

Educational Considerations:

- type of school attended (e.g., public, private, home-school)
- bilingual teacher or class
- separation from parents (in earliest school years)
- peer relationships
- type of grades earned
- scores on standardized tests (group tests from school record)
- attendance record
- grades skipped/repeated
- change in schools
- problems/successes
- relationships with teachers
- attitude toward school
- problems with homework
- interests, activities outside of school
- educational interventions (speech therapy, special education, etc.; what types of interventions have worked?)

Previous Psychoeducational Test Results

- referral questions
- test results
- diagnoses
- recommendations
- follow-up

Occupational History (adults)

- present and past employment, periods of unemployment
- presence or lack of appropriate training for the job (formal schooling or on-the-job)
- satisfaction with job
- relationship with work colleagues/supervisors
- status of retirement, alternate activities, or volunteer work

≡ Rapid Reference 3.6

Sample Topics for Medical and Psychological History

Medical History

- vision
- hearing
- illnesses
- injuries
- hospitalizations
- medications (current/past; name; dose; frequency)
- drug/alcohol use (current/past)
- cigarette use
- caffeine use
- eating habits
- sleeping habits

Psychological History

- current or previous diagnosis
- individual, family, or group therapy (past/present)
- drug or alcohol rehabilitation
- efficacy of past treatments

Previous Psychological Test Results

Past Records of Juvenile Detention or Incarceration

problems that led them to seek help. Sometimes, however, the duration of the problem is unclear. Did the problem begin in the past 12 months? Or in the past 2 weeks? If the problems have existed for the past 2 years, what led the person to come in *now?* Inquire about the duration and intensity of the problems. Some people reveal valuable new information when prompted with the question "Why did you seek an assessment *right now?*"

Obtaining Information about Touchy Subjects

Some topics are difficult to discuss. Examples include drug and alcohol abuse, sexual offenses, divorce, strained family relationships, and obesity. Often, taking a matter-of-fact approach is helpful (e.g., saying "these questions are a routine part of our evaluation"). You can acknowledge that some things you ask may be difficult to answer, but encourage people to respond to your questions openly and honestly. It is also helpful to alternate discussion of sensitive topics with straightforward, unemotional fact gathering.

≣*Rapid Reference 3.7*

Sample Topics for Family and Social History

Family History

- race of each parent (e.g., Caucasian, African American)
- languages spoken in home, by caretaker, in neighborhood, and by person
- siblings/stepsiblings and birth order
- marital status, past and present (if testing adult)
  —current relationship
  —if divorced, how long was marriage and when was divorce?
  —children from present or past relationships
- marital status of parents (if testing child)
  —if divorced, age of child at divorce
  —child custody and visitation arrangement
  —related difficulties
- parents' child-rearing practices
- has the problem affected the family?
- living situation
  —who lives with the child?
  —how long have they lived in the current residence?

Social Relationships

- quality of friendships
- sibling relationships (including stepsiblings and half siblings)
- other social supports

Family's Psychological or Educational History

- history of psychological problems in immediate family (e.g., mother diagnosed with depression)
- history of learning problems in other family members (e.g., father diagnosed with dyslexia)
- history of medically relevant problems in other family members (e.g., older sibling diagnosed with ADHD)

Individual's View of Self (or of child)

- self-concept
- strengths
- weaknesses
- hobbies and interests

During the interview, take notes about what the person says, but also observe how the person responds nonverbally. For example, did he seem defensive when asked about alcohol and drug abuse? Did she become embarrassed and blush when asked about how she disciplines her child? Did he become tearful when asked how he was doing in his math class? These additional bits of qualitative

≡ Rapid Reference 3.8

Example of a Boy's Educational History

Jason began kindergarten at Castle Hill School but remained there for only 2 weeks. Mrs. Jasper felt that the program was too structured for him, and so she moved him to Garden Park preschool. As a result of this change, his behavior improved, and he began to interact successfully with his peers. His preschool teacher noted that Jason spoke well and was good at drawing pictures. The following year he began kindergarten for the second time at Castle Hill School but stayed only from August to December. During this time, the kindergarten teacher raised concerns about his lack of attention. Mrs. Jasper then enrolled Jason in Harper Elementary School, believing that his difficulties with attention were because of his unhappiness at Castle Hill School. Prior to leaving Castle Hill, Jason was evaluated for special education but was not eligible for services. At that time it was reported that he could recite most of the alphabet but lacked sound-symbol relationships; he knew his shapes and colors and could count to 36, but he recognized numbers only up to 15. He then completed first and second grade at Harper Elementary. Both teachers noted problems with his attention. During these 2 years, he participated in a program called Reading Pals that was designed to promote early literacy.

Jason is currently in third grade in Ms. Mantell's class. In an interview, Ms. Mantell reported that he is easily distracted, even on academic tasks that are well within his capability. She noted that he rarely finishes assignments, and when he does complete a task, he has a tendency to rush through it and not notice his errors. Usually when she looks over at Jason, he is playing with a pencil or staring out the window. Ms. Mantell commented that Jason's attention is better when academic tasks are interactive, physical, or hands-on in nature.

information can prove invaluable when you are interpreting all results. On occasion, you may question the accuracy of the information provided during an interview. Usually, when you are unsure of the accuracy of an account, you can confirm the information by consulting another source.

Information from Different Sources

Mothers and fathers and parents and teachers may provide different (and conflicting) information about the same person. In fact, informants often disagree in their views of a child (Kamphaus & Frick, 1996). Compare the information provided by diverse sources and note all contradictions. For example, a teacher may state that a child exhibits aggressive behavior in school, but the parents may not report this type of behavior in the home. In another instance, the mother may have a higher tolerance for noncompliance than a father, leading to divergent opinions about whether the child is cooperative. Different expectations, interpersonal interactions, and situational factors can all lead to varied perceptions of the same person. Keep in mind that varied opinions about the same person do not mean that one person is right and the other is wrong. Differing perceptions often result because a certain behavior is only present in specific circumstances and because people vary in their perceptions of behavior.

You have to decide how to reconcile and report these differences when writing the results. In general, evaluators tend to weigh adult informants, such as parents and teachers, more heavily for observable behaviors (e.g., conduct problem behaviors) and tend to weigh child self-report more heavily for emotional problems (e.g., depression, anxiety; Loeber, Green, & Lahey, 1990). Perhaps that fact is not surprising given that adults report more conduct problems than do children (Kashani, Orvaschel, Burk, & Reid, 1985) and children report more emotional problems than do parents or teachers (Bird, Gould, & Stagheeza, 1992).

If you are evaluating a child, then the age of the child may affect how heavily you rely on the child's self-report in comparison to the parents'. As a child enters adolescence, parents invariably have less knowledge of his or her emotions and behaviors than they did when the child was younger. Therefore, adolescents may be better informants than their parents about certain topics, such as their emotional well-being, interests, fears, or feelings about school. Similarly, an elementary school teacher, who sees a child for many hours a day, will have more knowledge of certain behaviors than a child's junior high or high school teachers, who typically see the student for one class a day. In addition, as children develop cognitively, they are more capable of describing abstract concepts such as feelings and thoughts. Logically, then, the importance of a child's self-report increases with age, and the importance of information reported by parents or teachers decreases (Kamphaus & Frick, 1996). This generalization does not apply to factual developmental history or to situations where the child is incapable of providing an accurate self-report because of linguistic, emotional, or cognitive impairments.

When integrating information from diverse sources into your report, try to account for discrepant information and explain the reason for it. Rapid Reference 3.9 provides a father's brief summary of the educational experiences of Paul, his adolescent son. Paul's father believes that Paul could do the work if he wanted to, but Paul feels that he really needs more support if he is going to succeed at his school. Mr. Matthew attributes Paul's failure to a lack of motivation, whereas Paul attributes his current difficulties to a lack of support.

One reason for this discrepancy may be that Mr. Matthews only sees Paul on the weekends. He is the noncustodial parent, and Paul stays with him every other weekend. Mr. Matthews does not observe the amount of help that Paul needs on a routine basis to organize his materials and complete his assignments for school.

≡Rapid Reference 3.9

Example of a Father and Son's Discrepant Views

Paul was adopted when he was 2 days old. Mr. Matthews reported that as an infant he was extremely active. He spent an extra year in preschool because of difficulties sitting still and participating in groups. Paul has always gone to private schools that have a small student-teacher ratio and an advanced curriculum. His elementary school, Pine Ridge, provided small classes, individualized instruction, and close supervision. Paul was successful in elementary school, but in his first year at Westminster Preparatory Academy his grades have deteriorated considerably. Paul is currently failing all of his courses.

Mr. Matthews feels that the reason Paul is not doing well in school is because he is not prepared for his classes, which results in inadequate completion of homework assignments and poor test scores. He believes that if Paul would just try harder, he could perform well in all of his subjects without any extra help or tutoring.

In contrast, Paul reports that while he was at Pine Ridge he had tutoring three times a week. The teachers also made informal accommodations for him, such as letting him retake exams and working with him on a one-to-one basis. He believes that one main reason he is not doing well in his classes is that he needs extra time on all of his tests in school but is too embarrassed to ask for this accommodation. In the past when he was given more time, it was easier for him to focus his attention on the important aspects of the task. Paul believes that he needs a tutor or "homework coach" who can help him organize, prioritize, and complete his assignments. He also commented that the classes are too big at Westminster and the teachers don't have time for one-to-one help.

Paul's mother, Ms. Hoffman, corroborated Paul's perceptions. She noted that Paul has always struggled in school and required substantial outside tutoring to perform as well as he did at Pine Ridge. He currently does not have a tutor, nor is he receiving any special accommodations in school.

If you provide logical explanations for discrepant information, then the report will provide a more balanced picture of the person's functioning in the context of family and environment. Rapid Reference 3.10 provides a sample of the background section from Paul's report that contains conflicting information from his father and mother about his adjustment.

Identifying the Source of Information

When you write the background information, always reference the source of the information. If you write "Mrs. Jones reported that her husband is extremely depressed," such a statement may be interpreted quite differently by readers than if you write "Mr. Jones's psychiatrist reported that his client suffers from severe

Example of How to Present Conflicting Information

Parent rating scales. Paul's father and mother, who have been divorced for five years, completed the Behavior Assessment System for Children (BASC): Adolescent form, Parent Rating Scales. On the BASC, Paul's father, Mr. Matthews, rated the following behaviors as being significant concerns: lying to get out of trouble, rapidly changing moods, needing too much supervision, and tendency to act without thinking. However, his ratings also indicated that Paul has lots of ideas, compliments others, and has no trouble being social or making new friends. Nevertheless, the extent of his behavior problems at home resulted in a Behavioral Symptoms Index (BSI) that surpassed 91% of his peers; only 9% of adolescents in the United States were rated as high (negatively) in terms of their attention and adjustment problems by their parents. The BSI comprises the Hyperactivity, Aggression, Anxiety, Depression, Atypicality, and Attention Problems subscales.

In contrast, Paul's mother's ratings differed in that Mrs. Hoffman did not observe any indications of inattention, such as trouble concentrating, or impulsivity. Unlike Paul's father, she did not note concerns about lying or moodiness. She also did not feel that Paul required an inordinate amount of supervision. She described Paul as "sometimes" creative and "often" polite. His mother's ratings resulted in a BSI surpassing 52% of his peers, suggesting typical adjustment. One reason for this discrepancy in ratings may be that Paul lives primarily with his mother and only stays with his father every other weekend. Paul commented that he does not enjoy going to his father's house because the rules are too strict, there is no computer at the house, and he is not allowed to stay out later than 9 p.m.

Both Paul's father and mother rated his leadership skills as low. His father responded "never" and his mother "sometimes" regarding the following characteristics: good at getting people to work together, "self-starter," usually chosen as a leader, energetic, and involved in organized social clubs or groups. For someone of Paul's superior cognitive and academic skills, his ratings in leadership are highly atypical.

Teacher rating scales. To obtain a comprehensive measure of Paul's school behavior, his ninth-grade science and English teachers completed the BASC Teacher Rating Scale. The science teacher's ratings supported the evaluator's impression of an adolescent who is not depressed, overanxious, or demonstrating any significant learning problems. Conversely, he "often" is distractible, rushes through assigned work, is overactive, bothers other students, and demonstrates poor study skills. Paul's BSI score surpassed 88% of adolescents his age nationally. This score falls within the "at-risk" range (85% and above), suggesting a significant overall behavioral problem in the classroom.

Paul's English teacher also indicated that Paul shows no significant symptoms of depression or learning problems. In contrast, she rated Paul as "almost always" demonstrating behaviors that comprise the domains of attention problems, hyperactivity, and anxiety. These behaviors included bothering others who are working, frequently seeking attention, exhibiting difficulty in waiting his turn, insisting that he is not good at something, and often seeming nervous. Paul's BSI score surpassed 95% of adolescents his age nationally, which falls within the "clinically significant" range (95% and above), suggesting a severe behavioral problem in the classroom. Ratings provided by Paul's father, science teacher, and English teacher indicate that he has significant problems related to the behavioral symptoms of ADHD. In contrast, his mother's ratings indicated that Paul's adjustment is typical for adolescents of his age.

Adapted from M. Gerner (2003). Unpublished case report.

DON'T FORGET

Statements for Clarifying the Source of Information

According to....

Mrs. Hoffman said ...

Dr. Earle stated ...

Ms. Morgan, his second-grade teacher, revealed ...

Ms. Pereza's opinion is ...

Mr. Mohammad reported ...

The principal, Mr. Ortiz, acknowledged that ...

School records indicated ...

As mentioned by Dr. Zhu in a previous case report ...

Her psychiatrist, Dr. McGrew, noted ...

Colleagues of Ms. Whitney have complained to their supervisor that ...

depression." As another example, a mother may believe that her daughter is "just lazy" when the father interprets her behavior differently. To clarify each source's perceptions, provide specific information: "According to Mrs. Gomez, her daughter's refusal to clean her room stems from her laziness, whereas Mr. Gomez sees this behavior as an example of the power struggle between his wife and teenage daughter." Also, information from school records (e.g., report cards or standard scores on tests) can provide a more accurate account than a parent's or child's account of "what kind of student is Martha?" Examples of statements that can be used to clarify the source of information are listed in the Don't Forget box.

 TEST YOURSELF

1. **Well-written reports need to**
   (a) present critical pieces of history throughout the report.
   (b) avoid information that is not documented as factual by multiple sources.
   (c) obtain referral and background information from adults, not children.
   (d) answer the referral questions.

2. **In addition to the reason a person is being referred for an assessment, there are many other important pieces of information to gather about the referral question. Which of the following is *not* necessary to gather about the referral?**
   (a) intensity, frequency, and duration of the problem
   (b) when the problem started
   (c) why the person picked you for an evaluation
   (d) why the person came in now

(continued)

3. **Examples and brief anecdotes are a waste of time and space when writing the paragraph on reason for referral.** True or False?

4. **Generally, face-to-face interviews are better than interviews over the telephone when collecting information from teachers or parents.** True or False?

5. **Name several areas that can be included in the section on background information.**

6. **Because gathering information about touchy subjects may disrupt rapport, you should avoid asking questions about topics such as divorce and drug and alcohol history.** True or False?

7. **Which of the following is true when gathering information from a variety of sources?**

   (a) Information from parents, who live with the child, is believed over any information given to you by teachers.

   (b) Do not trust information from adolescents.

   (c) The age and maturity level of the child may affect how heavily you rely on the child's self-report.

   (d) Information from teachers is more reliable than that from parents because parents are more biased in their evaluations.

8. **Phrases that clarify the source of information, such as, "According to . . ." "School records indicate . . ." or "He acknowledged . . ." are needless wastes of words in a report.** True or False?

Answers: 1. d; 2. c; 3. False; 4. True; 5. see Rapid References 3.3–3.6; 6. False; 7. c; 8. False

Four

BEHAVIORAL OBSERVATIONS

This chapter focuses on the behaviors you observe during testing, as well as behaviors you observe in other settings (e.g., home or school). Its purpose is to help you describe and interpret important behaviors accurately.

OBSERVATIONS DURING THE ASSESSMENT

The testing environment differs from most other environments, in part because the interaction is most often one-to-one and thus more personal and focused than group interactions. In addition, the environment is carefully controlled to maximize the examinee's attention and performance. In other words, the testing is designed to elicit the person's optimal performance. Therefore, the observed behaviors may not be representative of a person's typical behaviors in another setting, such as a noisy classroom. You may suspect that the observed test behaviors are representative of typical behaviors observed in the home, school, or workplace, but you would want confirmation from others.

The behaviors observed during an assessment are, however, critical to understanding a person's test performance. For example, observing a student's behavior during the WISC-IV Arithmetic subtest will help you to determine whether the difficulties on this supplemental task were due to anxiety, lack of knowledge, inattention, or lack of effort. If Miranda was biting her nails and nervously twisting her hair during the subtest, you may assume that anxiety is affecting performance. In contrast, if she did not understand when to use certain mathematical operations (e.g., addition vs. subtraction), you would surmise that her difficulties are more likely due to a lack of knowledge, poor reasoning ability, or limited instruction.

Careful observation of behavior takes practice. New examiners are often so intent upon administering a test correctly and recording the responses that they have trouble attending to subtle behaviors. Be so thoroughly familiar with the test you are administering that you do not have to focus on how to administer or score it and can direct your attention to the person's comments, responses, and actions.

During the evaluation, take notes about what you are observing as you observe it. Because many evaluations last longer than two hours, you should not rely solely on memory. Take notes on the record form next to the section of the task you are administering. Include specific behaviors as well as any statements that may help you to understand and interpret an individual's test performance.

You will also find that at times you will want to quote a comment verbatim (e.g., "I have so much homework that I want to quit school"). During an evaluation, Mark, a third-grade student struggling with math concepts, commented, "I hate math and so does my mother." This comment may help you see that, albeit unintentionally, Mark's mother is actually reinforcing his negative academic self-concept about math performance.

Even if a behavior or comment does not initially seem relevant, you may find after the second hour of testing that the remark supports an important inference. Some behaviors are best understood when you consider errors and comments several hours or days later. For example, after examining your comments in the margins of the record forms, you may note that distractible behaviors only occurred during subtests involving the processing of language or during a specific academic subject, such as reading.

As you begin to plan what you will write in the Behavioral Observations section, compile a list of the behaviors you observed. For example, "she tapped her feet" or "she looked out the window" are sample statements that describe behaviors. As you review the list of behaviors and comments, attempt to categorize them into recurrent themes (e.g., behaviors indicative of persistence, inattention, positive self-concept). When a common underlying theme exists, provide an interpretation of the behaviors.

For example, you may find that several behaviors on different subtests seem to indicate inattention. If you observed that the child had difficulty following lengthy instructions and had trouble sitting still and remaining in the chair, then you can write a statement (and a supporting paragraph) about how these behaviors are indicative of problems with attention.

Your interpretation will help the reader understand the behavior. For example, the fact that "Claire tapped her feet during the Digit Span subtest" could indicate anxiety, boredom, or frustration, or it could even have been a technique for aiding in the recall of the numbers. Similarly, the statement "Maria looked off into space" may indicate distractibility, social avoidance, or failure to understand the requirements of the task. You have to interpret the behaviors. Ordinarily, do not interpret only one particular behavior in isolation, unless it is dramatic, such as when a child cries when trying to write a paragraph but responds appropriately to challenges on all other tasks.

Rapid Reference 4.1 provides examples of other behaviors and interpretations

≡ Rapid Reference 4.1

Samples of Behaviors, Interpretations, and How to Combine Them into a Statement

Behaviors	Interpretation	Statement in Report
Foot tapping, fidgety hands, twirling hair	Anxiety	José appeared anxious on tasks that required verbal responses, which was evidenced by his foot tapping, fidgety hands, and hair twirling.
Slouching in chair, averted gaze, silence	Resistance	Michelle was resistant to the assessment. Throughout the evaluation she slouched down in her chair and averted her gaze from the examiner, while often responding to the examiner's questions with silence.
Stacking blocks, spinning puzzle pieces, doodling with pencil on Coding booklet	Inattention and distractibility	Ian had trouble maintaining focus and attention during nonverbal items. He was easily distracted by the testing stimuli itself. For example, rather than copying a block design as the directions called for, he stacked the blocks on top of one another. He also spun the pieces to a puzzle around rather than putting them together and doodled with his pencil on a booklet meant for copying symbols.

and illustrates how to combine them to create a clear description of behavior. Figure 4.1 illustrates how to combine a paragraph of interpretations and a paragraph of behaviors into one cohesive description. The Don't Forget box reviews important points to remember when writing behavioral observations.

Although your behavioral observations will usually be consistent, sometimes they will contradict one another. When this occurs, attempt to resolve and explain any contradictory information. A child may seem anxious on certain tasks but relaxed on others. Explain then how differences in the types of tasks affected behavior. Before making broad generalizations about behavior, review the observed behaviors carefully. If ten behaviors support one interpretation, but one behavior seems contradictory, then propose a hypothesis about why the one behavior differed from the rest. If the person displayed frustration only during one problem-solving task and was calm for the rest of the evaluation, then describe

Interpretive Hypotheses	*Specific Behaviors*
Andy showed a strong ability to concentrate and remained focused throughout the evaluation.	Andy attended well on tasks even though he commented that they were "somewhat boring for him to do." On a task that required him to copy abstract designs with colored blocks, he had difficulty making the correct design but kept on trying and attempted to complete the design. When he did not know the answer to a problem, he said "I don't know." Failure to answer one question did not interfere with his attempting the next question.

Integrated Paragraph

Andy showed a strong ability to concentrate and focus on each task presented to him. His attention never wavered, even on tasks that he stated were boring. He also demonstrated stamina and persistence by working steadily on tasks that were challenging for him. For example, on a task that required him to copy abstract designs with colored blocks, Andy had difficulty making the correct designs but kept on trying and attempted to complete the designs. On other tasks, when he did not know the answer to a problem he said "I don't know." Failure to answer one question did not interfere with his desire to attempt the next question.

Figure 4.1 Combine Interpretive Hypotheses and Specific Behaviors

DON'T FORGET
....

Dos and Don'ts of Writing the Behavioral Observations Section

Don't	Do
1. List a string of behaviors without providing interpretive hypotheses.	1. Write a list of interpretive hypotheses about the person as soon as the session is over (without dwelling too much on specific behaviors).
2. List an array of hypotheses without providing behavioral examples.	2. Examine the specific notes of behaviors observed.
	3. Blend the interpretive hypotheses with specific behaviors to write paragraphs that integrate both interpretations and specific behaviors.

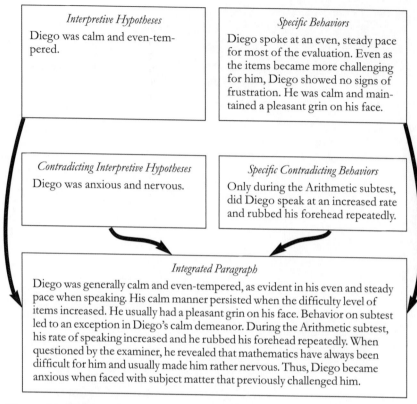

Figure 4.2 Writing about Contradicting Behaviors

this exception with a hypothesis about why the behavior differed on this particular task (see Figure 4.2).

You may address many different topics in the Behavioral Observations section of a report, although for different cases certain topics will be more important than others. The next Don't Forget reviews possible topics to include in this section that are discussed in more detail in the pages that follow.

Physical Appearance

Although it is not necessary to comment upon physical appearance, these observations can provide clues to an examinee's physical, psychological, and neurological functioning. When describing physical appearance, you will usually just write one or two sentences, such as "Victor is an attractive 4-year-old boy with dark coloring and straight jet-black hair" or "Martha is a tall, slender adolescent with a confident manner and an engaging smile."

DON'T FORGET

Possible Topics to Include in Behavioral Observations Section of Report

- physical appearance
- ease of establishing and maintaining rapport with examinee
- language style
- response to failures
- response to successes
- response to encouragement
- attention span
- distractibility
- activity level
- anxiety level
- mood
- impulsivity/reflectivity
- problem-solving strategy
- attitude toward the testing process
- attitude toward examiner
- attitude toward self
- unusual mannerisms or habits
- validity of test results in view of behaviors

You may note aspects of appearance such as the examinee's height, weight, and build (e.g., lanky, stocky, underweight) and also grooming. For example, was the examinee's clothing neat and clean or dirty and disheveled? If an adolescent boy comes to the session with shoes untied, one side of his shirt hanging out, and hair disheveled, you may begin to hypothesize about poor organizational skills or rebellion against adult authority. The same appearance for a 7-year-old, however, may suggest poor parental supervision. Similarly, if an adult client smells strongly of alcohol or appears "out of it," you will ask about alcohol and drug use (even if the client initially denied such use).

Ease of Establishing and Maintaining Rapport with Examinee

With some people, rapport is established easily, but with others it requires more time and effort. Some people are just slower to warm up and respond to new situations than others. Observe how the person relates to you. Is the person friendly, abrupt, shy, frightened, cooperative, aggressive, or respectful? Observe also how the relationship changes over the course of the evaluation. Typically, as individuals become more comfortable with you, they become friendlier, more talkative, and more relaxed.

Similarly, rapport is maintained easily throughout the assessment with some individuals, but for others, rapport may be disrupted. For example, if a child becomes unduly frustrated with a certain subtest, you may see that her attitude and motivation change for the remainder of the session. Be sensitive to changes in rapport, and be ready to pause or even stop testing when necessary to reestablish a good relationship.

Because different settings and cultures promote different values, beliefs, and behaviors, learn as much as possible about the culture and environment of the people you evaluate. For example, the amount of eye contact a person maintains with you during an evaluation is usually indicative of the level of rapport. Some cultural groups, however, consider it disrespectful to make or sustain direct eye contact with an authority figure.

Communication

The speed, pitch, volume, and rhythm of speech can make a person difficult or easy to understand. Both accents and regional dialects can affect a person's ability to understand or be understood. The ease of conversation also differs among individuals. Some people converse spontaneously, whereas others only respond when asked direct questions. Such differences may be attributed to linguistic difficulties or merely differences in style. Examine differences and errors in speech and language to determine whether they can be attributed to pronunciation, fluency, organization, or even memory. If on several items a person says, "Oh, I know what this is, but can't remember what it's called," the person may have word-retrieval difficulties.

Also consider the quality of the responses (e.g., detailed or brief, impulsive or reflective). Note how well the person pronounces words, uses words, conforms to rules of grammar, and maintains conversation. Also, observe nonverbal communication. Does the person use many hand gestures to make a point? Do the nonverbal behaviors seem appropriate for the situation? Does the person respond appropriately to your nonverbal communication?

Response to Failures

Good teachers try to avoid placing students at the frustration level where the content and material are too difficult to handle successfully. In testing, however, the goal is to cover the range of functioning or a person's operating levels from easy to difficult. Although tests are designed to minimize failure, in order to discontinue a subtest the person typically has to miss several problems or items in a row. As you administer a subtest, the questions move from an easy level to a frustration level where the items become increasingly more difficult. Some people do not seem to be bothered by errors or not knowing the answers, whereas others become sullen, angry, or frustrated. Observe how the individual reacts to difficult items: Some work harder, some seem to accept the fact that the items are too difficult, and some quit trying and may even refuse to go on.

Observe how the person's confidence level affects his or her response to items that are too difficult. People with high levels of confidence are able to state, "I don't know" without feeling incompetent. People with lowered levels of self-confidence may experience greater anxiety when they come to problems they cannot solve and may be more likely to criticize the test or their own abilities.

Response to Feedback

People also respond to praise and correction in various ways. Some people will smile when you say "Well done," whereas others do not seem to notice the praise. Some people are born with a predisposition to react more strongly and negatively to mistakes than others and are thus more likely to become frustrated during the evaluation (Brooks & Goldstein, 2001).

Some tests even include built-in feedback about performance. For example, on the WJ III COG, several tests require that the examiner provide corrective feedback when the examinee makes a mistake, a procedure that is followed as well on the KABC-II Atlantis subtest. Some people will try to learn from the feedback and incorporate the new learning into their next attempts. Others do not seem to profit from or even listen to the corrections.

People also react differently to verbal and nonverbal encouragement. Observe what type of reinforcement seems to motivate the person to put forth the most effort. As a general principle, remember to reward effort, not the correctness of the response. It is easy to get into a habit of saying "good" when a response is correct and saying nothing when a response is incorrect. Remind yourself to say "good" to both correct and incorrect responses, unless the person's response is clearly incorrect, such as a completely misaligned item on the WISC-IV Block Design subtest. Occasionally, praise the effort ("You are really working hard") instead of the response.

Attention

A person's attention can also vary throughout the evaluation. The person may be attentive during the beginning of the assessment but have trouble sustaining attention throughout the evaluation. Attention may also vary according to the type of tasks. For example, novel subtests may hold children's attention longer than subtests with familiar tasks (e.g., math computations), or subtests that use concrete materials to manipulate may sustain interest and attention better than those that have oral questions or pictures. Note the length of time that an examinee can sustain attention. Some people can work for several hours; some need a break after 30 minutes; and others need a break after 10 or 15 minutes. Children with severe problems in attention often require a great amount of redirection and reinforcement to keep them going on a task. In some situations, you will need tangible reinforcements, such as stickers, to keep the child engaged.

Some people are distracted by extraneous noise such as an airplane flying overhead or a conversation just outside the testing room, whereas others do not seem to be bothered. Observe how well the person attends to different types of instructions and tasks. For example, after you give directions for a task, the person may appear confused. Attempt to determine if the confusion stems from poor attention, trouble understanding the language, or difficulty determining exactly what to do. When a person asks you to repeat the instructions, this may indicate the person wasn't listening or that he or she was listening but did not understand the directions.

Activity Level

Observe a person's mannerisms and movements before, during, and after the tests to provide clues about anxiety level, boredom, impulsivity, and coordination. Observe what a person is doing as you first greet him or her. Is she sitting quietly reading a book, pacing around the room, or making conversation with the stranger next to her? During the testing, are his movements slow and deliberate, cautious and hesitant, fast and impulsive, or typical for his age? A person may tap a foot, tremble, or fidget, behaviors that may indicate fear, impatience, boredom, or hyperactivity. The examiner acts as the witness and needs to interpret the behavior for the reader of the report.

Interpret a person's activity level in regard to what is developmentally appropriate for that age. For example, one would not be surprised if a 2-year-old gets out of her seat six times in an hour, but one would be if the person were 20 years old.

Observing posture is also important. An adolescent may be slumped down in his seat almost to the point of sliding under the table. His posture may signify more than simply boredom and may more accurately depict a low self-concept and feelings of hopelessness.

Mood and Temperament

People's moods and temperaments vary. A person may be unresponsive or responsive. The person may seem happy to be participating or fearful of what the results may mean. In some instances, a person's mood is influenced by events that occurred earlier in the day, such as an argument with a parent prior to school. If moods change markedly during the evaluation, try to figure out what factors contributed to the mood change. Moods can also be perceived differently depending upon your own disposition.

People have different temperaments, which influence their response to the environment, their styles of learning, and their strengths and vulnerabilities (Brooks & Goldstein, 2001). Many believe that types of temperament are inborn and that even from birth children's temperaments vary considerably (Brooks & Goldstein, 2001; Chess & Thomas, 1996; Thomas, Chess, & Birch, 1968). Drs. Alexander Thomas, Stella Chess, and Herbert Birch, the pioneering researchers in this field, described temperament as the *how* of behavior. Two individuals may have the same capabilities and motives for completing a task, but they will differ in the intensity and rate with which they act, their moods, the ease in which they approach the task, and their readiness to begin a new activity.

Brooks and Goldstein (2001) reviewed and discussed the three patterns of temperament that Chess and Thomas (1996) described: the easy child, the slow-to-warm-up child, and the difficult child. Although all children do not fit precisely into these categories, these patterns provide a way to consider temperamental differences and the ways these differences can affect the evaluation and the establishing of rapport.

The easy child is a pleasure to evaluate, and both examiner and child find the experience to be enjoyable and pleasant. The child is cooperative and may even request to spend more time with the examiner doing more tests. The slow-to-warm-up child does not like out of the ordinary experiences and requires additional time to acclimate to new situations. This child will display hesitancy when beginning the evaluation. As a young child, he may cling to his parent when entering the office or clinic. The evaluator may describe this child as cautious or shy or as having difficulty taking risks. The difficult child is the most challenging to assess. Children with this type of temperament often have trouble with attention, motivation, and self-regulation. They also may become easily frustrated when they make mistakes. In some evaluations, you may not experience these difficult qualities because the interaction is one-to-one and positive in nature. Your goal is to help the person, and thus he or she may see you as an ally. As you describe behavior, consider the person's moods during the evaluation, as well as his or her temperamental style. As with other information, when contradictions exist (e.g., the child has been described as angry and hostile, but during the evaluation she is cooperative and friendly), attempt to explain why these perceptions vary.

Problem-Solving Strategies

Different approaches can be used for solving problems and responding to situations. Observe how the person attempts to solve problems and the types of strategies that he or she employs. For example, one person may try an approach that doesn't work and then quickly try another one. Another person may examine the problem carefully and proceed cautiously step by step.

Some examinees solve problems by talking themselves through the solutions. For example:

- "Come on. Put the large piece next to the small black piece—but be careful, don't mess up the other pieces."
- "I think that this red block should go beside the white triangular block to make the diamond shape complete."
- "That can't be right. It doesn't even look like what you showed me."
- "Let's see. That must go with that because they are both animals."
- "Because that nonsense word looks like a real word 'curb,' it must be pronounced as "furb.""

The format of a test can also affect a person's use of strategies. On an orally administered math test, some individuals can solve problems without using paper and pencil, whereas others can only produce the answers if they can write down the needed information. A reflective student may have trouble determining a good strategy when asked to perform a task rapidly without time to plan. This student's performance may be higher on tasks that are not timed.

Attitude Toward Self

People often reveal how they feel about the quality of their performance during an assessment. You may observe certain facial expressions (e.g., a rolling of the eyes or a grimace), or you may hear statements that the person makes (e.g., "I should really know this stuff"). Self-deprecating, derogatory, or boastful remarks often indicate a lack of confidence, whereas other behaviors such as blushing may be more subtle indicators of embarrassment or frustration.

Unusual Mannerisms or Habits

Some examinees (particularly those with psychological disorders) may display unusual behaviors such as flicking invisible specks of dust on the table, covering their ears or eyes, spinning a pencil or another object, or ritualistically picking up and putting down a paper clip before each response. Individuals with severe problems may even demonstrate self-injurious behaviors, such as biting on their hands when frustrated or banging their head. Ticlike movements (often of head, eyes, mouth, or cheeks) may also increase when a person is nervous. Be sure to note all odd mannerisms. Raymond, a young man who had been diagnosed with Asperger's syndrome, insisted upon counting all the tiles on the floor before beginning the evaluation.

Raymond also wanted to keep doing a particular type of problem he enjoyed. Although all math testing had been completed, Raymond insisted that he wanted to keep doing long division problems. When coupled with other information, these types of behaviors will often help you formulate an accurate psychological profile. With Raymond, for example, observation of these ritualistic, repetitive behaviors contributed to a clinical impression of Asperger's syndrome.

TOOLS TO ASSESS BEHAVIOR OBJECTIVELY

Some objective aids are available to help clinicians categorize children's behaviors during specific tests. Two instruments were designed to use during the administration of the Wechsler Intelligence Scale for Children–Third Edition (WISC-III): the Guide to the Assessment of Test Session Behavior (GATSB; Glutting & Oakland, 1993) and the Kaufman WISC-III Integrated Interpretive System Checklist for Behaviors Observed during Administration of WISC-III Subtests (K-WIIS; Kaufman et al., 1994). General test behaviors can be assessed with the GATSB and the scale provides standard scores on factor-based scales. The GATSB was normed during WISC-III administrations and has adequate psychometric properties. The checklist by Kaufman et al. includes both subtest-specific behaviors (e.g., obsessiveness when aligning puzzles in Object Assembly or giving opposites for Similarities) and general behaviors such as anxiety and distractibility. This checklist can be used to interpret the child's WISC-III score profile and to help generate an individualized case report. Although the WISC-IV has replaced the WISC-III, both the GATSB and the K-WIIS provide useful guidelines for assessing children's behaviors. These forms can be used during an administration of a Wechsler scale or with other test batteries as well. Rapid Reference 4.2 lists behaviors for some subtests (Comprehension, Block Design, Digit Span, and Symbol Search) from each of the four WISC-IV index scores.

Excerpts from the K-WIIS Checklist for Behaviors Observed During Administration of Several Wechsler Subtests

COMPREHENSION

Which of the following behaviors describe the child during administration of the Comprehension subtest?
✓✓✓

_____ 1. Do not know
_____ 2. Rarely elaborated on an initial response when queried or when asked for a "second reason"
_____ 3. Disagreed with basic premise of items or with society's expectations (e.g., "Paperback books aren't better than hard-cover books," "You want me to say 'give the ball back,' but personally, I'd keep it")

_____ 4. Attended closely to every question read by the examiner
_____ 5. Maintained good eye contact while the questions were read
_____ 6. Asked for repetition of at least two questions
_____ 7. Didn't seem to understand the wording of some questions
_____ 8. Was nervous and ill at ease
_____ 9. Complained about not having been taught the answers to one or more items
_____ 10. At least twice referred back to previous items while answering a later item
_____ 11. Gave up in frustration when an answer was not immediately known
_____ 12. Refused to guess if unsure of an answer
_____ 13. Gave too much detail or irrelevant information when giving reasons and explaining answers
_____ 14. Gave clear, concise responses to questions that were understood
_____ 15. Gave elaborations to answers or made spontaneous comments that suggested an enriched cultural environment

_____ 16. Gave responses or made spontaneous comments that suggested limited cultural experience

_____ 17. Gave some responses that indicated a good sense of humor

_____ 18. Mispronounced several words in the responses to items
_____ 19. Gave abstract answers to several questions

_____ 20. Gave concrete answers (description or specific examples to most items)

_____ 21. For several items, the answer seemed to be on the "tip of the tongue"
_____ 22. Gave at least two responses that suggested impulsive behavior

_____ 23. Gave at least two responses that suggested passive/dependent behavior

_____ 24. Gave at least two responses that suggested hostile behavior

BLOCK DESIGN

Which of the following behaviors describe the child during administration of the Block Design subtest?
✓✓✓

_____ 1. Do not know
_____ 2. Rotated at least two designs more than 30 degrees
_____ 3. Lost the square shape for some designs
_____ 4. Worked diligently with optimal concentration throughout
_____ 5. Spent extra time making sure that the blocks were aligned perfectly
_____ 6. Was too casual in approach and didn't sustain optimal effort

(continued)

_____ 7. Was overconcerned about the timed aspect of the task

_____ 8. Did not understand the importance of working fast

_____ 9. Was distracted by stimuli in the environment

_____ 10. Became very upset when unable to construct some designs

_____ 11. Was slowed down by apparent visual-motor coordination problems

_____ 12. Continued trying to solve at least one design after the time expired

_____ 13. Had trouble understanding the spoken directions of the task

_____ 14. Used the blocks in an inappropriate way (e.g., built a tower)

_____ 15. Was unaware that the blocks were placed incorrectly for some items

_____ 16. Quickly noted and corrected errors

_____ 17. Put blocks together impulsively for some items

_____ 18. Used slow, reflective approach to constructing designs

_____ 19. Used a trial-and-error problem solving approach for most items.

_____ 20. Used an organized, systematic problem-solving approach for most items

_____ 21. Displayed agile eye-hand coordination

DIGIT SPAN

Which of the following behaviors describe the child during administration of the Digit Span subtest?
✓✓✓

_____ 1. Do not know

_____ 2. Attended closely to every number read by the examiner

_____ 3. Insisted that the examiner repeat one or more items, even when told it wasn't allowed

_____ 4. Had difficulty attending to some items

_____ 5. Maintained good eye contact while the digits were spoken

_____ 6. Was distracted by stimuli in the environment

_____ 7. Daydreamed or otherwise seemed preoccupied

_____ 8. Didn't seem to try very hard

_____ 9. Was nervous and ill at ease

_____ 10. Complained that repeating digits backwards was "unfair," "stupid," etc.

_____ 11. Started to answer at least two items before all digits were spoken by examiner

_____ 12. Gave the right numbers, but in the wrong order for at least two trails

For the next two descriptions, enter the child's longest forward and backward spans—the number of digits in the longest span the child got right. (Note: It makes no difference whether the child got the span right on one trial or on both trials.)

_____ 13. Number of digits in longest forward span
0 2 3 4 5 6 7 8 9

_____ 14. Number of digits in longest backward span
0 2 3 4 5 6 7 8 9

SYMBOL SEARCH

Which of the following behaviors describe the child during administration of the Symbol Search subtest?
✓✓✓

_____ 1. Do not know

_____ 2. Responded to most items by looking at the Target Group once, scanning the Search Group efficiently, and marking "YES" or "NO" without referring back to the Target Group

_____ 3. Spent extra time with each item, making sure not to make an error

_____ 4. Worked diligently with optimal concentration throughout

_____ 5. Was too casual in approach and didn't sustain optimal effort

_____ 6. Was overconcerned about the timed aspect of the task

_____ 7. Did not understand the importance of working fast

_____ 8. Was distracted by stimuli in the environment

_____ 9. Was slowed down by apparent visual-motor coordination problems

_____ 10. Held pencil awkwardly

_____ 11. Had to be reminded to continue after coming to the end of a page

_____ 12. Had trouble understanding the spoken directions for the task

_____ 13. Made three or more errors

_____ 14. Responded to most items by going back and forth from the Target Group to the Search Group (sometimes several times per item) before marking "YES" or "NO"

_____ 15. Displayed agile eye-hand coordination

WRITING BEHAVIORAL OBSERVATIONS

When you are ready to begin writing this section of your report, keep in mind a few points:

- Determine the behaviors that you should describe.
- Describe the specific behaviors and use examples.
- Explain to the reader your interpretive hypotheses about the behaviors indicated.
- Support these hypotheses with specific examples.
- Organize your thoughts logically.

You will observe numerous behaviors. Some will lead to increased understanding of the person, whereas others will not. For example, a young girl may have rubbed her eye during one subtest. Originally you thought this behavior may indicate fatigue, but instead she remarked that something was in her eye; this behavior is not worth commenting upon in the written report. To select what is important, look at your list of behaviors and note the ones that are most consistent. The behaviors that are left standing alone (i.e., not supported or corroborated by other behaviors or data) are usually the ones that are the least relevant. As you write about the behaviors observed, select words that clearly depict what you observed. Specific descriptions will improve your communication. For example, writing "Tom's attention was good during most of the evaluation, but on occasion he did not pay attention" does not help the reader understand how Tom behaved during the evaluation. A more thorough description of behavior would be:

> In general, Tom was attentive and cooperative throughout the testing session. On occasion, he showed a puzzled expression, indicating that he did not understand the test questions. He needed to have several questions repeated two to three times before he was able to respond. When the test items were repeated, he was able to respond appropriately. At times, he appeared to be distracted, and on three occasions, he asked questions that were unrelated to the task.

Similarly, simply writing "He was tired" does not provide as clear a description as writing "His continual yawning and eye-rubbing were indicative of fatigue." As we suggested earlier, you should attempt to couple descriptions of behavior with interpretive statements. See Rapid Reference 4.1 for examples of how to pair behavioral observations with interpretations.

Some writers attempt to describe how the assessment went by writing, "first . . . , second . . . , and then . . ." or "in the beginning," "after an hour," and "by the end." For example, the examiner may write, "In the beginning of the evaluation, Charlotte was quiet and reluctant to respond to questions. She would nod her head and provide simple 'yes' or 'no' responses. After the first two nonverbal subtests had been completed, Charlotte became more responsive and answered questions willingly in complete sentences. By the end of the evaluation, Charlotte was openly discussing topics of interest, such as the fact that her pet cat, Whiskers, had recently been bitten by a rattlesnake."

Include the sequence of the behaviors when it is meaningful. In Charlotte's evaluation behaviors observed early in the testing pertained to a gradual establishment of rapport. In another situation, initial behaviors may relate to an ill-at-ease feeling about the testing situation; behaviors observed near the middle of a testing session may relate to a need for a break; and behaviors noted at the end of the session may relate to fatigue or boredom.

In most instances, a step-by-step account of what happened is not as useful as are paragraphs that are organized by clear-cut themes. One paragraph may have the theme of attention; another may describe the person's problem-solving abilities; and yet another may describe the person's level of motivation and persistence.

Influences of Behavior on the Assessment

In the Behavioral Observations section, note any behaviors that may influence interpretation of the test data. For example, if an adult were extremely tired because she worked a double shift before the testing, you would want to reschedule the assessment because clearly the results may not indicate her true capabilities. Similarly, if an adolescent is so guarded that he won't reveal even the smallest amount of personal information, then the information obtained during an interview about his emotional functioning is likely to be of questionable validity.

Statement Describing the Validity of the Test Results

Typically, report writers include a statement at the end of the Behavioral Observations section that indicates the reliability and validity of the results. If results are valid (and also reliable), you may say: "Because he was motivated and attentive throughout all sessions, the results of the present assessment appear to be a valid and reliable summary of Joe's present performance levels." A statement reflecting questionable results would be "The results of the present assessment may not be a valid indication of Mary's current level of functioning because at the end of the assessment she remarked that she had forgotten to take her medication." Because the validity of the results is most often brought into question by behaviors observed during the assessment, such statements are logically placed in the Behavioral Observations section; however, the statement may also be placed at the beginning of the Results section, as certain behaviors can clearly impact the results.

If you feel that the results of the assessment are invalid or a portion is invalid, clearly explain what happened to invalidate the results. Do not report invalid data. For example, imagine that when you were evaluating a young boy on several measures of oral language, he refused to respond. Because he would not cooperate, you do not know what this boy is capable of answering. Thus, the scores on the oral language subtests would provide misleading information about his present level of language. His refusal to respond, however, does suggest underlying emotional or psychological problems.

CAUTION

Sample Factors That May Lead You to Question the Validity of Data

- Although Vicky repeatedly said she feels fine, she nearly fell asleep during the assessment.
- Although he denied it, you suspect Richard had been drinking alcohol.
- The individual was extremely guarded, depressed, anxious, or unresponsive.
- You suspect your client has an undiagnosed hearing loss.
- The individual complained about the setting (e.g., too noisy).
- The individual complained about physical factors (e.g., hungry, tired).

OBSERVING IN NONTESTING ENVIRONMENTS

Clinical observations during an assessment are essential, but, whenever feasible, supplement them with observations made in a natural setting. Observations in everyday life settings such as a classroom, a playground, a cafeteria, the home, the workplace, or a retirement home provide information about a person's typical behaviors. Although naturalistic observations are easier to obtain for children and adolescents than for adults, they are important for anyone who is assessed, regardless of age. Information gathered from a naturalistic setting can verify the teachers' and parents' reports of a child's behavior (or an adult client's self-report) and can also provide a comparison to the behavior you observe in the structured testing environment.

Observational systems can be designed to meet your particular needs for a given assessment. At times you may want to have more quantitative information about behaviors, and at other times qualitative components of behavior may be most important. Generally, a trained observer will either record a variety of behaviors or focus on one or two specific problematic behaviors. The referral question and other test data help determine the types of information to be gathered from the observation.

When observing behaviors in a naturalistic setting, consider these general guidelines. An effective observation is planned carefully and systematically. Before beginning, determine several key components of the observation, including what behaviors will be observed, where the observations will take place, and how the behaviors will be recorded. In defining the behavior or behaviors that will be observed, be as specific as possible. Clear and concise definitions of behavior will help distinguish the target behaviors from other similar behaviors. For example, you may define cooperative behavior by focusing on the specific behaviors involved in cooperation, such as taking turns during games or working together to build something. Other types of behavior are easier to define, such as hitting or crying. Rapid Reference 4.3 lists several behaviors that can be observed using an observational system.

In addition to observing a person's behaviors, you may find it helpful to observe and record the antecedents to the behaviors. For example, if the targeted constellation of behaviors includes aggression, and you observe the child grab-

≡Rapid Reference 4.3

Sample Behaviors Targeted during Observation

ADHD	Conduct Problems	Social Competence	Depression
Off task	Noncompliance	Solitary play	Talking
Fidgeting	Destructiveness	Cooperative play	Playing alone
Vocalization	Aggressive play	Compliments	Negativism
Plays with objects	Insults, threats	Smiling	Frowning
Out of seat	Aggression	Rule making	Complaining
	Arguing	Turn taking	Whining
	Teasing		
	Yelling		
	Humiliating		

Source: Kamphaus and Frick, 1996, p. 185. Copyright © 1996 by Allyn & Bacon. Adapted with permission.

bing a toy out of another child's hands, you would also want to record that the other child seemed to start the incident by first grabbing the same toy. Such an antecedent-behavior pattern is quite different from one in which there was no apparent instigating incident that prompted aggression.

Once you have determined what behaviors will be observed, decide where the observation will take place. If the setting is a school, numerous possibilities exist. If the referral question has to do with how the child is functioning in academic situations, then the best place to observe the child would be during academic classes—possibly during one of the child's worst subjects and during one of the child's best. However, if the referral question has more to do with a child's social functioning, then a less structured atmosphere, such as the playground, would provide more useful observations.

Home observations can be more challenging than school observations, because it is difficult to blend into the background and be unobtrusive. Some people behave in a manner that is far from natural when being observed (e.g., parents may give much more praise and attention to their child than usual, or children may be unusually cooperative). If observations take place in the home, then certain rules may help get the most from the observations. Such rules may include a ban on television watching or talking on the telephone during the observation. During a home observation, ask family members to create a typical situation, such as the parents giving directions to their son to perform a chore or to begin his nightly homework, so that you can observe how the child reacts.

Once you have decided what behaviors to observe and where those behaviors will be observed, then you need to determine how to collect and record the data based upon the behaviors of interest. Three basic categories of data collection are event recording, duration recording, and time sampling. An additional type of recording is narrative or anecdotal recording; this type of data collection is qualitative rather than quantitative.

Event Recording

The simplest of all the recording methods is event recording. All that is required is recording the number of times that a target behavior occurred during a certain interval. Event recording is best suited for behaviors that have discrete beginnings and endings (e.g., being out of seat, hitting). Behaviors that persist for longer periods of time are not as well suited for event recording because it is difficult to delineate when one behavior began and another ended (e.g., solitary play, thumb sucking, reading, listening). The best types of behaviors to record with event recording are brief, low-frequency behaviors (Keller, 1986; Shapiro, 1987).

Duration Recording

Event recording provides data about how frequently a behavior occurs, but duration recording provides data about how long a behavior occurs. During an observation, the length of time of a behavior from beginning to end is recorded. Like event recording, the behavior targeted for the duration recording must be discrete. That is, it must have a clearly distinguishable beginning and end. Crying, temper tantrums, and thumb sucking are good examples of behaviors whose duration can be recorded. Event and duration recording may be used in combination to collect thorough information about both the frequency and the duration of behaviors.

Time Sampling

Time sampling (sometimes referred to as interval recording, interval sampling, or interval time sampling) records behavior within specified intervals of time. The presence or absence of the target behavior in an interval is tallied. Three types of time sampling techniques are available: whole-interval recording, partial-interval recording, and momentary recording (Kamphaus & Frick, 1996; Shapiro, 1987). Rapid Reference 4.4 distinguishes among these different types of interval recordings, and Figure 4.3 provides an example of a time sample recording.

Rapid Reference 4.4

Types of Interval Recording

Whole-Interval Recording	Partial-Interval Recording	Momentary Recording
A behavior is recorded when it occurs at the beginning of the interval and lasts throughout the entire interval.	A behavior is recorded only once during an interval, regardless of how long it lasts or how many times it occurs.	A behavior is recorded if it is present only during the moment when a time interval ends.
Example: Coding out-of-seat behavior in 20-second intervals.	*Example:* Teacher divides the day into 15-minute intervals and notes whether hand raising occurred during the time segment.	*Example:* During 60-second intervals, record whether a child is displaying hand flapping at the end of each interval.

Referred child: <u>Malena</u> Date: <u>February 2, 2003</u>

Comparison child: <u>Samantha</u> Start time: <u>9:30 AM</u>

Class: <u>Mrs. Vasquez</u> End time: <u>9:33 AM</u>

Behavior	Total	Child	10	20	30	40	50	60	70	80	90	100	110	120
On-task	4	Malena	X	X	O	O	O	O	O	X	O	X	O	O
	11	Samantha	X	X	X	X	X	X	X	X	O	X	X	X
Passive off-task	4	Malena	O	O	X	X	O	O	O	O	X	O	O	X
	1	Samantha	O	O	O	O	O	O	O	O	X	O	O	O
Disruptive off-task	4	Malena	O	O	O	O	X	X	X	O	O	O	X	O
	0	Samantha	O	O	O	O	O	O	O	O	O	O	O	O

Figure 4.3. Example of Time Sampling Record

Note. The 3-minute partial interval record includes twelve 10-second observation periods that are each followed by a 5-second pause for recording data. During the 3 minutes, three behaviors were recorded for the target child and comparison child: on-task, passive off-task, and disruptive off-task. An X in the box indicates that the behavior was observed, and an O in the box indicates that the behavior was not observed. The referred child, Malena, was off-task in eight of the twelve intervals, with half being passively off-task and the other half being disruptive off-task behaviors. In comparison, Samantha was off-task only one time out of the twelve and had no disruptive off-task behaviors.

Narrative Recording

This type of recording is different from those discussed earlier because it is not quantitative in nature. Rather, narrative recording provides a running description of a person's natural behavior. You do not need a specific time frame or coding criteria for particular target behaviors. Narrative recording can include both directly observable behaviors and inferences based upon the behaviors observed.

To complete a narrative recording, try to time your observation so that you will view a representative sample of behavior. Some people find it useful to conduct their observations at different times throughout the day. The narrative itself may include a description of the setting, the people in the setting, and the ongoing action. Note the behavior of the person being observed in detail, including what he or she says and does and what others say and do in response. Narratives can be recorded in writing or on a tape. Rapid Reference 4.5 provides an example of a narrative recording.

PUBLISHED OBSERVATIONAL SYSTEMS

In this section we review some prominent assessment systems.

≡ Rapid Reference 4.5

Sample Narrative Recording

As she ran over to the dress-up chest in the classroom, Abby excitedly declared, "I'm gonna be Ariel today, and you be Flounder." Her friend, Ella, who had been quietly following Abby, frowned and replied meekly, "I don't want to be Flounder, I wanna be a mermaid too."

Abby quickly grabbed the sparkly princess costume that was lying in the dress-up chest and put it on over her clothes. She appeared to be standing her ground about the roles that she and her friend were going to play. She turned away from Ella and said proudly, "I'm Ariel, queen of all the mermaids." Then she did a little dance in a circle with her arms floating over her head. Abby appeared oblivious to Ella's feelings as she danced around.

Ella looked distraught and almost tearful. Her head hung low as she quietly sifted through the other dress-up clothes hoping to find another princess costume. She occasionally glanced up at Abby, who was still gleefully dancing as queen of the mermaids. At the very bottom of the dress-up chest, Ella found another dress. It wasn't as fancy or sparkly as the princess costume that Abby put on, but it was a dress nonetheless, and she put it on.

"Come on, do the dance of the sea with me!" Abby commanded Ella. Ella obliged but was clearly not happy with the situation. Abby bounded with excitement and enthusiasm, and she grabbed Ella's hands, forcing her to dance around in a circle with her. Frustrated with Ella's lack of enthusiasm, after a few moments of swinging around in a circle with her, Abby let go of Ella's hands, letting the centrifugal force make them each fly backward and then fall to the ground. Abby laughed wholeheartedly, and Ella began to softly whimper and cry.

Behavioral Assessment System for Children-Student Observation System

Reynolds and Kamphaus (1992) developed and published a short observational system that is designed for use in a classroom setting. Their Student Observation System (SOS) is part of the comprehensive Behavioral Assessment System for Children (BASC). In a 15-minute time frame, the BASC-SOS targets 65 behaviors that are categorized into 4 groupings of positive/adaptive behaviors and 9 groupings of problem behaviors. These 13 categories are defined in Rapid Reference 4.6.

Within the 15-minute observation period, observers record a child's behaviors in thirty 30-second intervals. A momentary time-sampling approach is used to record data, so at the end of each 30-second interval, the child's behavior is observed and recorded for 3 seconds. Recording the observed behaviors is simplified via use of a checklist of behaviors, and additional information is recorded in narrative fashion at the end of the observation.

≡Rapid Reference 4.6

Categories from the BASC-SOS

Category/Definition	Example of Specific Behaviors
Response to Teacher/Lesson (appropriate academic behaviors involving teacher or class)	Follows directions Raises hand Contributes to class discussion Waits for help on assignment
Peer Interaction (appropriate interactions with other students)	Plays with other students Interacts in friendly manner Shakes hands with other student Converses with others in discussion
Work on School Subjects (appropriate academic behaviors that student engages in alone)	Does seat work Works at blackboard Works at computer
Transition Movement (appropriate non-disruptive behaviors while moving from one activity to another)	Puts on/takes off coat Gets book Sharpens pencil Walks in line Returns material used in class
Inappropriate Movement (inappropriate motor behaviors that are unrelated to classroom work)	Fidgeting in seat Passing notes Running around classroom Sitting/standing on top of desk
Inattention (inattentive behaviors that are not disruptive)	Daydreaming Doodling Looking around room Fiddling with objects/fingers
Inappropriate vocalization (disruptive vocal behaviors)	Laughing inappropriately Teasing Talking out Crying
Somatization (physical symptoms/complaints)	Sleeping Complaining of not feeling well
Repetitive Motor Movements (repetitive behaviors that appear to have no external reward)	Finger/pencil tapping Spinning an object Body rocking Humming/singing to self
Aggression (harmful behaviors directed at another person or property)	Kicking others Throwing objects at others Intentionally ripping another's work Stealing

(continued)

Category/Definition	Example of Specific Behaviors
Self-Injurious Behavior (severe behaviors that attempt to injure oneself)	Pulling own hair Head banging Biting self Eating or chewing nonfood items
Inappropriate Sexual Behavior (behaviors that are explicitly sexual in nature)	Touching others inappropriately Masturbating Imitating sexual behavior
Bowel/Bladder Problems (urination or defecation)	Wets pants Has bowel movements outside toilet

Source: Reynolds & Kamphaus, 1992. Copyright © 1992 by American Guidance Service. Adapted with permission.

The simplicity and brevity of the BASC-SOS are assets. Because the method of data collection is direct observation rather than parent or teacher report, unique and valuable information may be gathered from the BASC-SOS. Unfortunately, psychometric data and norms are not available for this instrument. Thus, the lack of reliability and validity data needs to be considered when interpreting the behaviors observed and recorded with the BASC-SOS.

Child Behavior Checklist–Direct Observation Form

Achenbach (1986) developed and published an observational system in conjunction with Achenbach's Child Behavior Checklist (CBCL). In addition to its observational system, the CBCL has report forms for the parent and teacher, plus a child self-report. The CBCL Direct Observational Form (DOF) is a structured method to record observed behaviors of a child during a 10-minute period. The CBCL-DOF was designed for use in a classroom or other group setting. Although the observation is only 10 minutes, Achenbach (1986) recommends observing a child on three to six separate occasions and averaging the ratings so that a representative sample of behavior is obtained.

Three types of information are gathered on the CBCL-DOF: (1) a narrative description, (2) binary coding of on-task behavior, and (3) a 4-point Likert rating of specific behaviors. The narrative description notes the occurrence, duration, and intensity of specific problems during the 10-minute observation. The binary coding of on-task behaviors requires the observer to note whether the child's behavior is on-task or off-task at the end of each minute. The final type of information gathered on the CBCL-DOF is a rating of 96 behaviors. A 4-point scale is used to record whether the behavior was present or not (0 = behavior was not observed to 3 = definite occurrence of behavior with severe intensity, or behavior lasted longer than 3 minutes).

The ratings of the 96 problem behaviors can be summed to calculate a Total Problems score. In addition, two broad-band scores (Internalizing and Externalizing) and six narrow-band scales (Withdrawn-Inattentive, Nervous-Obsessive, Depressed, Hyperactive, Attention-demanding, and Aggressive) can be calculated. The scores obtained from the CBCL-DOF can be used in combination with the teacher, parent, and self-report forms of the CBCL for a multimodal assessment of a child.

The reliability and validity of the CBCL-DOF have been demonstrated in some samples. For example, interrater reliability has been shown to be high for the Total Problems scale in a residential treatment center (.96) and in a sample of boys referred for special services (.92; Achenbach, 1982; Reed & Edelbrock, 1983). The interrater reliability in a sample from an outpatient psychiatric clinic was lower (.75; McConaughy, Achenbach, & Gent, 1988). In an examination of the interrater reliability for individual items in a sample of 25 boys, Reed and Edelbrock (1983) found generally high correlations between observers, with most values above .80. However, some items were much lower (e.g., nervous, high-strung, or tense = .20; picks nose, skin, or other parts of body = .52; and compulsions, repeats behavior over and over = .53).

The discriminant validity of the CBCL-DOF Total Problems scale was shown by distinguishing normal from disturbed children (McConaughy et al., 1988; Reed & Edelbrock, 1983). The Externalizing, On-Task, and Total Problems scores differentiated children with internalizing and externalizing problems (McConaughy et al.). In contrast, the Internalizing scale did not demonstrate the same discriminant validity in the study.

Similar to the BASC-SOS and other observational systems, the CBCL-DOF does not provide norms to which a child's scores can be compared. Although norm-referenced data are not available, the information obtained from the structured observation can be compared to the CBCL reports of parents and teachers, as well as the child's self-report. Overall, the CBCL-DOF is easy to use and provides good clinical information about a child's behavior in a school (or group) setting.

Controls for No Norms in Structured Observations

As we have noted, one limitation of the BASC-SOS and the CBCL-DOF is that no normative data exist to which a child's behaviors can be compared. Thus, it is difficult to know whether the observed child's particular behaviors are truly unusual in the setting in which he or she was observed. A well-trained observer with some understanding of child development can get a sense of how peculiar the behaviors are given the child's gender and age. However, added observation of other nontargeted children can provide baseline information about what is typical for similar children in any particular setting.

One or two children of the same age and gender as the child may provide a frame of reference for the observation. Ideally, you should observe these additional children at the same time as the subject (e.g., using the BASC-SOS or CBCL-DOF). The data obtained about the other children's behaviors will provide baseline information about how children are responding in a particular environment. For example, if you observe that the target student has six out-of-seat episodes during the observation period and the other two nontarget children each have seven or eight of the same episodes, then the student's six out-of-seat behaviors are not atypical. However, if the other two children do not get out of their seats at all, then the subject's six out-of-seat episodes may be interpreted as excessive. Thus, your observation can turn into an experiment with an N of 2 or 3. Changing your observation from a case study to a mini-experiment will provide helpful baseline data for interpreting the person's behavior.

 TEST YOURSELF

1. **The Student Observation System (SOS) and the Direct Observational Form (DOF) are useful forms because**

   (a) they provide a normative base against which a child's behavior can be compared.

   (b) behaviors may be readily noted by marking a checklist.

   (c) they contain every behavior that a child would exhibit in a classroom setting.

   (d) they are both more reliable than most standardized parent reports of behavior.

2. **The Behavioral Observations section of a report should essentially list behaviors observed during each test administered. The interpretation of those behaviors is then included later in the Test Results and Interpretation section.** True or False?

3. **List several categories of behaviors that may be included in the report.**

4. **Specific examples of behaviors may significantly enhance the description of global behavioral characteristics.** True or False?

5. A step-by-step, sequential account of what happened during the assessment is the most useful type of organization for the Behavioral Observations section of a report. True or False?

6. Data from naturalistic settings can be collected in each of the following manners except what?

    (a) dolby recording

    (b) event recording

    (c) duration recording

    (d) time sampling

7. A mini-experiment may easily be created by using a structured observation checklist to observe the child and one or two well-selected comparison children. True or False?

8. A person with a difficult temperament will always be difficult to evaluate. True or False?

Answers: 1. b; 2. False; 3. physical appearance, rapport, language style, response to failure, response to successes, response to encouragement, attention, activity level, mood, problem-solving strategy, attitude toward examiner and testing process, attitude toward self, unusual mannerisms or habits; 4. True; 5. False; 6. a; 7. True; 8. False

Five

TEST RESULTS AND INTERPRETATION

The Test Results and Interpretation section contains data from the tests that were administered, as well as an insightful interpretation of the data. This section integrates and interprets the scores in combination with all relevant qualitative and quantitative data. Interpretations are supported by multiple sources of data, including (1) scores from the various tests administered; (2) behavioral observations, both during the evaluation and in other contexts; and (3) history and background information, including scores earned on tests administered previously. The focus is in on providing a comprehensive picture of the *individual,* not the test scores. The amount and type of information will vary according to the particular referral question, the environment of the individual, and the type of evaluation (e.g., neuropsychological, speech/language, special education). This chapter focuses upon writing the Test Results and Interpretation section of a report and reviews several basic principles of organization, means of addressing consistencies and inconsistencies in data, and ways to describe and report test scores.

PRINCIPLES OF ORGANIZATION

Adhering to the following basic principles will enhance the organization of your report.

- Decide on a basic format.
- Use subheadings.
- Move from global to specific.
- Move from standardized to informal results.
- Use global themes to organize.
- Use contrast to organize.

These basic principles are discussed in the sections that follow.

Decide upon a Basic Format

Three basic formats for reporting results are discussed in this section: domain by domain, ability by ability, and test by test. Various combinations of these formats can also be used. Some evaluators write their test interpretation by integrating data from all measures under subsections that correspond to domains (e.g., intelligence, achievement, emotional functioning, vocational), whereas others organize results by specific abilities (e.g., memory, visual-spatial ability, oral language, visual-motor), and still others organize this section into subsections according to the specific tests that were administered (e.g., WAIS-III, MMPI-2, CAS, KABC-II, WJ III). All three formats present the evaluator's conclusions from both qualitative and quantitative data and inform the reader of the main findings. Rapid Reference 5.1 lists the three different ways to organize the Test Results and Interpretation section and presents sample headings.

Domain by Domain

This type of organizational format is often used in school settings where the evaluation is designed to assess both intellectual and academic functioning. Typically,

---

≡ Rapid Reference 5.1

Ways to Organize Test Results

Domain by Domain	Ability by Ability	Test by Test
Separate paragraphs are written on each domain of interest. Each paragraph may include data from multiple tests.	As in the domain-by-domain approach, specific abilities can be used to organize this section. Multiple tests can be used to describe the specific abilities.	Separate paragraphs describe the results of each individual test. A summary paragraph at the end then integrates the main findings across measures.
Sample Headers:	**Sample Headers:**	**Sample Headers:**
Intelligence Achievement Adaptive Behavior Social/Emotional Functioning	Memory Reasoning Visual-Spatial Ability Expressive Language Receptive Language Visual-Motor Ability	WISC-IV WJ III CAS KTEA-II VMI Vineland MMPI-II

intellectual or cognitive results are described first, followed by performance on measures of achievement. Depending upon the referral question, the report may also describe other domains, such as oral language, social functioning, behavior, adaptive behavior, or vocational aptitudes.

Ability by Ability

This organizational format is the most complex because the evaluator synthesizes information across tests and observations. This type of format is often used in neuropsychological evaluations and in-depth evaluations for learning disabilities.

Test by Test

In this organizational format, the evaluator discusses the results on each test that was administered. Typically, the tests are arranged from the most comprehensive assessment instrument to the tests measuring fewer abilities, or the tests are arranged by domain (e.g., measures of oral language are followed by results on behavioral rating scales). Although the test-by-test format is often the easiest to write, it is more difficult to integrate findings and conclusions from a variety of sources. The Don't Forget box provides a reminder of ways for organizing results.

Whether the organization of the section is domain by domain, ability by ability, or test by test, you may vary the order of the information presented, unless you work for a clinic or an agency that has a standard format for reporting results. A few additional guidelines can help you to arrange your results in a coherent, concise manner.

Use Subheadings

Depending upon the amount of detail included in your report, you will want to include one or more levels of subheadings to help you organize the information. Similar to the major headers used in other parts of the report (i.e., Referral, Background Information, Behavioral Observations, Test Results and Interpretation, Diagnostic Impressions, Summary, Recommendations), these subheadings specify the information that will be included within each paragraph. The types of subheadings will vary according to the referral question and the approach used for organization (e.g., domain by domain or test by test). Sample subheadings to place in the Test Results and Interpretation section for a report organized do-

DON'T FORGET

Ordering Results

Moving from the global to the specific, from comprehensive instruments to ones measuring narrower abilities, or from results from standardized measures to informal results, provides a logical flow of information.

main by domain include Cognitive and Linguistic Abilities (e.g., Oral Language, Memory, Processing Speed), Achievement (e.g., Reading, Math, Written Language), Motor Coordination (e.g., Fine- and Gross-Motor Coordination), Emotional Functioning, and Family Functioning.

In a detailed report of academic performance, you may include additional levels of subheadings (e.g., under the broad heading of Reading, you could have subsections on Basic Reading Skills, Reading Rate and Fluency, and Reading Comprehension). If the report is organized test by test, the headings will be the names of the tests that were administered, and the subheadings can be the various factors measured by the test (e.g., Short-Term Memory) or subscales or composites (e.g., Attitude toward School or Anxiety).

Move from Global to Specific

Most report writers find it helpful to place the most global information first, followed by specific details, or to discuss the most comprehensive instruments followed by ones that measure only one or two narrow abilities. For example, if the main data are about intellectual abilities, then the global IQ is reported first, followed by factor scores and then subtest strengths and weaknesses. In psychoeducational assessments, descriptions of cognitive abilities are presented first and then followed by sections on achievement. In neuropsychological reports, general abilities are often described (e.g., memory), followed by performance on specific types of memory tasks (e.g., short-term memory, visual memory, spatial memory). In a clinical assessment of personality functioning, the data from the most comprehensive instrument often start the report (e.g., MMPI-II or MCMI-III), followed by less comprehensive instruments (e.g., Incomplete Sentences or the Thematic Apperception Test [TAT]). Typically, the main themes are derived from the most comprehensive instruments and further supportive data are obtained from other instruments that measure fewer abilities.

Your major conclusions can go in the first or last paragraph. If your main findings are in the first paragraph, then the subsequent paragraphs will provide data to support these conclusions. In contrast, if you prefer to give your conclusions in the last paragraph, each paragraph in the Test Results and Interpretation section will contribute to building your case.

Move from Standardized to Informal Results

In a psychoeducational report, you should move from the results of standardized instruments to results obtained from informal assessments and observations. Rapid Reference 5.2 provides an example of what you may write.

≡ Rapid Reference 5.2

Example of Moving from Standardized to Informal Results

Manuel scored in the Low range in basic reading skills. His word identification ability was in the Very Low to Low range (Letter-Word Identification test standard score [SS] = 69, 2nd percentile), whereas his ability to sound out phonically regular nonwords was in the Low Average range (Word Attack SS = 87, 19th percentile). On the Illinois Test of Psycholinguistic Abilities-3 (ITPA-3), his ability to apply regular phoneme-grapheme rules to pronounce and spell phonically regular nonwords (Sound-Symbol Processing SS = 86, 16th percentile) was better than his ability to recognize and recall English spelling patterns (e.g., silent e rule, words never end in v) in both reading and spelling (Sight-Symbol Processing SS = 61, below the 1st percentile). Although both abilities are below average, Manuel's ability to apply phonics rules to reading and spelling is more advanced than his ability to recognize and reproduce common English spelling patterns. This discrepancy between abilities can most likely be attributed to gains from specific phonics instruction in the resource room.

Sections of the Brigance Inventory of Basic Skills were given to help provide more in-depth assessment in reading and spelling. This criterion-referenced test revealed that Manuel's instructional level for reading recognition (words in lists) was Preprimer but below this level for oral reading of passages. He knew 15 out of 21 initial consonant sounds and 8 out of 30 initial blends (e.g., st) and digraphs (e.g., sh). His accuracy on the first-grade spelling test was 60% but only 20% on the second-grade test. Manuel confused short vowel sounds, particularly i and u. He did not apply word attack skills for reading long vowel sounds unless prompted. He confused the letters b and d and the names of the letters s and c.

Use Global Themes to Organize

You can sometimes use your central findings or the main themes as a way to organize your report. The two most common types of findings are (1) advanced, typical, or limited performance; and (2) specific talents or difficulties in one or more cognitive, linguistic, academic, social, or emotional domain. Specific themes will emerge as you consider the referral question and explore the consistencies and inconsistencies among the data. Most of the discussion then will center upon the specific questions or themes.

For example, the purpose of an evaluation may be to determine Jen's eligibility for a gifted and talented education program and, depending on the outcome, consider ways to adapt and enrich the curriculum to challenge her. As you interpret the test results, you will also consider findings from background information, such as Jen's stating that she does not find middle school very engaging and that she is bored by the lecture approach used by most of her teachers. Furthermore, her mother has noted that the curriculum is not sufficiently challenging for Jen, that Jen has not been assigned any significant projects or reports this year, and that she has already mastered the eighth- and ninth-grade math curricula via a computer-based tutoring program through Stanford University.

Jen's performance on the WJ III Tests of Cognitive Abilities indicated very advanced cognitive functioning in almost all areas assessed. Given these findings and her high academic grades, you may conclude that she meets the criteria for the Gifted and Talented Education Program (GTEP) in this district. Class placement and appropriate curriculum for Jen may then be determined at the next meeting of the GTEP team.

As another example, teachers may have expressed concern about Ben's erratic school performance. All teachers noted that Ben has difficulty starting and finishing assignments and that he rarely completes homework. Observations in Ben's class indicated that he often leaves his seat without permission and fails to listen to teacher directions. During the assessment, you note that Ben can only focus for a short time on a task and then requests to switch to another activity. Results collected from a rating scale and checklist also indicate that behaviors such as inattention to work, not listening to others, and not following directions at home or in school are common. Although you may discuss other results from the assessments (e.g., level of academic functioning), you would organize the report around the theme of Ben's ability to sustain attention to relevant classroom activities.

Use Contrast to Organize

You can sometimes use contrast as an organizing factor for the Test Results and Interpretation section (Tallent, 1993). For example, in an assessment of emotional functioning if a client appears one way in one setting (e.g., aggressive and hostile) but another way in another setting (e.g., fearful and anxious), you can write back-to-back paragraphs that contrast these apparent contradictions. Similarly, in a psychoeducational assessment, you can follow a paragraph on expressive language with a paragraph on receptive language to easily convey the contrast (or similarities) between the two language modalities. In a neuropsychological assessment, you may have a specific section that compares and contrasts different types of memory—for example, memory span versus working memory.

As an example, in a neuropsychological report, the evaluator explained differences on tasks of visual-spatial functioning in this way:

Juliette's abilities in the area of visual-spatial functioning were within the Average range with no obvious weaknesses (WISC-IV: Picture Completion, 37th percentile; Block Design, 37th percentile; Object Assembly, 25th percentile; WJ COG III Visual-Spatial Thinking, 56th percentile; Spatial Relations, 77th percentile; Picture Recognition, 36th percentile). In contrast, Juliette's ability to combine visual-spatial processing with a motor response when copying simple geometric shapes was within the Below Average range on the Developmental Test of Visual-Motor Integration (VMI, 16th percentile), and significantly impaired when attempting to copy a complex geometric figure on the Rey Complex Figure Test and Recognition Trial (RCFT, 1st %). Thus, her visual-spatial functioning appears adequate when tasks are relatively simple and structure is provided, but it seems problematic on more unstructured, visually complex tasks that require a motor response.

You may also use the contrast between past and present data to organize the results. For example, if Juanita comes for an assessment with a report detailing her functioning prior to her rehabilitation treatment, you will convey to the reader her level of functioning after her treatment. In a paragraph, you will describe her pre-rehabilitation functioning from the earlier report, follow that information with results from the current assessment, and compare her pre- and posttreatment levels. Even if different assessment measures were used, you may compare and contrast specific areas of functioning. For example, you can compare overall visual-motor skills pre- and posttreatment (perhaps they were Below Average and now are Average) or contrast her clarity of speech pre- and posttreatment. You will want to explain why differences exist between current and previous functioning. For example, if Casey's previous assessment describes his severe depression and the current assessment reveals no change in his emotional status after 6 months of psychological counseling, try to determine why the treatment has been ineffective.

CONSISTENCY OF THE FINDINGS

Before writing this section of the report, consider how the data fit together. For some individuals, all data converge on the same main point, but for others, data are contradictory and interpretation challenges even the most competent writer. Consider the following four questions:

1. How are the findings consistent?
2. What patterns of data support the common themes?
3. Which data are contradictory?
4. How can you explain the contradictions?

The Don't Forget box provides a reminder to explore how the findings are consistent or contradictory.

How Are the Findings Consistent?

Regardless of the type of assessment, both the qualitative and the quantitative results of the evaluation will suggest to you common themes about the person. Begin by looking for consistencies in the patterns of scores and reported and observed behaviors. You may detect one or more major themes. To help keep track of the themes, you can create a data chart, such as the one shown in Table 5.1.

As noted in the data chart, your conclusions will be based on several samplings of data. If only one subtest score is low, you will need to find other data to support or negate the importance of this finding. For example, you would not hypothesize that a child has poor social judgment based solely on one low score, on the WISC-IV Comprehension subtest, for example. A person can obtain a low score on this subtest for a variety of reasons that have nothing to do with social judgment (e.g., poor verbal expression, poor verbal reasoning ability, or limited experiences).

Similarly, do not note that a child has poor social skills or poor attention based on only one 10-minute observation during one academic subject. You need more information. For example, you may have three pieces of converging data about a child: He performed poorly on the Comprehension subtest, he displayed poor social skills during a classroom observation, and his parents report that he is unable to maintain friendships. Viewed together, these findings suggest difficulty with social skills. Sometimes, even two pieces of data provide enough support for a hypothesis, if the quality of evidence is strong. Figure 5.1 reiterates the need for forming diagnostic hypotheses based on more than one piece of data.

What Patterns of Data Support the Common Themes?

Examine all data sources for further evidence to support interpretive hypotheses. Look for consistency across (1) test scores, (2) behavioral observations, (3) background information, and (4) previous assessment data. When reporting common themes, attempt to link together cognitive and academic test results, as well as formal and informal test results, with various bits of qualitative information.

Table 5.1 Sample Data Chart for Julia, Age 16

Hypothesis	Tests/Subtests Supporting	Behavioral Observations	Background Information	Supplemental Test Data
Slow processing speed and slow reading rate	• Visual Matching • Digit Symbol-Coding • Symbol Search • Reading Fluency • Test of Word Reading Efficiency	• Approached tasks in a hesitant manner • Skipped a row of numbers • Placed finger under text when reading	• Mother said that Julia has trouble finishing tests. • <u>Contradictory data:</u> Julia reported that she completed most sections of the SAT within the time limits.	Performance on Nelson Denny much higher on untimed (90th percentile) than timed format (10th percentile).
General difficulty with numbers and math	• Letter-Number Sequencing • Arithmetic • Digit-Symbol Coding • Digit Span	• Looked anxious during subtests with numbers • More motor activity during these subtests • Asked: "How many more tests have numbers?" • Did not know common math concepts (e.g., number of feet in a yard).	• Julia and her mother report that math has always been difficult. • Mother said that Julia has trouble balancing checkbook and making correct change.	KTEA-II Comprehensive Mathematics Applications (5th percentile)

First Piece of Data		Second Piece of Data		Third Piece of Data		Interpretation
Johanna has a low score on a test of visual-motor integration	+	No other data	+	No other data	=	Not enough data to support poor visual-motor integration
No other data	+	Johanna's mother provides a drawing of Johanna's depicting component parts not well integrated	+	No other data	=	Not enough data to support poor visual-motor integration
No other data	+	No other data	+	Johanna's teacher reported that she has extreme difficulty with handwriting	=	Not enough data to support poor visual-motor integration
Johanna has a low score on a test of visual-motor integration	+	Johanna's mother provides a drawing of Johanna's depicting component parts not well integrated	+	No other data	=	**Two pieces of information support poor visual-motor integration**
Johanna has a low score on a test of visual-motor integration	+	Johanna's mother provides a drawing of Johanna's depicting component parts not well integrated	+	Johanna's teacher reported that she has extreme difficulty with handwriting	=	**Three pieces of information support poor visual-motor integration**

Figure 5.1 Support Interpretations with More Than One Piece of Data

For example, in describing background information, the evaluator had noted the first-grade teacher's comment that Andrea had extreme difficulty learning and retaining numbers. In describing her cognitive abilities, the evaluator had noted Andrea's difficulties on tasks involving short-term memory and working memory on both the Stanford-Binet-V (SB5) and the Cognitive Assessment System (CAS). In the Test Results and Interpretation section, under the subheading of Mathematics she wrote:

> On formal math testing, Andrea performed within the Low Average range on tests of computation (WJ ACH III: Calculation SS 82, 11th percentile; Math Fluency SS 84, 14th percentile), while performing in the Low range on a test assessing her ability to apply math concepts (WJ ACH III Applied Problems SS 75, 5th percentile). Informally, she was able to count from 1 to 23, but she could only identify 12 of these numbers when they were presented in random order on index cards. It is likely that her marked weaknesses in both memory span and working memory relate to her difficulties recalling number symbols and number names. Her ability to apply math concepts is strongly influenced by the fact that she often directs her attention toward recalling specific information (symbols, names, facts) rather than to thinking through solutions to problems.

Which Data Are Contradictory?

As you examine the data, note any contradictions, and search for explanations for these findings. Contradictions may exist among the data, between the data and teacher or parent reports, or between the data and behavioral observations. Sometimes what you have measured may not be in line with the job expectations or the school curricula. For example, a teacher may refer a student who is struggling tremendously with math in the classroom. The results of your evaluation indicate that the child's math scores are all in the Average range. After examining the classroom math curriculum, you determine that the types of mathematical skills you assessed differ from the skills being taught in the classroom.

In some cases, you will find that several data points lead to one hypothesis, whereas others lead to the opposite conclusion. Clinical observations during the administration of the KABC-II Learning/Glr and Sequential/Gsm Scales and low scores on these scales suggest that Tony, an adolescent male, has attentional problems, but other information suggests that he is suffering from depression. Mary's mother describes her as hostile and uncooperative, but her teachers describe her as polite, hard working, and respectful; during the administration of the Differential Ability Scales (DAS) and the KTEA-II, she was defensive and agitated when she believed questions were unreasonably difficult, but she was otherwise cooperative and pleasant throughout the testing sessions. Regardless of whether one or numerous pieces of data diverge from the main hypotheses, you need to attempt to explain the inconsistencies.

How Can You Explain the Contradictions?

In order to integrate the data and draw appropriate conclusions, you need to address contradictions in the data. You may find that a person has an expansive vocabulary but then struggles on vocabulary tasks that involve longer oral stimuli, such as listening to lengthy sentences and providing a missing word at the end. In some cases, your behavioral observations will help you explain unexpectedly low test scores (e.g., Rafael commented that he was "hungry and having a hard time focusing" during the WAIS-III Letter-Number Sequencing subtest. Because his scores on all other subtests involving memory and/or working memory were in the Average range, this relatively low subtest score is most likely attributed to difficulty concentrating, rather than poor memory).

As another example, Dan, a first-grade student, obtained a low scaled score on the supplemental WISC-IV Word Reasoning subtest, but all his other scores on subtests involving vocabulary and acquired knowledge were in the High Average range. When considering the school schedule (recess at 2 p.m.) and Dan's behaviors during this subtest (he responded to most items with "Don't Know"), the evaluator realized that this low score was most likely because Dan did not want to miss recess.

In other cases, a pattern across tests may explain apparent contradictions in the data. For example, her second-grade teacher described Kiana's memory as "poor," but not all of your test data support this description. Closer examination of her SB5 and KABC-II test scores reveals that only her memory for verbal material is poor, and her memory for visual stimuli is typical for children her age. As another example, a child may obtain low scores on some timed tests but average scores on others. When you look more closely at the data, you realize the low scores involved rapid retrieval of words (WJ III Retrieval Fluency and Rapid Picture Naming), whereas the average scores were on tests involving rapid scanning and matching of visual symbols (WJ III Visual Matching, Decision Speed, and Pair Cancellation). Other factors to consider when examining inconsistent data are listed in Rapid Reference 5.3.

≡Rapid Reference 5.3

Where to Look for Explanations for Divergent Information

- Look at behavioral observations before, during, and after the subtest or test that yielded inconsistent data.
- Consider the type of stimuli (e.g., verbal vs. nonverbal, complex vs. simple, auditory vs. visual, timed vs. untimed)
- Consider the environment (e.g., Were the behaviors consistent during the assessment but different from those observed at school? Is inattention a problem at school, but not at home? Does the mother report oppositional behaviors, but not the teachers?)
- Determine whether any situational factors during the assessment such as anxiety, fatigue, poor attention, or lack of interest contributed to the divergent test scores.

Integrate the findings in your Test Results and Interpretation section by addressing the four questions mentioned at the beginning of this section. To transition between descriptions of findings that are comparable, use cohesive ties and phrases such as *similarly, furthermore,* or *in addition.* To transition between discussions of data that differ from the main findings, use phrases noting dissimilarity, such as *on the other hand, in comparison, in contrast,* or *however.*

INTERPRETATION AND REPORTING OF SCORES

The Test Results and Interpretation section usually contains scores, but the scores can instead be reported at the end of the report in summary tables. In interpreting and reporting scores, keep in mind the following principles: (1) examine all levels of score information; (2) focus on the individual, not the test scores; (3) describe what the person could and could not do; and (4) report scores so they are easy to understand. These topics are discussed next.

Examine Global, Factor, and Subtest Scores

Your data will include scores that are based upon combinations of several subtests, as well as scores that are based on the subtests themselves. In interpreting the test and subtest scores, the total scores, such as a Full Scale IQ or a Total

Achievement score, are some times the least helpful. It is rarely possible to understand functioning by only examining global scores. Stern (1938) commented about the limited utility of a global IQ score:

> To be sure there has been and there still is exaggerated faith in the power of numbers. For example, "an intelligence quotient" may be of provisional value as a first crude approximation when the mental level of an individual is sought; but whoever imagines that in determining this quantity he has summed up "the" intelligence of an individual once and for all, so that he may dispense with the more intensive qualitative study, leaves off where psychology should begin. (p. 60)

Because of its global nature, we encourage examiners to begin the Test Results and Interpretation section with the person's Full Scale IQ (if administered) or a similar composite score, create confidence bands around this score, convert the scores to percentile ranks, and provide a descriptive label. However, as Kaufman (1994) notes, "Beginning test interpretation with the Full Scale IQ does not elevate this global score into a position of primacy. Rather, the Full Scale IQ serves as a target at which the examiner will take careful aim . . . in effect, trying to declare the Full Scale IQ ineffectual as an explanation of the child's mental functioning" (p. 99).

More information is obtained from partial, domain, factor, or cluster scores than from any global score. Once you have considered the factor scores, analyze the person's performance on the various subtests that contribute to the factor score to check for consistent and inconsistent performance. If significant differences exist among the subtests, consider the narrow ability that each subtest is measuring. Attempt to determine the meaning of discrepant scores by viewing this score in light of all other qualitative and quantitative information.

The following quotation from *Standards for Educational and Psychological Testing* (APA, 1999) describes how broad-based scores or combined scores on different narrow abilities can obscure the meaning of the test results.

> Because each test in a battery examines a different function, ability, skill, or combination thereof, the test taker's performance can be understood best when scores are not combined or aggregated, but rather when each score is interpreted within the context of all other scores and assessment data. For example, low scores on timed tests alert the examiner to slowed responding as a problem that may not be apparent if scores on different kinds of tests are combined.

Once you understand the pattern of scores within the context of observed behaviors and pertinent background information, you can consider the consistencies in your findings and formulate a diagnostic hypothesis that is based on all of the acquired information.

Focus on the Individual and Not the Test Scores

Compose your sentences so that they convey results about the person, not the tests or scores. In a discussion about report writing, Dr. Lynne Beal succinctly explained this principle: "We need a paradigm shift in how we think about psychological assessments and how we write psychological reports. We must move away from writing reports on how children score on various tests, to writing about children's abilities, strengths, and needs. Writing about children's abilities makes reports more understandable to parents and teachers, and leads more directly to describing students' strengths and needs for developing educational plans" (personal communication, April 15, 2003). The same principles apply to adults as well, when educational plans are not usually relevant to the reasons for referral.

Similarly, write about the person's abilities, or about the kinds of personality or behavioral traits displayed, and not about what the specific tests, scales, or subtests measure. For example, write "Ophelia displayed a weak range of general knowledge, which was supported by her relatively poor performance on tests that required her to define words and answer questions about general information (KABC-II Verbal Knowledge and WJ III COG General Information test, 10th percentile and 7th percentile)." Do not write "Ophelia performed relatively poorly (10th and 7th percentile) on the KABC-II Verbal Knowledge and WJ III COG General Information subtests, both of which measure vocabulary and acquired knowledge."

In another example, the following sentence inappropriately places the focus on the tests, not the person: "The contrast between her score at the 5th percentile on WISC-IV Vocabulary and the 75th percentile on Peabody Picture Vocabulary Test-III (PPVT-III) suggests that Amanda's receptive vocabulary is better than her expressive vocabulary." A more person-oriented description would be "Amanda's receptive vocabulary appears to be more advanced than her expressive vocabulary. On a test that required her to listen to a word and select one of four pictures (PPVT-III), she scored at the 75th percentile. In contrast, when she was required to define words that she heard (WISC-IV Vocabulary subtest), her score was at the 5th percentile."

It is also best to focus upon the abilities or traits that a test or subtest measures rather than relying on the test's name to communicate what is being measured. Some test and subtest names (e.g., WJ III Analysis-Synthesis, KABC-II Atlantis

≡ *Rapid Reference 5.4*

Example of How to Describe What the Person Could and Could Not Do

The Bayley Scales of Infant Development-II was administered to Greg. His successes and failures ranged from 12 months to 17 months. His performance on tasks that did not require language was more advanced than his performance on those that measured receptive and expressive aspects of language. On the Bayley-II Behavior Rating Scale, Greg's Orientation/Engagement was in the Average range for his ability level, whereas his Emotional Regulation was somewhat Below Average because of occasional silliness. Motor Quality was nonoptimal, although he was able to pick up and use the toys and objects given to him.

Greg was able to imitate scribble strokes with a crayon, and he rolled a car appropriately to indicate movement. At this time, he was unable to identify parts of a doll's body such as hair, mouth, eyes, and nose. When shown a comb and asked to comb the doll's hair, he combed his own, illustrating that he understood the use of a comb. Greg showed interest in turning the pages of a picture book, and he found hidden items fairly easily. He enjoyed viewing his reflection in a mirror and also delighted in trying to see the examiner. He was able to systematically place nine cubes in a cup and three pegs into a form board. Overall, Greg watched materials being manipulated and, with mild encouragement, attempted most, but not all, tasks.

and Rover subtests, SB5 Position and Direction) do not communicate what was measured to readers who are unfamiliar with the tests.

Describe Exactly What the Person Could and Could Not Do

In many cases, you will want to describe exactly what the person could and could not do. You can begin by describing the assessment and then provide specific examples of what the person was able to do. Rapid Reference 5.4 provides an example of what an evaluator wrote in an assessment of a preschool boy with cognitive delays.

Report Scores so They Are Easy to Understand

Report scores in a way that communicates directly, without jargon and without attempting to impress the reader with your level of sophistication. In some situations, it is appropriate to write a few sentences to explain the meaning of the reported scores. Rapid Reference 5.5 illustrates what you may write at the beginning of the Test Results and Interpretation section.

≡ *Rapid Reference 5.5*

Explain the Meaning of the Reported Scores

On the attached score summaries, Mary's academic abilities measured by the components of the WJ III ACH are described as standard score (SS) and SS ranges created by 68% confidence bands (SS ± 1 SEM).

	Standard Score Range						
	<70	**70–79**	**80–89**	**90–110**	**111–120**	**121–130**	**>131**
Descriptive category	Very Low	Low	Low Average	Average	High Average	Superior	Very Superior

The percentile rank (PR) indicates where Mary's score would fall within the scores of 100 or 1,000 students of the same school grade and month. For example, a PR of 75 would indicate that her score was higher than 75 out of 100 grade-peers in the norm sample, whereas a percentile rank of 0.1 would indicate her score was higher than only 1 out of 1,000 grade-peers. The grade equivalent (GE) indicates the median raw score of students in that month and year of school. The Relative Proficiency Index (RPI) is a qualitative score indicating Mary's expected level of proficiency on similar tasks if her average grade-peers had 90% success. RPIs above 96/90 suggest that Mary will find the task to be easy, whereas RPIs below 75/90 suggest that she will find that type of task to be difficult. The following discussion of results is based upon grade norms.

In other reports, you may prefer to use descriptive classifications of the scores, rather than the scores themselves (e.g., Above Average). On tests for which scores are given, usually confidence intervals are available. Because tests contain measurement error, a range of scores (rather than a single score) best represents a person's abilities. For example, write "Jeffrey, age 4, obtained a WPPSI-III Full Scale IQ of 107 ± 3," or "Jeffrey obtained a WPPSI-III Full Scale IQ of 107 (103–111 with 90% confidence)," or "The chances are 90 out of 100 that Jeffrey's WPPSI-III Full Scale IQ is within the range of 103–111." You may select a level of confidence from 68% to 99%. The choice is based upon how confident you want to be. A more stringent level of confidence leads to a wider confidence interval. In many instances, psychologists choose to report intelligence quotient scores with a 90% level of confidence, whereas in others, such as achievement test results, the 68% level is deemed sufficient. Some evaluators choose to define confidence intervals more explicitly in their reports. Markwardt (1991) provides the following example:

Because no test score can be perfectly accurate and any student might score higher or lower if tested again on another day, it is said that the "true" score can only be estimated. To account for the possible variation in test results, a range of score has been calculated for your child. (This range is written in parentheses following the test score obtained by your child.) In interpreting the test results, you should think of your child's score as falling somewhere in that range. (p. 2)

Because tests provide different types of standard scores, the wide range of means and standard deviations can be confusing to readers. Most standardized tests yield scores with a mean of 100 and standard deviation of 15. Others have a mean of 50 and a standard deviation of 10. In addition, on many tests the factors have a mean of 100 and a standard deviation of 15, but the subtests have a scaled score of 10 with a standard deviation of 3.

Most people, professionals and laypersons alike, find that percentile ranks are the most understandable metric. You can easily convert standard scores into percentile ranks by using Table 5.2 or consulting the manual of a given test.

Table 5.2 National Percentile Ranks and IQs Corresponding to Scaled Scores

Percentile Rank	Scaled Score	Corresponding IQ
99.9	19	145
99.6	18	140
99	17	135
98	16	130
95	15	125
91	14	120
84	13	115
75	12	110
63	11	105
50	10	100
37	9	95
25	8	90
16	7	85
9	6	80
5	5	75
2	4	70
1	3	65
0.5	2	60
0.1	1	55

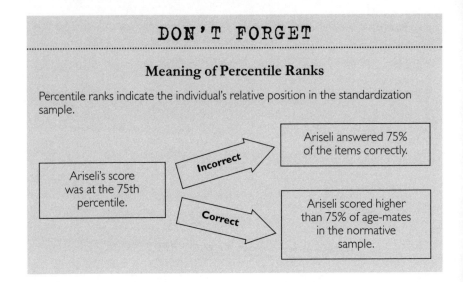

DON'T FORGET

Meaning of Percentile Ranks

Percentile ranks indicate the individual's relative position in the standardization sample.

| Ariseli's score was at the 75th percentile. | Incorrect → | Ariseli answered 75% of the items correctly. |
| | Correct → | Ariseli scored higher than 75% of age-mates in the normative sample. |

Sometimes people confuse percentile ranks with the percentage correct (e.g., thinking that the 75th percentile means 75% correct). Thus, be careful to explain that a score in the 75th percentile means that the person did better than 75% of the normative group, not that the examinee got 75% correct (see Don't Forget box).

In addition to the standard score, confidence interval, and percentile rank, descriptive categories are also useful. The descriptive categories vary greatly according to each test, so be careful to apply the correct category according to the test that you are using. For example, the Wechsler scales use categories of Very Superior to Extremely Low, whereas many of the Kaufman instruments use categories of Well Below Average to Well Above Average or Lower Extreme to Upper Extreme.

Sometimes report writers place scores within the interpretive section of the report, making it easy for the reader to associate the interpretation with the obtained test scores, as shown in Rapid Reference 5.6.

Scores are also provided in a Psychometric Summary (usually at the end of the report). The scores that are listed in the Psychometric Summary are usually grade or age equivalents, percentile ranks, and standard scores. Because they do not have any meaning, raw scores or the number of items correct are rarely included.

Various neuropsychological tests, however, do not yield standard scores (e.g., verbal fluency, grip strength, tactile form recognition), and in these cases the raw

≡Rapid Reference 5.6

Integrating Scores Within the Interpretive Section

Phonemic Awareness and Auditory Processing.

Frankie had significant difficulty on all tasks, both formal and informal, that measured phonemic awareness. These skills are not necessary for oral communication but are critical for the development of basic reading and spelling skills. They include, but are not limited to, blending together separate sounds into a word (e.g., /c/ /a/ /t/ is *cat*), saying the individual sounds in a word (e.g., the sounds in *cat* are /c/ /a/ /t/), and omitting sounds from words (e.g., *flat* – /l/ = *fat*). All of Frankie's phonemic awareness scores were in the Very Low range.

Cluster	GE (Grade Equivalent)	Easy to Difficult	RPI	PR	SS (±1 SEM)
Auditory Process (Ga)	K.9	K.1 to 3.1	60/90	5	76 (71–81)
Phonemic Awareness III	K.5	<K.0 to 1.5	30/90	0.4	60 (57–64)

scores are listed. Generally, tables with clearly labeled columns (subtest, standard score, percentile rank, etc.) are the best way to summarize the scores. Also, clearly indicate the titles of the tests on the top of the score tables, and do not use subtest or scale abbreviations (except in parentheses after the full name has been spelled out), since abbreviations often confuse readers unnecessarily. Figure 5.2 shows an example of a table of scores from a psychometric summary.

Clearly label title of test

Wechsler Adult Intelligence Scale–Third Edition (WAIS-III)

Include confidence intervals and indicate % of confidence

Scale	IQ	90% Confidence Interval	Percentile Rank
Verbal Scale	128	123–131	97
Performance Scale	130	123–134	98
Full Scale	133	129–136	99

Factor Index Scores

Factor	Index	90% Confidence Interval	Percentile Rank
Verbal Comprehension	129	123–133	97
Perceptual Organization	135	126–139	99
Working Memory	124	117–128	95
Processing Speed	108	99–115	70

Label each column with a header

Subtest Scaled Scores

Subtest	Scaled Score	Percentile Rank	Subtest	Scaled Score	Percentile Rank
Vocabulary	16	98	Picture Completion	13	84
Similarities	13	84	Digit Symbol-Coding	11	63
Arithmetic	13	84	Block Design	18	99.6
Digit Span	15	95	Matrix Reasoning	15	95
Information	16	98	Picture Arrangement	14	91
Comprehension	13	84	Symbol Search	12	75
Letter-Number Sequencing	14	91	Object Assembly	14	91

Only report scores that are compared to the normative group (not raw scores)

Figure 5.2 Sample Table from a Psychometric Summary

Wechsler Adult Intelligence Scale–Third Edition (WAIS-III)

TEST YOURSELF

1. **The Test Results and Interpretation section should contain data from**
   (a) only the tests administered during the current evaluation.
   (b) both the tests administered during the current evaluation and supportive background information and behavioral observations.
   (c) only data that support your hypotheses.
   (d) tests administered plus any background information or behavioral observations that you did not mention in earlier sections of the report.

2. **Which of the following provides enough data to document an anxiety disorder?**
   (a) Annika's self-reported anxiety attacks
   (b) Annika's extreme elevation on the Anxiety scale of the MMPI-II
   (c) Annika's observed anxious behaviors during the testing, including excessive motor activity, stuttering, rapid breathing, and so on
   (d) Annika's extreme elevation on the Anxiety scale of the MMPI-II, her self-reported anxiety attacks, and observed anxious behaviors during both testing and school observation

3. **If you feel strongly that Monique has difficulties with tasks requiring short-term memory, but the test results do not support this belief, you should**
   (a) ignore the test data that point to Monique's intact short-term memory and expound upon the fact that her background information leads you to believe she must be suffering from poor short-term memory.
   (b) state that the test data are in direct conflict with what was reported by Monique and determine possible explanations for the contradiction.
   (c) report that Monique's test data must be invalid because they do not support what your clinical intuition is telling you.
   (d) make a big point out of the background information and try to minimize the importance of the psychometric data.

4. **Which of the following illustrates more person-centered language?**
   (a) Hector is experiencing a deep depression, which was evident in both his extreme elevation on the Depression scale of the MMPI-II and his frank discussions with his mother about suicidal thoughts.
   (b) The MMPI-II revealed an extremely elevated score on the Depression scale, which suggests that Hector is extremely depressed.
   (c) Suicidal thoughts and elevation on the Depression Scale of the MMPI-II are diagnostic indicators of major depression, both of which are positive for Hector.

(continued)

5. **As long as common themes are present throughout most of the results, you can ignore the data that diverge from the main findings in the written report.** True or False?

6. **The order of the test results can vary from report to report.** True or False?

7. **Which of the following scores should not ordinarily be reported along with percentile ranks?**
   (a) Standard scores
   (b) Stanines
   (c) Confidence intervals
   (d) Raw scores

8. **Usually, the domain-by-domain and ability-by-ability formats are more difficult to write than the test-by-test organizational style.** True or False?

9. **Percentile ranks are an easily understood metric.** True or False?

10. **Standard scores can be converted into percentile ranks.** True or False?

Answers: 1. b; 2. d; 3. b; 4. a; 5. False; 6. True; 7. d; 8. True; 9. True; 10. True

Six

DIAGNOSTIC IMPRESSIONS AND SUMMARY

S ome reports include a Diagnostic Impressions section as well as a Summary section, and others do not. Diagnostic impressions or clinical implications may be included within the summary section of the report at the end of the Test Results and Interpretation section or in a separate section with its own heading. Although these sections may be combined for clarity, we will discuss them separately. This chapter focuses on how to (1) report your diagnostic impressions and (2) write clear, effective summaries that will lead to the recommendations.

DIAGNOSTIC IMPRESSIONS

After all the data have been analyzed, you will usually form a diagnostic impression about the individual that is based on multiple pieces of data. In addition to the recommendations, clinical impressions—whether formal diagnostic classifications or more descriptive impressions—can be some of the most important information provided by the report (Wolber & Carne, 2002), because they may help explain why an individual has trouble performing tasks or exhibits certain behaviors. When writing a diagnostic impression, you will want to (1) describe data that support the diagnosis, (2) provide enough data to support the conclusion, (3) use a diagnostic code when appropriate, (4) consider the setting of the individual, and (5) consider whether you are qualified to make a diagnosis.

Describe the Data That Support the Diagnosis

When a diagnosis is based partly on data from test scores (such as in the case of mental retardation, a specific reading disability, or giftedness), then explicitly describe the test scores that contributed to making the diagnosis. For example, in discussing a child who appears to have a specific reading disability, you could write "Kara's performances on tests of reading were significantly poorer than would be predicted from her overall intellectual ability. This discrepancy between her WISC-IV Full Scale IQ of 125 and her WIAT-II reading scores (Reading Comprehension SS = 80 and Word Reading SS = 85) are supportive of superior intellectual abilities, in contrast to specific difficulties in reading." You would also include any additional data that further support this diagnosis, such as "Kara's language arts teacher also reported that she reads very slowly in class and often has difficulty pronouncing words. Furthermore, her parents indicated that Kara becomes easily frustrated with her reading homework and often attempts to hide her assignments. Both the test scores and teacher and parent observations indicate persistent difficulties in reading."

Patterns of elevations or depressions in subtests may also provide support for a diagnostic hypothesis. You may write "Michael's depressed mood, lack of energy, insomnia, feelings of hopelessness, and weight gain over the past month are in accordance with his elevated scores on the Beck Depression Inventory and Major Depression Scale of the MCMI-III. This combination of elevations on tests of depression and the constellation of specific depressive symptoms indicates a diagnosis of Major Depression, Single Episode, *Diagnostic and Statistical Manual of Mental Disorders,* fourth edition, text revision *(DSM-IV-TR)* Code 296.2x."

Provide Enough Data to Support the Conclusions

Faulty diagnostic statements occur when not enough data exist to support the conclusion. For example, one report contained the following statement: "Eduardo's inattention was evident in his low scores on subtests that comprise the Working Memory Index of the WISC-IV. He performed equally poorly on tests of oral arithmetic, sequencing letters and numbers, and recalling lists of digits. His low performance on these subtests indicates a pattern of behavior that is consistent with a diagnosis of ADHD." Although poor performance on these subtests may provide some support for a diagnosis of ADHD, without further data it does not provide sufficient evidence for the diagnosis. Additional supportive information from outside the evaluation would be needed to draw this conclusion.

Although some data are more important than others, most of your findings will support your main conclusions. If contradictions exist in the data, provide explanations that explain these inconsistencies. If you cannot resolve the contradictions, do not make a diagnosis, but instead describe the contradictory data and explain why definitive conclusions cannot be reached at this time.

In some instances, the data are not

CAUTION

Do not make a diagnosis when the data are contradictory.

contradictory, but more information is needed before an accurate diagnosis can be made. For example, if the referral question asks whether Samantha has a learning disability but the data are insufficient or inconclusive, then explicitly state that fact. As an example, the evaluator may write,

> Findings consistently reveal Samantha's motor difficulties and poor social skills. Additionally, school anecdotal records and current teacher reports indicate that she is easily overstimulated and has trouble switching from one activity to another. Although her overall profile suggests that she has nonverbal learning disabilities, this type of profile and the accompanying behavioral characteristics can also be present in a host of other low-incidence neurological disorders. Therefore the Assessment and Planning Team should view her current profile as a *preliminary finding* that requires further neurological and neuropsychological evaluation before an accurate differential diagnosis can be made.

Use a Diagnostic Code When Appropriate

Some referral questions request that a specific diagnosis be supported or refuted. In these instances, evaluators record a code from the *Diagnostic and Statistical Manual of Mental Disorders,* fourth edition, text revision (*DSM-IV-TR;* American Psychiatric Association, 2000) or the *International Statistical Classification of Diseases and Related Health Problems,* tenth revision (*ICD-10;* World Health Organization, 1992). Reports from medical or forensic settings often require that the formal *DSM-IV* or *ICD-10* codes be used. These codes and classification systems are regularly updated, so it is important to make sure that you use the most recent edition. Whether the code is written in sentence or tabular format is a matter of style (see Rapid Reference 6.1 for an example of each). In some cases, all five diagnostic categories of the *DSM-IV* system may be

DON'T FORGET
....

DSM-IV Multiaxial Classification System

Axis I: Clinical disorders, Other conditions that may be a focus of clinical attention

Axis II: Personality disorders, Mental retardation

Axis III: General medical conditions

Axis IV: Psychosocial and environmental problems

Axis V: Global assessment of functioning

Source: American Psychiatric Association, 2000. Copyright © 2000 by the American Psychiatric Association.

≡ *Rapid Reference 6.1*

Diagnostic Implications Stated in Sentences or Tables

Sentence Format	Tabular Format		
Mrs. Munson's symptoms fit the classifications of Anxiety Disorder, Not Otherwise Specified (300.00) and Alcohol Dependence (303.90). Although she has tendencies toward paranoid thinking, she does not exhibit disturbances in her basic thought processes.	Axis I	300.00	Anxiety Disorder, Not Otherwise Specified
		303.90	Alcohol Dependence
	Axis II	V71.09	No diagnosis
	Axis III		None
	Axis IV		Threat of job loss
	Axis V	GAF = 55	

included (see Don't Forget), whereas in others, the first two are sufficient. Axis I and Axis II are the most commonly used in psychological and personality assessments.

Axis V refers to the Global Assessment of Functioning (GAF), a rating of overall psychological functioning ranging from 1 (persistent danger of severely hurting self or others) to 100 (superior functioning in a wide range of activities). Midrange ratings of 51–60 indicate moderate symptoms, and ratings of 41–50 indicate serious symptoms. For example, Jessica, a 15-year-old, has a history of social isolation and severe depression. She has attempted to commit suicide five times with plans that had a high potential of lethality. She has few friends and reports that she worries excessively, has difficulty concentrating in school, and is unhappy about her weight. She refuses to take psychotropic medicine. On Axis V, Jessica's GAF was 30.

In contrast, Ryan, a 17-year-old, has a history of early learning difficulties and was diagnosed with ADHD in first grade. He received many interventions throughout his childhood, including tutoring and educational therapy. Although he presently has weaknesses in reading comprehension and spelling, he is emotionally stable and is quite successful in sports. He continues, however, to be disorganized about his schoolwork and to procrastinate in completing assignments. On Axis V, Ryan's GAF was 60.

At times the Diagnostic Impressions section will include several diagnoses or a synopsis of several concerns. As an example, in a neuropsychological evaluation, Rider and Goldstein (2002) provided the following Diagnostic Impression section:

> Rolanda was referred due to a difficult time with attention and concentration in the classroom. Behaviorally, she is occasionally uncooperative in the classroom. Results from the CAS indicated that Rolanda's intellectual functioning as a measure of higher-order thinking abilities falls in the borderline range. Her verbal abilities are one standard deviation below her non-verbal abilities. Rolanda possesses average working memory, non-verbal reasoning and learning capacity, while her planning and attentional skills are markedly deficient. The patterns among scores suggest a verbal language disability, especially on tasks involving meaning and comprehension. If this pattern continues, school will become increasingly more difficult.
>
> By history and current report, Rolanda has difficulty developing self control at home, and, to somewhat a lesser degree, in the classroom. While Rolanda's inattentiveness is at least partially attributed to her neurocognitive profile, her overall pattern of behavior is consistent with a diagnosis of Attention-Deficit Hyperactivity Disorder, Not Otherwise Specified. This diagnosis is made when clinical symptoms are subthreshold, but significant impairment exists.
>
> Children with Rolanda's cognitive profile, particularly those experiencing comprehension and complex thinking problems, often experience anxiety and frustration as they struggle to interpret the increasing demands required by maturity. Rolanda acknowledges worrying about school and finds it difficult to keep her mind on schoolwork. She believes that others can do things at school more easily than she and frequently worries about a variety of aspects of her life. Though the current symptoms and severity are subthreshold for a diagnosis of Generalized Anxiety Disorder, it is the examiner's impression that Rolanda's worries at times do, in fact, cause impairment. A diagnosis of Anxiety Disorder, Not Otherwise Specified appears warranted.

A diagnosis may be qualified with several terms: initial, deferred, principal, additional/comorbid, rule out, admitting, appears warranted, tentative, suggestive of, working, final, discharge, or in remission. In addition, the level of severity of the diagnosis can be specified: mild, moderate, or severe (see *DSM-IV-TR* for definitions).

The evaluator may write: "Overall, her performance on this evaluation was consistent with characteristics of a mild Reading Disorder (*DSM-IV* 315.00) and a moderate Disorder of Written Expression (*DSM-IV* 315.2)." If diagnostic criteria are no longer met, then the following descriptive labels may be used: in partial remission, in full remission, or prior history. Each diagnostic class in the *DSM-IV* has a not otherwise specified (NOS) category, which can be used when the full diagnostic criteria are not met or when there is an atypical or mixed presentation. As examples, the evaluator may write "Axis I: Rule Out Eating Disorder, NOS" or "*DSM-IV* 315.9, Learning Disorder, NOS." In cases where a diagnostic code does not apply, the evaluator may write "Axis II: V71.09 No Diagnosis" or simply "None."

Consider the Setting

The diagnosis may also differ based upon the setting. A clinical or medical diagnosis may be described differently in a school setting. In some cases, it is helpful to explain differences in meanings in diagnostic labels and to predict possible future diagnoses. As an example, a clinical psychologist may write:

> The findings of this evaluation, parental observations, and Reid's history suggest a diagnosis of Asperger's Disorder (*DSM-IV-TR* 299.80). In the school setting, the relevant special education diagnosis that subsumes Asperger's Disorder is Autism (A), because it falls within the autism spectrum. It is important, however, to understand that Reid does not demonstrate the severe cognitive impairments that are typically associated with classic autism. His language is more functional than that of many autistic children. In addition, in classic autism the child may exhibit highly stereotyped motor mannerisms, as well as marked distress when a change occurs in the environment.
>
> While Reid shows some difficulty adjusting to change, this difficulty is most related to his interest and overfocus on a topic or activity. Although in earlier years there were repetitive motor behaviors (e.g., rocking, head banging), these behaviors are no longer present. In addition, in classic autism individuals may show severe self-isolation and no social regard whatsoever, whereas in Asperger's disorder there may be motivation for approaching or interacting with others. Reid shows difficulty comprehending nonverbal gestures and he lacks social and emotional reciprocity, but he wants to interact and play with other children. (Adapted from M. Gerner; unpublished case report)

The psychologist goes on to explain that the prognosis is better for a child with Asperger's:

> Children with Asperger's Disorder often have a more positive prognosis than those with classic autism, and as adults many are capable of gainful employment and personal self-sufficiency. Nevertheless, throughout the developmental period children with Asperger's can continue to need help

with interpreting social situations. They are also more at risk for depression and anxiety-related problems, which can significantly affect school and educational progress, because feelings of social isolation or excessive worry about routines and preoccupation with their own restricted areas of interest can alienate peers.

In the concluding paragraph of the Diagnostic Impressions, the psychologist notes that the final diagnosis will be made by the school team, advises the team to consider an additional diagnosis, and alerts the team to possible problems in the future:

> The Multidisciplinary Team, which includes Reid's parents, will make the final determination of his eligibility for special education as a student who appears to have Asperger's Disorder or the school-age diagnosis of Autism (A). At the present time, Reid is able to function academically in his first-grade setting and there is no need for "pull-out" special education services. The Team also may wish to add a diagnosis of Other Health Impairment (OHI) related to Reid's medically documented Attention-Deficit/ Hyperactivity Disorder. If subsequent academic weaknesses begin to emerge associated with Reid's weaknesses in visual-motor integration, a later diagnosis might also include Specific Learning Disability (SLD).

In other private settings, such as medical, psychological, and forensic evaluations, an individual, not a team, makes the diagnosis, and a formal diagnostic classification is often expected.

Describe Your Clinical Impressions

If a formal diagnostic classification is not included, then state a clear clinical impression. If the results suggest that the person does not have a specific disability (e.g., no learning disability is present), then state that there is presently no evidence of that disability. The results may indicate that the person does not meet the criteria for a specific impairment but does show need for specific supports. For example, the evaluator may write "Although Jordan's level of cognitive functioning does not meet the criteria for mental retardation, her low level of adaptive functioning is of primary importance in determining her ability to live independently. Because she is unable to adequately perform basic housekeeping duties, including cooking and cleaning, she is best suited for a supervised housing situation."

In some types of reports—psychoeducational, educational, or speech-language evaluations—report writers often explain the nature of the problem but do not make a formal diagnosis using a *DSM-IV* code. As an example, the report may state:

Results of formal and informal assessments indicate that Patrick has severe difficulty with spelling. This difficulty with spelling appears to be primarily related to a weakness in orthographic awareness, the ability to recall letters and letter strings. His frequent letter and number reversals, difficulty spelling exception words (words with an irregular spelling pattern), and trouble recalling letter forms are all indicative of impaired recall of spelling patterns. In addition, his difficulties learning to spell are unpredicted, given his advanced oral language and phonological awareness abilities.

In some situations, the evaluator may rule out certain conditions rather than arriving at a definitive diagnosis. The referral question may center upon whether the person does or does not have a specific disorder. For example, Rosa's grandparents and school counselor referred her for an evaluation because all three had observed motor and facial tics and occasional inappropriate vocal outbursts. Rosa's grandmother had recently read an article about Tourette syndrome, and she was fearful that Rosa might have this syndrome. Assessment results and clinical impressions indicated, however, that Rosa did have motor and facial tics but did not display any other characteristics or symptoms consistent with the diagnosis of Tourette syndrome.

In other situations, an evaluator may support one clinical impression over another. For example, Tabbatha, a second-grade girl, was referred for poor handwriting. Her teacher felt that Tabbatha had a severe problem with fine-motor skills. Tabbatha's mother, however, believed that her handwriting was poor because she was always in a hurry to get tasks done and could only focus her attention for brief periods of time. Further examination of quantitative and qualitative information indicated that Tabbatha has adequate motor skills. On timed tests, Tabbatha's writing was barely legible, but on untimed tasks, her handwriting improved. Other findings corroborated that the poor handwriting was more a reflection of impulsivity than a lack of motor control. Tabbatha commented that she just wanted to get her work done fast and she did not care how it looked.

Determine Whether or Not You Are Qualified to Make a Diagnosis

Always consider what types of diagnoses your professional role and training qualify you to make. Unfortunately, a title does not guarantee that the evaluator has the necessary expertise to diagnose a specific condition. Some medical doctors do not have experience with children who are referred for an ADHD diagnosis, whereas others are pediatric specialists who have advanced training in ADHD. As a general rule, when you feel that the symptoms and characteristics of the individual being tested fall out of your realm of knowledge and expertise, do not make a diagnosis; just describe what you have observed and suggest the need for a referral to the appropriate specialist.

In cases where evaluators describe what they have observed, the observations in the report can then be used by another professional as a piece of contributing evidence toward the formulation of an accurate diagnostic impression. For example, the evaluator may observe and report on Ben's difficulties listening to teachers, following directions, and completing assignments. She may gather additional information from teachers and parents from rating scales indicating problems with attention as well as social difficulties because of impulsive behaviors. All findings lead to a clinical impression of ADHD. Ben's pediatrician then uses this report, the data collected from the school setting, a review of developmental history, observations of Ben, and interviews with the parents to help determine medical treatment options.

Finally, keep in mind that diagnostic impressions are just that—impressions. They may suggest future performance, but they do not rule out a different diagnosis at another time. Your evaluation provides a snapshot of a person at one point in time during one period of development. Future assessments may provide further support for your conclusions or suggest that the findings from the past are no longer accurate or applicable.

SUMMARY

This section of a report can be the most influential because in some instances it may be the only section of a report that is carefully read. Some readers, particularly those who have to read many reports, skip immediately to the Summary to quickly ascertain the main findings. Others will read the entire report and then use the summary for reference after the first reading. Thus, the summary often becomes the focal point of the report.

Inclusion of a Summary Section

Although the Summary section of reports is well established in the writing practice of psychologists and related professionals, some evaluators do not include one (Bradley-Johnson & Johnson, 1998; Sattler, 2001; Tallent, 1993). Some reasons for not including a summary are (1) it encourages a reader to ignore the body of the report, (2) it is redundant, and (3) it makes reports unnecessarily longer.

A Summary section is, however, a natural way to conclude a report, and different approaches fit different professionals with different purposes. If you end your report with a summary, make sure that there is adequate support for all statements within the body of the report.

Contents of the Summary Section

Although you will integrate data and discuss interpretations in the Test Results and Interpretation section (as we suggest in Chapter 5), you need to review and integrate key ideas from *each part* of your report in the Summary section. If the main sections of the report are well written, then writing a summary is easy. In a well-written report, the key ideas for each section are easy to gather by scanning the opening and closing sentences of paragraphs, which often convey the main points. When preparing to write the Summary section, first review the key points of each section by rereading the paragraphs' opening and closing sentences. You may want to write down brief points on Post-It notes that capture the main concepts of prior sections. When writing your summary, you can then place the notes in order and quickly prepare a coherent summary.

Briefly, reiterate the reason for referral, pertinent background information, behavioral observations, interpretive results, and clinical impressions. Diagnostic impressions or clinical implications can also be included in the Summary section of a report. Do not use the same wording as in other sections of the report or readers will feel that they are rereading the report. Make sure to rephrase the information and keep it shorter than the original explanation. Figure 6.1 displays the key features of a summary.

How to translate pertinent information into the summary paragraph is exemplified by Joy's case in Rapid Reference 6.2. When writing the summary, the eval-

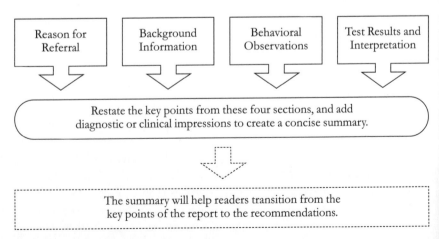

| Reason for Referral | Background Information | Behavioral Observations | Test Results and Interpretation |

Restate the key points from these four sections, and add diagnostic or clinical impressions to create a concise summary.

The summary will help readers transition from the key points of the report to the recommendations.

Figure 6.1 How to Formulate a Summary

Rapid Reference 6.2

Example of How to Translate Pertinent Facts into the Report's Summary

Pertinent Information from Joy's Report	Summary Section of Joy's Report
Reason for referral: difficulty learning and retaining math skills despite long-term math tutoring; referred by parents	"Joy was referred for an evaluation by her parents, who were concerned about her difficulties learning and retaining math skills and concepts despite long-term tutorial support. In addition, Joy's anxiety regarding math has developed into school phobia. She frequently refuses to go to school and has bouts of despair. Currently she is receiving therapy to help her cope with anxiety and fear of math activities in school. In contrast, Joy does quite well in all other academic subjects. Results of this evaluation indicate a specific math disability. Joy requires educational programming in math facts, math concepts, and procedures."
Background information: anxiety concerning math, school phobia, tutoring twice a week for two and a half years in math, and therapy for school phobia	
Behavioral observations: advanced conversational proficiency; stated she couldn't remember how to do certain math problems and hated anything involving numbers	
Interpretive results: Above Average performance in all other academic areas, Low performance in math; Weaknesses apparent in memory, visual-motor coordination, visual-spatial skills, and knowledge of math concepts and procedures	
Diagnostic impressions: specific math disability	

≣*Rapid Reference 6.3*

Sample Template Illustrating Typical Wording of a Summary

"(Examine name) is a (_____)-year-old child who is currently in the _____ grade at (name of school). She was referred for testing by _____ to assess her current (intellectual, academic, emotional, behavioral, personality) functioning. Her current level of intellectual ability falls within the _____ range. Strengths were noted on tasks that required abilities to _____. In contrast, weaknesses were noted on tasks that required _____. These findings are consistent with parental and teacher reports. Overall, her performance on this evaluation is consistent with a diagnosis of _____."

uator focuses upon Joy's persistent difficulties with math. Because the summary will lead directly to the recommendations, it highlights the main points that will be addressed in the recommendations. Rapid Reference 6.3 provides a sample template to illustrate the typical wording of a summary.

Some cases are more complex than others and will require more detail than the example provided. The summary attempts to explain how the various issues interrelate and contribute to an individual's observed difficulties. The following example, adapted from Mather and Jaffe (2002), illustrates a summary of a case with multiple issues:

Gregory Blackhawk is a 7-year-old Navajo boy with ocular albinism, which causes nystagmus and reduced acuity. He was referred for an evaluation because of low academic performance in reading, writing, and math. Both the visual impairment and his limited attention make the validity of formal test scores questionable. Because the majority of his test scores are within the Average range, one can conclude that Gregory has intellectual ability, including oral language comprehension, *at least* on par with second-grade children. Formal and informal test results and analysis of error patterns strongly suggest that Gregory has a learning disability that affects his ability to recognize symbols and symbol patterns, which, in turn, seriously impairs his ability to learn basic reading, writing, and arithmetic skills. Gregory's visual impairment compounds but does not cause these disabilities. Additionally, rating scales, information provided by Gregory's teachers, and examiner observations describe behaviors consistent with a diagnosis of Attention-Deficit/Hyperactivity Disorder, Inattentive type. The combination of these three disabilities causes severe learning difficulties. Nevertheless, Gregory's intellectual and language capabilities suggest that if he receives appropriate, intensive intervention, he can be successful in reading, spelling, and mathematics.

This summary then leads directly to the Recommendation section.

Main Principles for Writing Summaries

Observation of several main principles can help you write effective summaries. In general, attempt to keep your summaries short; do not introduce any new material, avoid vague and ambiguous statements, and describe what the person can, as well as cannot, do. These key principles are discussed briefly in the following sections.

Keep It Concise

Do not attempt to restate everything that was said in earlier sections. Summaries should rarely exceed one page in length and often can be accomplished in one paragraph. In most instances, the reason for referral can be summarized in one or two sentences, key points from the Background Information section can be summarized in one to three sentences, and the key behavioral observations can be described in one to three sentences. Depending on the complexity of the assessment, the summary of the Test Results and Interpretation section can range from a couple of sentences to one or two paragraphs. Often, multiple key findings can be combined into one sentence.

Do Not Include New Material

Do not include any new information in the summary. If new information is introduced in this section, then readers will not know how you arrived at a specific conclusion (see the Caution). When readers read the summary, they should think, "This provides a clear synthesis of what I just read," not "How did the evaluator reach these conclusions?"

Avoid Vague and Ambiguous Summaries

When summaries do not draw definitive conclusions, readers may assume that the answers to the referral ques-

CAUTION

Do not add new information or interpretations of the data in the summary.

Humm…Why does this report conclude with a diagnosis of depression when it was not mentioned before?

tions are unknown or that the examiner's skills are inadequate. Neither impression is desirable. Avoid concluding with a vague statement (e.g., "The results seem to indicate that Irving has a possible tendency toward acting in a somewhat negative manner"). As we noted when discussing diagnostic impressions, if the data you gathered seem unreliable or incomplete, then simply write a clear, unambiguous statement that conveys to the reader that definite conclusions cannot be determined at this time because the available data were insufficient, unreliable, or incomplete.

Describe What the Person Can and Cannot Do

Oftentimes, in the Summary section it is easy to focus solely on the concerns that prompted the evaluation and overlook areas of strength. For example, Steven, a ninth-grade student, was referred for continued difficulties in reading and writing, as well as concerns regarding his general apathy toward school and homework. Although these concerns were confirmed, the evaluator was also able to document Steven's significant strengths on tasks involving nonverbal reasoning and visual-spatial thinking, abilities highly related to vocational success.

You may also want to start this section with statements about what the person can do, followed by a statement regarding what he or she cannot do. Consider these examples:

- In mathematics, Hannah was able to solve word problems involving basic math facts, and she understood basic math concepts. In contrast, she experienced difficulties with more advanced concepts related to fractions and measurement.
- Rosa has strong verbal intelligence, excellent rote memory skills, and good attention. However, she has difficulty making transitions in the classroom and misses social signals that her classmates would immediately discern.
- Steve's intellectual ability falls in the Superior range. He demonstrates advanced performance across a wide array of cognitive and academic tasks. Despite these strengths, Steve feels anxious and overwhelmed when taking timed examinations.
- Becky functions within the Above Average range on measures of oral language and verbal abilities as well as on nonverbal, visual-spatial tasks. In contrast, Becky experiences difficulty when having to attend to and process visual detail with ease, accuracy, and speed.

✎ TEST YOURSELF ✎

1. **Which of the following statements is *false*? The summary should**
   (a) only include information that was already mentioned in the body of the report.
   (b) avoid drawing vague or ambiguous conclusions.
   (c) only summarize the results section, not the reason for referral and background sections.
   (d) be approximately a paragraph to a page long.

2. **If you are not sure of a formal diagnosis, then it is best to let readers draw their own conclusions rather than writing that the data do not lend themselves to a particular diagnosis or that the data are inconclusive.** True or False?

3. **Diagnostic labels, such as those provided by the *DSM-IV* or *ICD-10*, are usually more descriptive than clearly stated general clinical impressions.** True or False?

4. **If contradictions are present in the data, you should provide explanations for the diverging pieces of data so that the final diagnostic impressions are not viewed as faulty.** True or False?

5. **Most people read the body of the report and skip the summary and diagnostic impressions because they simply restate already read facts.** True or False?

6. **It is acceptable to introduce new information in the Summary section as long as you explain why you are reporting the additional findings.** True or False?

7. **The Summary section may include diagnostic and clinical impressions.** True or False?

8. **In psychological and personality testing, the most commonly used classifications of the *DSM-IV* code are**
   (a) Axis I and Axis II
   (b) Axis II and Axis III
   (c) Axis III and Axis IV
   (d) Axis I and Axis IV

9. **In *DSM-IV*, the Global Assessment of Functioning (GAF) score provides a rating of**
   (a) general academic functioning.
   (b) overall psychological functioning.
   (c) overall social and emotional functioning.
   (d) overall behavior and personality rating.

10. **On the GAF, ratings below _____ suggest a serious problem.**
    (a) 80
    (b) 70
    (c) 60
    (d) 50

Answers: 1. c; 2. False; 3. False; 4. True; 5. False; 6. False; 7. True; 8. a; 9. b; 10. d

Seven

PERSONALITY ASSESSMENT

by Rita W. McCleary

This chapter discusses the specifics of documenting personality testing. After discussing general principles of effective report writing, it concludes with a fully annotated evaluation that exemplifies them. A personality report answers specific questions posed by the referring clinician and, very often, by the patient him- or herself. It interprets an individual's personality functioning across a variety of circumstances, represented by different tests and clinical observations. How it is written and how the results are presented to the individual constitute a powerful intervention, typically within the context of ongoing psychotherapy, but also occasionally for the purposes of residential placement and/or other sorts of planning. Above all else, a good personality report furthers our understanding of a person's individuality by using language that is clear, vivid, and persuasive.

FUNDAMENTAL QUALITIES OF A PERSONALITY REPORT

In writing a report for a personality assessment, the following factors are considered fundamental:

- Psychologists serve as consultants in the assessment.
- A personality report is an interpretation.
- Psychological testing is an intervention.
- The diagnostic understanding of personality is dynamic.
- The "level of personality functioning" helps organize the report.
- Identifying the person's strengths is as important as conceptualizing weaknesses.
- Comprehensive personality reports describe the *range* of an individual's functioning.
- Writing personality reports for children and adolescents is challenging.
- Good prose is necessary for a good personality report.

Each of these fundamentals is discussed in the sections that follow.

Psychologists Serve as Consultants in the Personality Assessment

Psychologists asked to conduct psychological testing serve as consultants to whomever makes the referral. They are consulting psychologists with a special expertise in formal evaluations in intellectual, personality, and perhaps neuro-psychological functioning. They ascertain what tests to administer and whether testing for this particular person makes sense in the first place. Perhaps most important, they provide feedback about their findings that attempts to answer the referring clinician's questions and make recommendations for ongoing treatment.

Historically, treatment teams within institutional settings requested comprehensive psychological testing, including a Wechsler intelligence scale and personality measures, often as part of an initial psycho-diagnostic workup. The consulting psychologist gathered relevant information about the patient, helped the team clarify how his or her evaluation could further the aims of the patient's care, and later presented his or her findings and recommendations to the team. Jon G. Allen's 1981 article, "The Clinical Psychologist as a Diagnostic Consultant," is an excellent discussion of this model.

With the changes in lengths of hospital stay and the economics of mental health care in particular, however, few hospitals can afford such consultations. Increasingly, referrals for personality testing, especially for adults, come from individual clinicians and their patients. This makes the psychologist's role as a consultant even more critical.

A good personality report is written for good reasons. This includes at the outset the appropriateness of the referral. For instance, can personality measures reasonably answer the questions posed? Is the person sufficiently stable to undergo such an evaluation? What is his or her level of drug and alcohol use? Has he or she ever had testing before and, if so, when and with what results? What is the psychiatric history? Answering each of these questions will allow the psychologist to determine whether psychological testing for this individual makes sense at present.

Equally important, though, consulting psychologists must consider who wants to read the finished document and why. Perhaps more than any other type of testing, personality assessments are time consuming, emotionally taxing, and expensive. Consultants should make sure that

DON'T FORGET

Before you begin writing, consider these questions:

- What questions are you answering?
- Who are you writing for?
- How will the testing be used?

they know that the evaluations will get used—and how they will be used—before undertaking them. The Don't Forget box reminds you to consider how the testing will get used and presents other questions to consider before writing a personality report.

Just as psychotherapists routinely ask prospective clients why they have sought treatment *now,* testing consultants should ask referring clinicians about the timing of their request for testing. Are they at the beginning of a treatment and having difficulty with a diagnosis, or are they years into a therapeutic relationship and feeling in need of a fresh perspective? Is the therapist hoping to use the testing to persuade the person to consider some auxiliary mode of treatment or to refer the patient on to a residential facility or hospital-based program? The timing of a referral informs its use as much as the specific questions posed by the referring clinician.

As complicated as it can become at times, personality reports must now also aim to respond to the *client's* queries as well as to the referring clinician's. Individuals rarely request testing for themselves, but, unlike a decade ago, the evaluator must now assume that they (or—even trickier—their parents) will read the results. It is also increasingly likely that adult clients will pay out of pocket for some significant portion of the assessment's cost. Since the persons tested are both the subject of study and the report's primary audience, it is critical that the referral questions make sense *to the clients.*

A Personality Report Is an Interpretation

The role of consulting psychologists with expertise in psychological testing is to analyze and integrate multiple sources of data. These data include a variety of standardized measures, the person's history and current treatment, and the consultant's own clinical observations of and interactions with the person. Examiners are responsible for sifting, cross-referencing, evaluating, and synthesizing these converging sources of information and making interpretations that fit them best. It is neither sufficient nor acceptable to provide interpretations of individual tests. It is *completely* unacceptable to string together a series of computer-generated reports of, for instance, the Rorschach and the MMPI-2. Rather, the written personality report should encompass *all* of the data and provide a comprehensive psychological profile or character analysis of the person being evaluated.

There is a great deal of interesting and important debate about whether personality measures are *objective* or *subjective.* They are both and neither. Some measures, such as the Wechsler intelligence scales, generate impressively reliable and valid data recorded in terms of norms and statistics. Others, such as the TAT, are rarely scored but rather are evaluated according to established principles of organization, coherence, and content, in light of the clinician's extensive experience with the instrument. For the purposes of assessing personality, however, both the Wechsler scales and the TAT, as well as the Rorschach, MMPI-2, projective drawings, and other measures, represent more or less standardized observations of behavior across a variety of situations—tests—with different levels of structure and expectation. How diagnostic consultants weave these observations together into a portrait of an individual with strengths and liabilities, conflicts, blind spots, and longings requires a level of clinical hypothesizing and conceptualization that goes beyond reporting "data" in any simple sense.

Good personality reports, like other good clinical reports, create narratives that rest upon carefully gathered information (e.g., history, demographics, intellectual profile, and test scores), while also organizing, making sense of, and breathing life into the facts of the case. David Shapiro's classic book *Neurotic Styles* (1965) remains unsurpassed in arguing for and exemplifying how psychodiagnosticians draw upon their clinical experience, knowledge of psychopathology, and developmental and personality theories to generate plausible explanations of why this particular person views and responds to the world in these particular ways.

Exner (1974) developed his Comprehensive System for the Rorschach as if it were atheoretical, much as the most recent *DSM-IV* constructs diagnoses as if they were purely descriptive. Although most psychological testers use Exner's system—and the *DSM-IV*—all should strongly challenge their assumptions. A value on thinking hypothetically and especially metaphorically is inherent in their work as psychologists (if not as human beings). Whether or not they make it explicit, mental health professionals are continually trying out various conceptualizations as we strive to understand our cases. We also rely upon more or less established theoretical repertoires that we have found useful in the course of work.

In the 1940s and 50s, when psychological testing became established in the United States, consulting psychologists grounded personality reports in ego psychology and psychoanalysis. (See, for example, Rapaport, Gill, and Schafer's [1945–1946] *Diagnostic Psychological Testing* or Schafer's [1954] *Psychoanalytic Interpretation in Rorschach Testing*.) In the case reports accompanying *Intelligent Testing with the WISC-III* (1994), Kaufman uses developmental theory as well as expert knowledge of intellectual and personality measures to make sense of a young child's abilities. This author draws most frequently upon ego psychology, object relations theory, attachment theory, and interpersonal psychoanalysis in an effort to find unifying themes and characteristics in psychological test data.

Test data need not fit into a particular interpretative schema. Unlike many psychologists of the 1950s, most psychologists today do not think that one theory is uniformly best or most true to human nature. Rather, they find themselves trying out various theoretical constructs on the data at hand. They establish a dialectic or conversation between their observations and interpretations. Does Shapiro's hysteric "fit" systematic observations of this individual? Might this individual's difficulty with relationships best be conceived in terms of early attachments? Sometimes a concept illuminates the data; it allows one to develop a useful interpretation. Sometimes it does not, and the examiner must try another perspective (McCleary, 1992). Sometimes, of course, *no* plausible interpretation emerges of some aspect of the testing, and the report needs to state just that.

The Diagnostic Understanding of Personality Is Dynamic

The diagnostic understandings generated by a comprehensive personality report and a *DSM-IV* diagnosis represent different types of information, and they are obtained and used differently. *DSM-IV* diagnoses collate descriptions of behavior into diagnostic categories that are primarily used in the management of symptoms (mania, psychosis, binge eating, and so forth; see Don't Forget box). The diagnostic understanding section of a personality report, instead, interprets the underlying dynamic that organizes and motivates manifest behavior, whether this be an unresolvable conflict between one's self-concept and ideal self, an inability to read another's nonverbal cues, or an unrelentingly pessimistic view of the world that results in distortions of perception and reasoning (see Don't Forget).

In general, personality testing is ill suited for a determination of *DSM-IV* Axis I diagnoses. Establishing whether a person suffers from bipolar illness, for example, includes getting a thorough history of any manic and depressive episodes, a good medical history and recent examination, and a history of past and current drug use. Personality testing, with the possible exception of self-report inventories such as the MMPI-2, does not significantly contribute to the information needed.

Frequently, however, a diagnostic understanding of personality functioning complements and enriches a *DSM-IV* diagnosis. A psychotherapist

> **DON'T FORGET**
> ....
> *DSM-IV* diagnoses are *descriptive* and obtained by
> - systematic, formal interviewing about symptoms
> - gathering a detailed history, especially of the present illness
> - carefully observing behaviors

treating an individual suffering from a major affective disorder, for instance, might ask for testing to determine whether and to what extent her patient suffers from psychosis or under what conditions the patient is most likely to act upon her suicidal tendencies. In other cases, personality assessments provide insights into how individuals experience and cope with their Axis I illnesses. Less commonly, but importantly, analyzing a patient's personality dynamics challenges an Axis I diagnosis. With testing, for example, a psycho-diagnostician might come to understand an individual

> **DON'T FORGET**
>
> The diagnostic understanding of personality is *dynamic* and includes the
>
> - full range of an individual's functioning, from best to worst, across a variety of circumstances
> - individual's defenses and coping strategies
> - quality of thought processes
> - nature and quality of affects and moods
> - level and quality of representations of self and others
> - underlying motivations that organize an individual's actions

provisionally diagnosed with Attention Deficit Hyperactivity Disorder (ADHD) as someone who defends against anxiety with flights of attention that mimic, but are not the same as, ADHD.

Identifying the Level of Personality Functioning Helps Organize the Report

Many personality reports are organized by a characterization of personality organization as either neurotic, borderline, or psychotic. "Level of personality functioning" or "organization" characterizes people's abilities to think clearly, make reasonable decisions, and act moderately in different types of situations represented primarily, but by no means exclusively, by the WAIS-III, the TAT, and the Rorschach. The WAIS-III is a relatively neutral task with a clearly defined end point, the TAT a more open-ended and interpersonally demanding task, and the Rorschach a very ambiguous and emotionally stressful one. No matter what their intelligence, level of education, and creativity, individuals will respond differently to these differing expectations and degrees of structure. Their capacities for perception, affect regulation, information processing, judgment, and decision making will fluctuate by a little or a lot.

An individual whose functioning remains steady, with the exception of relatively discrete conflicts (for example, around gender identity) is probably neurotic. An individual who confuses boundaries between self and others and between fantasy and reality regardless of a situation's clarity is psychotic. And a person whose functioning fluctuates between these higher and lower levels, usually in response to emotional demands, is borderline.

Having such a format for a report is helpful and perhaps indispensable. The danger, though, is relying on it to such an extent that evaluators forget to translate overly familiar concepts into terms that their particular audiences will understand. This was not such a problem in an earlier era, when psychologist-consultants provided written reports only to other clinicians, abbreviating and simplifying their findings for verbal feedback sessions with patients. As readers of test reports have shifted away from hospital-based clinical teams and toward outpatients who expect copies of their reports, however, writing for an intelligent but *non-specialized* reader has become essential. Much more translation of previously acceptable psychological language is necessary.

This author's (Rita W. McCleary) evaluation of a hospitalized patient illustrates how I used to write about an individual's level of personality organization. A 44-year-old man was hospitalized after he became intoxicated and set his shirt on fire in an apparent suicide attempt. His wife and associates reported that in the weeks leading up to his hospitalization he had started drinking excessively and appeared emotionally distraught. Once in the hospital, however, the patient denied feeling depressed or suicidal. His primary clinician referred him for testing to assess his level of personality organization, his potential for suicide, and his capacity for impulse control, memory, and judgment.

Writing a report for this patient's hospital clinicians, I first characterized him as "a man in acute distress." Responding to the referral questions, I subsequently elaborated how and when Mr. X became psychotic and his high risk for self-harm outside of a structured and predictable environment. "His insistence on his comfort with himself and his life—apart from this hospitalization—provides only the thinnest veneer over his near-constant sense that his life is outside his control." I continued,

Mr. X's personality is organized at a borderline level as evidenced by his easy susceptibility to perceptual distortions, faulty reasoning, affective instability, ill-considered actions, and overly self-referential representations of others. He uses a variety of maneuvers to distance himself from his emotions, including intellectualization, minimization, detachment, avoidance, and projection. None of these defenses reliably protects him at present, hence his extreme diffuse anxiety and precarious cognitive and affective organization. At times, the peculiarities in Mr. X's thinking and perceptions reach psychotic proportions.

In the hospital context of several years ago, I felt confident that I could discuss my findings using well-established clinical terminology. As will become clear in the full case discussion at the end of this chapter, I presently think that when individuals are likely to read their reports such terminological short-cuts too often become off-putting and confusing.

Identifying Patients' Strengths Is as Important as Conceptualizing Their Weaknesses

By definition, psychotherapy patients suffer from some sort of psychological distress or disorder. Clinicians most often request personality assessments to clarify the nature and extent of these disabilities. Thus, to contend that testing is equally valuable for identifying how patients function *best* may sound counterintuitive. It becomes less so when one considers the ultimate aim of psychotherapeutic interventions: to expand the range of a person's healthy functioning while decreasing his or her susceptibility to seemingly irrational feelings and actions.

Psychologists, especially less experienced ones, frequently have difficulty recognizing patients' assets. When they test patients who have had multiple hospitalizations and provide disturbed TAT stories and psychotic Rorschachs, pathology seems more interesting and important than health. Yet if a person is *completely* taken over by illness we can have no hope for his or her improvement. An evaluation of such an individual could only confirm an unrelentingly chronic course, a sometimes necessary conclusion. In the absence of any positive qualities—moments of clarity, connection, desire, humor, reflection, and so forth—a report will not contribute to new perspectives and interventions.

It takes practice and open-mindedness to credit psychiatrically ill individuals with their *highest* level of functioning, ascertained from the *entire* testing situation. Out of eagerness to apply his or her expertise in Rorschach interpretation, for example, a psychologist-consultant might overlook something as simple as a patient's willingness to undergo an evaluation, perseverance in spite of frustration, and good use of the consultant's gentle encouragement. More specifically, evaluators should actively seek out the person's best abilities for perception, thought, decision making, interpersonal relatedness, and regulation of emotions, fantasies, and impulses, while paying attention to the particular contexts in which positive attributes can be maintained.

An assessment might establish, for example, that an easily disorganized individual is most able to remain focused and engaged when he knows very specifically what is expected of him and is under minimal pressure to work quickly. Already this information suggests a preliminary treatment plan that includes a

> # DON'T FORGET
>
> ....
>
> *Strengths* provide the building blocks for an assessment's treatment recommendations. These include but are not limited to
>
> - willingness to undergo testing
> - problem-solving strategies
> - sense of humor
> - sensitivity to the examiner's needs
> - real-world accomplishments
> - capacity for self-correction

therapist's establishing with the patient clear ground rules for therapy appointments, his or her willingness to alternate structuring activities with quiet waiting, and a capacity to interpret and respond to the patient's momentary disorganization as a meaningful communication of distress.

Not incidentally, patients appreciate evaluators' attention to their strengths. Patients more than anyone fear negative test findings, ostensible proof that they are bad, defective, guilty, or hopeless. Learning that experts value their positive qualities can have a tremendously salutary influence on their treatment (see the Don't Forget box).

Comprehensive Personality Reports Describe the Range of Functioning

Generally speaking, *DSM-IV* diagnoses categorize psychiatrically impaired individuals in terms of their *worst* functioning or symptoms. A comprehensive diagnostic understanding, by contrast, presumes that personality is not static. People have characteristic ways of interacting with the world that adapt, shift, become diverted, or break down in response to changing demands, challenges, organizations, and desires. We obtain a *dynamic* diagnosis by evaluating the quality of a person's thinking, mood, interpersonal relatedness, fantasy life, and actions across such differing circumstances.

To work effectively, psychotherapists need to understand empathically their clients' unique difficulties and create common ground around strengths. An individual's psychological strengths and weaknesses outline personality functioning or organization. The *range* of emotional states, problem-solving strategies, self-regulatory capacities, and behaviors *between* these points fleshes out and animates a psychological portrait. Most psychotherapists will discern the breadth of their clients' functioning over the initial weeks of treatment. When requested, though, psychological testing should detail the scope of personality dynamics with an eye toward making specific and applicable treatment recommendations.

All individuals fare better or worse psychologically depending on their circumstances, but the particular situations that allow for optimum functioning vary from person to person. An open-ended and emotionally demanding situation may cause one individual to feel anxious and incompetent while providing another with incentives with which she can flourish. The majority of people, for example, stay most alert, calm, and capable when engaged in goal-directed pursuits and in control of setting their own pace. A significant few, though, excel when flying by the seat of their pants, competing intensely with others, or being forced to deal with unexpected crises.

How can psychologist-consultants, working from their offices, evaluate functioning across such an array of situations? By recognizing how the different challenges and demands of the WAIS-III, MMPI-2, TAT, and Rorschach create different sorts of circumstances for people. While each person will respond individually to each test, the tests themselves are standardized. Psychologist-consultants observe and make clinical inferences about how each person responds to these well-defined administrations and carefully note whenever the person deviates from the norm.

Generally, the Wechsler tests approximate structured and emotionally benign situations in which the expectations are clear and the interpersonal climate is relatively free of stress. The MMPI-2 and other self-report inventories are even more structured, but they ask for personal information and require (or allow) people to complete them on their own. The TAT adds choice and the stress of interpreting pictures that are frequently disquieting. It is also more interpersonally demanding, both because individuals must tell stories *to* the examiner and because they are asked to make inferences about the emotional states, motivations, and relationships of the characters in their stories.

The Rorschach is less structured still. The pictures are ambiguous, and people must draw upon their inner resources to discern meaningful percepts. Even relatively trusting people, moreover, have trouble believing that there are no right or wrong answers. Making matters worse, just when they think they have finished, the examiner asks them to review every response again and to state clearly how they saw what they did. This unforeseen demand calls for flexibility, even greater trust in the examiner's good intentions, and an ability and willingness to put into words and share a predominantly private experience.

A discussion of the range of people's functioning falls easily into four parts: (1) when and how they function best; (2) the limits to their highest functioning, even under optimal circumstances; (3) what pulls them away from their best functioning; and (4) what circumstances result in their faring worst. Often answers to specific referral questions, about a patient's psychotic potential or risk for suicide, for example, fit best in one or another part of this analysis.

Psychological Testing Is a Clinical Intervention

Personality assessment is a highly specialized type of extended clinical interview, which is greatly enhanced by the extent of consulting psychologists' clinical expertise. Conducting themselves as clinicians allows them not only to answer many of a patient's questions and concerns prior to beginning an evaluation, but also to write up and provide feedback about their findings in ways that are most likely to communicate them well. The person's responses to the evaluation become integral both to the test data and to how examiners interpret these data for use. Paying attention to the ways in which testing stimulates the person's fears, narcissism, curiosity, or antipathy, in other words, guides the examiner's rhetoric as well as conclusions.

Another, more general way of stating this is that when psychologist-consultants are asked to conduct a personality assessment their responsibility is to present the diagnostic information they gather clearly, specifically, and persuasively to their audience. This means using what they come to know about their audience to guide how they write for and talk to *them*. The primary goal of writing—and verbally discussing—a personality report is to communicate findings effectively to the referring clinician(s) and the person referred (see the Don't Forget box).

Having agreed that the reasons for testing a particular patient at this particular time are valid, testing consultants view themselves as collaborating with the referring clinician(s) to orient, shift, or enhance the treatment. They consult with the clinician before, during, and after the testing, doing all they can to use the clinician's unique relationship with the patient to make what they write and say accessible to them both.

Whenever possible, testing consultants should also include the referring clinician in the feedback session with the person referred. This underscores that they are working together to enhance the person's mental health. Aligning themselves with the primary clinician in such an immediate way places consultants' feedback in this psychotherapeutic context. Meeting as a mini-team also invites the person him- or herself to become more engaged in the diagnostic process. This frequently helps him or her feel less anxious about, more able to hear, and more comfortable exploring what the psychologist-consultant is saying. Consultants might also feel reassured in a joint feedback session in which the primary clinician repeats, rephrases,

---

DON'T FORGET

The Rhetoric of Report Writing

- Consider how the person's personality dynamics will affect how he or she interprets the report.
- Use language that is clear, specific, and persuasive.
- Provide verbal feedback to the client and referring clinician together whenever possible.

or reexamines the findings, as needed. Although examiners should invite individuals to call if they have subsequent questions or concerns, the value of an assessment resides in the *ongoing* and *collaborative* use of the written and verbal reports with their primary clinicians.

The Challenges of Writing for Children and Adolescents

One could write a separate chapter on the obstacles to writing test reports simultaneously suitable for both clinicians and their clients. Young children, most obviously, should not read their personality evaluations, although providing them with age-appropriate verbal feedback is essential. Their parents will request written reports, however, and most of the rhetorical recommendations made in this chapter apply.

Parents have an added layer of defensiveness, about which psychologist-consultants must remain sensitive. Many fear that their children's difficulties reflect negatively on them, and sometimes they do. Only in an ideal world could an examiner say what needs to be said in a nonoffensive, nonjudgmental, *and* accurate way. Psychologist-consultants, in collaboration with referring clinicians, must often make difficult compromises.

Adolescents undergoing testing pose even more difficult issues, much as conducting individual psychotherapy with them does. Parents have both legal and moral grounds for wanting information about their adolescents' functioning, at least until their children reach age 16, if not 18. By the age of 13 or 14, though, most teens need and deserve some amount of privacy and separateness from their parents. To complicate matters further, troubled teens and their parents are very likely to misunderstand, mistrust, and dislike one another. Adolescents often believe that psychotherapy is a punishment for their unacceptable behaviors, that the psychologist is colluding with their parents, and, by extension, that the testing will be used against them.

There are no easy resolutions to these conflicts. Sometimes, when relationships between adolescents and their parents seem too estranged, destructive, or otherwise dysfunctional, you may choose to decline a testing referral unless or until some form of family counseling is established. In similar cases, you may insist on having parental permission to discuss their child's evaluation with all relevant clinicians, educators, and so forth to make implementation of the report's recommendations more likely.

Feedback sessions in tandem with the referring clinician, always desirable, are imperative for adolescents and their parents. The adolescent's psychotherapist, psychologist, or counselor already has experience mediating and setting boundaries around the adolescent's relationship with his parents and will, one hopes, continue to do so with regard to psychological test results. Do your best to persuade older adolescents to attend an initial feedback session separately from their parents, to give them an opportunity to ask questions and express concerns more freely. Such a private meeting demonstrates respect for adolescents as young adults and minimizes their fears that authority figures are talking behind their backs and trying to control them.

Another consideration that affects how reports are written is the generally wider audience a child's or adolescent's personality evaluation is likely to have. Specifically, personality reports are often sent to schools, where the confidentiality of records is far less stringent than in private offices. If the primary purpose of the assessment is school-related—to determine a child's eligibility for social and emotional supports, for example—the examiner must make his or her case without betraying information best left within a therapeutic context. A father's alcoholism, mother's affair, or brother's suicide may have profound consequences for the child or adolescent, but it remains the family's prerogative, not the psychologist-consultant's, to choose what and how much to disclose. Fortunately, word-processing programs let evaluators block-delete sections of the report they agree are not suitable for school records.

None of these provisos precludes making every reasonable attempt to write clearly and specifically. Whether they are written for patients and therapists, parents, educators, or the clinical staff at a treatment facility, remember that reports are always interventions and as such aim to communicate, persuade, and influence decision making.

Good Reports Are Written in Good Prose

A well-written report offers a fresh perspective on a person's inner life. Conveying what makes a person tick succeeds best when the language used is lively, descriptive, and original. In the course of an evaluation, psychologist-consultants take extensive histories and make very careful observations. Their goal is to write up this information in a way that conveys a person's particular individuality. As they prepare to write, supervisors often encourage their students to attempt to see the world through their patient's eyes, to feel what it is like to live as this person, and then to put those insights into words. Most supervisors would strongly discourage students' use of overly theoretical language, which, among other things, emphasizes the distance between themselves and their clients. The style of prose in reports differs from the style endorsed in the APA's guidelines for journal articles and dissertations.

Although many psychological and educational reports are written in the third person, the analysis of personality report writing in this chapter takes the possibly controversial position that testing consultants should write about their interactions with testing patients in the first person. They should also avoid using the passive voice whenever possible (see Chapter 2 for more discussion of passive vs. active voice). For example, instead of writing "The examiner met with Ms. X for three appointments, and the patient was encouraged to ask about the testing before she began," this author would write, "*I* met with Ms. X three times, and *I* encouraged her to ask about the testing before *we* began." These simple modifications make reports easier to read and follow. At a more conceptual level, this author is committed to the view that test data include information that examiners gain directly from interacting with clients. Their observations of how people make them feel, the responses they elicit, their conversation before and during the formal tests, and what the examiners can infer about emotional states throughout add invaluably to their interpretations of TAT stories and Rorschach responses. Writing as if "the examiner" were someone—anyone—else masks the source of this information and its obvious relevance to the person's modes of relating, most notably to the evaluators.

It might seem as if striving to communicate the particulars of an individual's personality would preclude consultants relying upon theory in their interpretations of their test data. This is not the case. As stated earlier, well-established theories, concepts, and metaphors are ways that testing consultants gather together test results and identify the patterns and dynamics of a person's functioning. Optimally, there is a creative tension between the two. Examiners try out a concept on the data at hand and assess how well it accounts for the data. Conceptualizing a case should shed light on people's personality rather than obscuring their personality in over-generalizations.

Rather than continuing this general discussion of how to write effective personality reports, I provide the following example to illustrate the recommendations I am making.

CASE ILLUSTRATION

As in all cases presented in this book, the names and identifying information have been changed to protect confidentiality. The following report was written at the request of a colleague, Stacey Corcoran, and her patient, a single woman in her early 40s, Elizabeth R. Ms. R has reviewed this report and has given permission to include it in this chapter. Alongside the report, Rapid Reference boxes call out important information about how and why each section was written as it was.

PSYCHOLOGICAL EVALUATION OF ELIZABETH R [BY RITA W. McCLEARY]

Background Information and Reason for Referral

Ms. R is a Caucasian woman in her 40s who completed all but one semester of college (see Rapid Reference 7.1). She reported receiving excellent grades but noted that she figured out by age 22 that she wanted to work independently (see Rapid Reference 7.2). She presently co-owns a successful business with her brother. Ms. R is the oldest of three children born and raised in New England. Her parents are retired and in relatively good health, and they now reside in Florida. Although they were never diagnosed or treated, Ms. R stated that she thinks both her maternal grandmother and her father have suffered from depression. She also characterized her brother, to whom she is very close, as having a hard time psychologically, not unlike herself.

Ms. R began individual psychotherapy with Stacey Corcoran in January to better understand her difficulties with intimacy and commitment, as well as to better manage her intense anxiety (see Rapid Reference 7.3). In discussion with me, she described herself as being an "overachiever" with "high energy" who sometimes wonders how she manages everything she does. Both she and Ms. Corcoran requested psycho-

⟫Rapid Reference 7.1

There is no reason to write an extensive introduction in Ms. R's case. I wrote this report for her and her therapist's use in psychotherapy and established early on that Ms. Corcoran had already taken a good history. My primary goal in the introductory paragraphs was to frame Ms. Corcoran's referral questions in a way that Ms. R would find relevant and engaging.

⟫Rapid Reference 7.2

The Referring Clinician's Concerns

Ms. Corcoran told me that her patient was simultaneously extremely anxious and very ambivalent about seeking help. Although Ms. R talked animatedly and at length about her difficulties, Ms. Corcoran felt she maintained too much control over her narrative. Ms. Corcoran noted Ms. R's well-established defenses, in particular her strong tendency to submerge her psychological issues in bodily preoccupations (bulimia, bodybuilding, and breast augmentation). Ms. Corcoran also felt frustrated by Ms. R's refusal to consider medication because of the possibility it posed of weight gain. A written, comprehensive personality report, we agreed, might serve as a touchstone, something that would lead back to Ms. R's reasons for psychotherapy when the work became stuck or derailed.

logical testing to identify how best to understand and ameliorate her long-standing relational patterns and sometimes crippling anxiety. Ms. R asked specifically if testing could uncover the "unconscious fears" that inhibit her making "conscious choices" (see Rapid References 7.4 and 7.5).

Ms. R has had therapy previously, most recently about 10 years ago. At that time she had suffered from bulimia "nonstop" for a decade. This therapy enabled her to control her

≡ Rapid Reference 7.3

The Client's Referral Concerns

By integrating Ms. R's questions with her therapist's in "Reasons for Referral," I underscored the importance of Ms. R's willing involvement to the evaluation and treatment. I used her understanding of her conflicts and dilemmas to emphasize testing, and psychotherapy, as *collaborative* relationships of a sort Ms. R wanted in general but with which she had had little success.

≡ Rapid Reference 7.4

Flag key points for later integration. The second sentence of my introduction acknowledges Ms. R's preference for working independently and her readiness to walk away from previous commitments, sometimes impulsively. I noted that one semester shy of graduating from college, probably with honors, she dropped out. My task in this section of the report is not to uncover the story behind this dramatic change, of course. Rather, it is to flag it, as a preliminary illustration of the diagnostic understanding that will follow.

Similarly, in my final introductory paragraph, I pair Ms. R's earlier history of "nonstop" bulimia with her current investment in bodybuilding and recent cosmetic surgery. Extensive discussions and interpretations do not belong in the introduction. Including information that will later be interpreted, however, makes for a coherent and persuasive report.

≡ Rapid Reference 7.5

Not every detail obtained needs to be reported. I chose *not* to mention Ms. Corcoran's concerns about her patient's refusal to take medication until the Recommendations section of the report. In part, this was because determining whether and what type of medication to prescribe is not an appropriate reason for personality testing. Collecting a history and identifying manifest symptoms is far better. Mostly, though, I did not want to intensify Ms. R's anxieties about therapeutic relationships by framing the testing report as ostensible evidence for how Ms. Corcoran was right and her patient wrong. Rather, I aimed primarily to understand what motivated Ms. R's exhausting need to "manage everything" in ways that would promote therapeutic exploration. I could then suggest medication as one possible means of coping more effectively in a way that emphasized that the decision remained hers.

eating disorder, although she has had some relapses, most recently this past summer. In other respects she reports having good health. She competes in fitness and bodybuilding and denies any substance abuse. Ms. Corcoran told me that Ms. R had breast augmentation surgery this past December. Ms. R was on no psychoactive medications at the time of the evaluation.

Tests Administered

Wechsler Adult Intelligence Test, Third Edition (WAIS-III)
Minnesota Multiphasic Personality Inventory–Second Edition (MMPI-2)
Sentence Completion Test
Projective Drawings
Rorschach
Thematic Apperception Test (TAT)
Object Relations Inventory

Diagnostic Understanding

The extent to which Ms. R strives to know herself psychologically is both dazzling and disarming (see Rapid Reference 7.6). At least when she is with others, she

≡Rapid Reference 7.6

Should behavioral observations be placed in their own section? Some clinicians do not write a separate Behavioral Observations section. Instead, they just interpret the person's dress, manner of interacting with the examiner, mood fluctuations, and conduct during the testing per se as data to be interpreted with the person's history, course of treatment, and, most importantly, test results. The underlying premise is that they need not separate their observations from their diagnostic understanding of the person's personality functioning.

Except in Ms. R's report, this author (McCleary) almost always does create a separate Observations section. Despite a strong commitment to integrating and interpreting data, I am persuaded that the most helpful reports bring a person alive for their readers. Examiner's selectively describing their perceptions and experiencing of clients helps them achieve this aim.

My interactions with Ms. R, though, so perfectly illuminated my diagnostic understanding of her that it made little sense to describe them separately from the body of the report. Certainly, I could have used an Observations section to describe her appearance and other quirks of her presentation, but I decided these did not significantly enliven my conclusions. For the purposes of this chapter, the lack of a visual correlate to my psychological portrait of Ms. R helps to protect her identity—a bonus, if an atypical one.

closely monitors her thoughts and feelings, as well as others' actual and imagined responses to her. She plays with competing images and insights, sometimes humorously, other times defensively. Ms. R places a high value on her rich emotional life, but she acknowledges that her passionate nature and constant self-examination exhaust her. When I asked her to describe herself during our third and final testing session, she observed:

> I would say there are probably not many people who think as intensely or are as intense as I am. I am on high drive, overdrive, driven! [She took a tissue as she started to weep.] I'd say I was a very passionate, sensual, creative, expressive woman who's equally delighted and tortured by her feelings [pauses and sighs]. I have a very hard time in revealing myself to people in totality and yet I crave being the thing I can't do, so I'm constantly at odds with myself.

The results of my evaluation consistently support Ms. R's self-evaluation. She feels split in two—between delight and torture, distrust and desire, fear and ambition. She lives with conflicts and confusions that all too often threaten to unravel her sense of herself as a whole person. (The Don't Forget box suggests how to begin a discussion of a client's personality functioning.)

Pondering her test data, I found myself wondering if I could say anything to Ms. R that she had not already thought of herself. More than once she commented plausibly on the relevance of a TAT story or a Rorschach response to her "intimacy issues." At other times I felt as if she were daring me to do better than she. Near the end of the Rorschach, Ms. R challenged me directly. Having exclaimed, "I see a penis!" she laughingly continued, "Actually, I see a few of them if you want to get real about it! [She tossed the card down.] I've given you pubic

---

DON'T FORGET

Begin the Diagnostic Understanding section with a "W" paragraph. Psychodiagnosticians should begin a discussion of personality functioning by imagining themselves under a person's skin and seeing the world through his or her eyes. Characterizing a person's most fundamental attitudes and assumptions in this way is analogous to a response on the Rorschach, scored "W," that accounts for all aspects of the blot. Such an initial summary of findings is useful for several reasons: (1) It underscores the consultant's efforts to provide a psychological portrait that captures a person's individuality; (2) it requires a synthesis of diagnostic materials; and (3) rhetorically, it is more likely to grab a reader's attention successfully than the more technical analyses of defenses and conflicts that follow.

bones, penises, and angels, and a few bear rugs; let's see what you do with that!" At no time during the many hours we spent together did I doubt that Ms. R longed for me to help her feel less tormented. Gradually, though, I also realized that her compulsion to see and feel and do everything on her own protects Ms. R as much as it prevents her from gaining the intimacy she longs for (see Rapid References 7.7 and 7.8).

Ms. R's quick intelligence, wit, and verbal fluency are indisputable assets. She

---

≡ Rapid Reference 7.7

The "W" Paragraph About Ms. R

My "W" response to Ms. R comprises two paragraphs and draws upon my experience of her and some of our conversation, both observations and much of the test data. I was not kidding when I wrote in the second paragraph that "I found myself wondering if I could say anything to Ms. R that she had not already thought of herself." She had provided me with a rich and varied protocol accompanied by a running commentary that revealed the impressive extent to which she had already identified and analyzed key aspects of her personality. Stymied at first, I ultimately decided that my feeling of having nothing new to offer her revealed something essential about Ms. R.

≡ Rapid Reference 7.8

Revealing Some of the Examiner in Analyzing the Client

I could have written my second paragraph in a less self-revealing but, I think, less effective way in view of the referral questions. I could have simply reported Ms. R's self-analyses and apparent challenge for me to do better in an Observations section, without recording how these affected me. Or I could have made a more general interpretation, such as "Ms. R feels torn between her wish for help and her defensive need to take care of herself; she longs for intimacy but also avoids it." Neither of these alternatives, however, conveys as vividly Ms. Corcoran's difficulty connecting with her painfully anxious patient at the same time that Ms. R both longs for and fears such a bond.

In effect, what I tried to communicate to both Ms. Corcoran and Ms. R was my understanding of their impasse from my own "inside" view of it. I offered my firsthand experience of Ms. R's dilemma to let her know how it affected me and, by extension, her therapist. In effect, I hoped to help her feel more comfortable thinking *together* with Ms. Corcoran about how they in some sense share her conflicts about control and intimacy. Whether conceptualized as role-responsiveness, countertransference, or reenactment, the conflicts that dominate Ms. R's inner world simultaneously construct an interpersonal reality.

uses them, however, in a variety of high-level defenses against becoming too deeply involved with others. As much as she wants to love and feel loved, Ms. R scarcely distinguishes this desire from a wild, destructive, and potentially deadly passion. For her, falling in love brings the risk of feeling inadequate, ugly, threatened, and frighteningly out of control. Intellectualization, a professed faith in things working out, and a self-defying confrontation of what scares her help Ms. R to avoid the very relationships she wants (see Rapid References 7.9 and 7.10).

Of a TAT picture of a young woman leaning against a doorway with her head in her hand, for instance, Ms. R told the following story, after a lengthy pause:

This woman is in some sort of classroom or some sort of learning or educational environment and everyone else has left. Something doesn't make

≡ Rapid Reference 7.9

Don't use technical jargon to describe personality functioning. I did not characterize Ms. R's personality organization as borderline, although I could have. Borderline has become an overused diagnostic label that is too frequently confused with Borderline Personality Disorder, even by clinicians. Moreover, any associations Ms. R might have had with the term—on the edge, marginal—would have probably seemed pejorative.

I could have detailed evidence for Ms. R's borderline personality organization in terms of her "inconsistent control over her impulses, poorly integrated representations of self and others, defensive use of intellectualization and avoidance, and a counterphobic embrace of self-defeating behaviors." She would probably have responded negatively. For most people who are untrained in certain psychological theories, these terms and phrases sound off-putting and vaguely threatening. One could argue that even psychologists talking among themselves might question using language that creates such distance between themselves and their clients.

≡ Rapid Reference 7.10

Analyze personality organization with comprehensible terms. Writing a more comprehensible and communicative report does not relieve evaluators from analyzing personality organization, of course, even though evaluators are often tempted to minimize serious pathology for fear that clients who read about it will feel angry, depressed, or hurt. Balancing honesty and accuracy with an appropriate level of sensitivity sometimes seems impossible. In the third, fourth, and fifth paragraphs of my Diagnostic Understanding section on Ms. R, I provide information about her defensive use of her intelligence, her erratic emotions, her harsh view of herself, and her self-defeating behaviors, but in a style that flows from the section's introduction instead of shifting to more technical terminology. I also lead with her most positive and adaptive qualities, her "quick intelligence, wit, and verbal fluency."

sense. Instead of leaving, she's decided she's going to grab a chair and sit down and just wonder or contemplate. She just wants a few minutes alone to try to put a few pieces together.

Ms. R wept as she developed her story and said at the end that it was hard for her (see Rapid Reference 7.11). She concluded it "happily," although still crying, with the woman "figuring it out [viz.] that whatever she chooses it's all going to be okay." Later she identified this as her favorite TAT story in part because "in that one I just left the classroom, left everyone else, and just went down into deep places no one else wanted to go. And it wasn't easy, but I know I'm going to be fine, better than fine."

In her narrative, Ms. R explicitly identifies herself with a woman striving painfully and ultimately successfully to figure herself out—alone (see Rapid Reference 7.12). She wants to put the pieces of her self together intellectually, relatively freed from the intense passions that usually dominate her life. Although Ms. R credits the general support of an impersonal

---

≡Rapid Reference 7.11

Convey understanding for the person's dilemma. Individuals undergoing testing almost always know that they feel disturbed—and disturb others—even those angry adolescents who protest that their parents made them seek help. Psycho-diagnosticians might have to reassure clients routinely that they are not mind readers, that at best they will provide new perspectives on thoughts and experiences of which the individual is already to some extent aware. Most people suffering from lapses in reality testing, for instance, know that at times the world makes no sense to them. The examiner's challenge is to phrase these sorts of findings in ways that convey understanding and sympathy for the person's dilemma.

≡Rapid Reference 7.12

Use the client's words to exemplify your point. In Ms. R's case, I showcased her favorite TAT story to demonstrate my understanding of her dilemma. The story featured a protagonist with many of Ms. R's strengths: intelligence and love of learning, determination, discipline, and self-reliance. Ms. R ended her story on a note of self-affirmation and hope. Without detracting from its positive qualities, my interpretation of Ms. R's story brought its subtext to light. I emphasized that although the protagonist figured out "that whatever she chooses it's all going to be okay," she had to "leave everyone else" and go "into deep places no one else wanted to go." The plot of Ms. R's story echoed themes I found throughout the testing. It exemplified the defensive use of her intellect to avoid passions and relationships that frighten and overwhelm her. I introduced my interpretation on territory Ms. R had established, extending images and metaphors that she had created.

"learning environment," she does not imagine herself working with a teacher or collaborator. The character in Ms. R's story believes that no one *wants* to explore her innermost life with her. In view of the testing as a whole, I believe that Ms. R feels terrified by the possibility that someone might try. This clearly has implications for her psychotherapy, as well as for her interpersonal relationships generally. It is to her credit—as well as evidence of her counterphobic pursuit of what frightens her—that Ms. R participated in this evaluation with candor and openness (see Rapid Reference 7.13).

In fact, Ms. R does best in situations like, but not limited to, educational environments, in which she can work relatively independently and for which specific sorts of learning or achievement are the goal. She has strong intellectual abilities, especially in the verbal realm, and is very highly motivated to do well. She is extremely adept at solving a variety of problems and enjoys working quickly and efficiently. Not surprisingly, Ms. R is also someone who places a high value on self-sufficiency and thinking for herself. She is unafraid to challenge authority when a particular situation calls for it and is capable of finding innovative ways to achieve her objectives. Ms. R's anxiety does not significantly impair her functioning in these sorts of circumstances (see Rapid Reference 7.14).

Even at her best, however, Ms. R experiences feelings of inadequacy that inhibit the range of situations in which she might otherwise participate. Open competition makes her self-conscious. She feels afraid that others find her lacking and tends to avoid activities that involve comparing her abilities directly with theirs. She becomes easily resentful of what she experiences as external pressures to excel in socially conventional ways, and this resentment only intensifies her tendency to question authority.

After completing the TAT, for example, Ms. R identified as her least favorite a story she had told to a picture of a little boy staring at a violin. In her story, the

---

Rapid Reference 7.13

Identify both strengths and weaknesses in the results. Ms. R's strengths became evident from her history and presentation, prior to the formal evaluation. Notwithstanding her acute anxiety, years of bulimia, and multiple, near-disastrous love relationships, her successful management of her own business established a very high level of motivation, determination, planning abilities, focus, frustration tolerance, and relatedness to others—at least in certain circumstances. During our meetings, moreover, Ms. R spoke in a lively, intelligent, and appealingly self-deprecating way, even though she felt so nervous that she had to wipe the sweat from her palms. Once we began the testing, she demonstrated evident pleasure at solving intellectual problems, often using innovative strategies.

≡ Rapid Reference 7.14

Begin to consider how to link strengths with treatment recommendations. The sixth paragraph begins, "Ms. R does best in situations like, but not limited to, educational environments [like, but not limited to, the WAIS-III], in which she can work relatively independently and for which specific sorts of learning or achievement are the goal." The report goes on to specify the strengths that become evident under these circumstances: Ms. R's intelligence, articulateness, high motivation, creative and efficient problem solving, self-sufficiency, and independence. Anticipating (but not yet writing) "treatment recommendations," I could begin to consider how Ms. R's desire to do well, creative problem solving, and verbal facility might become great assets for her psychotherapy.

Even in the best situations for her, however, Ms. R feels uncomfortable with open competition and fearful that others will find her lacking. She defends herself from feeling criticized by blaming what she experiences as external pressure to conform. The report as a whole makes clear that this conflict—between wanting others' recognition and defiantly rejecting her own desire—is central to Ms. R's psychological life. To emphasize its importance, and to frame it in her own words, I quoted her first and least favorite TAT story, about a young boy burdened by "all of the 'shoulds'." That Ms. R is likely to experience many of her psychotherapist's interventions as criticisms and demands begins to make treatment planning more challenging.

Overall, the report states, in more open-ended and interpersonally demanding situations Ms. R adopts as her own the old adage "the best defense is a good offense." Her attitude toward others, we can assume, will pose particular problems for her open-ended, collaborative, and emotionally demanding therapeutic relationship. Ms. R's psychological need to stay busy further hinders her making a strong connection to her clinician.

child debates whether or not to practice. He eventually chooses not to and "never becomes good at the instrument." Later, Ms. R commented that this story "reminded me of all the 'shoulds,' all the things that you should do, the battles, and the shame if you don't choose the right 'should.' Yeah, I just look at this picture and think, 'I've got to, I have to, I've got to, I have to.' But I don't really want to!" Even though Ms. R repudiates the struggle to make socially rewarded choices, she is not freed of it. She cares too much about how others might evaluate her even as she claims to defiantly opt out.

Ms. R does less well as situations become more open-ended and interpersonally demanding. As her preference for operating independently is curtailed and she feels increasingly inferior and alienated from others, her resentment and rebelliousness grow. At these times Ms. R adopts the adage "the best defense is a good offense." She accentuates her willingness to break some rules and make her own path in order to distance herself from, and thus feel more in control of, the humiliating sense of herself as a failure.

≡ *Rapid Reference 7.15*

Explicit references to theoretical concepts generally do not add to reports. I do not usually include theoretical concepts explicitly in personality reports. The concept of preoccupied attachment, however, seemed to characterize perfectly Ms. R's insecurity about others' emotional availability, for two reasons. First, the visual image of a preoccupied child "determinedly maintaining [her] level of play, no matter what" captured my sense of Ms. R's inner world much more than the theory per se. Like that child, who ignores her mother's comings and goings, Ms. R remains engrossed in activity. She remains separate in order to stay emotionally safe. By sharing my image of the preoccupied little girl, I attempted to bridge the gap Ms. R typically maintains between herself and others.

Even if Ms. R resisted my invitation to connect emotionally, though, she could still appreciate intellectually the concept of preoccupied attachment. Like the woman in the TAT story who stayed in the classroom after everyone else had left, Ms. R might later piece the ideas offered by the report into her experience of her life.

Ms. R also keeps herself busy. I found myself thinking of both Melanie Klein's "manic defense" and the more contemporary notion of "preoccupied attachment" as I considered what motivates Ms. R's compulsion to keep pushing herself (see Rapid Reference 7.15). Briefly put, in the past decade the developmental psychologist Mary Main has reworked Ainsworth's classic studies of the "strange situation" and developed a classification system for how mothers and infants relate to each other. She argues that securely attached children at 18 months will play happily in unfamiliar situations as long as their mothers stay with them, will cry when their mothers leave, and will greet their mothers joyfully when they return. "Preoccupied" toddlers, instead, minimize the effect of their mothers' presence or absence by determinedly maintaining their level of play no matter what. Main hypothesizes that these children's busyness provides them with an important means of managing their insecurity about their mothers' emotional availability, at the expense of fully developing relationships with others. I think that Ms. R's self-described "driveness" functions similarly, as a way of keeping herself safe—and separate—from the negative assessments and rejections she presumes others intend for her.

The good news is that Ms. R has not succeeded in disengaging from her desires to feel loved and nurtured. This desire brought her into psychotherapy and provides a basis for her to hope that she will figure out her "intimacy issues." The bad news, though, is that Ms. R has almost no internalized experience of feeling loved *for herself*. As a result, she fares worst in situations in which the ways that others feel for her are paramount. In a funny way, she might feel happier if she did

≡ Rapid Reference 7.16

Additional client narratives support the main points. Although the report illustrates Miss R's worst level of functioning with yet another TAT story, let me reiterate that I base my interpretations of each level from *multiple* observations and sources of data. However, TAT stories are particularly compelling because they directly demonstrate how individuals talk to a clinician (the evaluator) about the origins and fates of feelings and relationships. Using personal narratives to illustrate more general interpretations of their dynamics minimizes an individual's common apprehension that clinicians see hidden aspects of their personalities and/or impose their views more or less arbitrarily.

not care so much about other people and if she were the type of person who kept herself apart, a loner. Even though Ms. R certainly functions best when operating on her own, she also feels lonely. When she becomes intimately involved with someone else, however, she feels unhinged. Living "constantly at odds with [her]self," as she put it, creates a fundamental instability that most threatens to defeat her, sadly, when she feels in love.

Ms. R's dilemma—of wanting to feel loved and valued, but fearing the destruction she believes such loving can cause—is illustrated in another TAT story (see Rapid Reference 7.16). To a picture of a woman holding another woman who is slumped on a stairway, she said,

> This woman looks like she possibly fell down the stairs or collapsed and the woman above her either is picking her up . . . actually she looks like she's strangling her [Ms. R laughs], but she doesn't have the passion on her face as if she's strangling, there's no sign of struggle, and there's no emotion that she'd indicated that the person was loved or valued . . . This could almost be a nursing home and this is an attendant or nurse.

When I pushed her to choose which story she wanted to tell, Ms. R opted for the impersonal one, a story about a nurse helping an elderly woman who fell and who will "get a little more time on the planet." She pulled back from the disturbing story involving a love that has the power to make one feel murderous. Ms. R made a similar connection between love and loss of control, though, when I asked her to describe her mother. With humor, as well as resignation, she told me that her mother, a "passionate" woman, "has loved me wildly and driven me crazy, at the same time!"

Intimacy threatens Ms. R in several ways: The intense emotionality of it distorts her ability to perceive herself and her circumstances realistically and flexibly; it exposes her extremely negative sense of herself; her feeling out of control of it fuels her ever more desperate and risky attempts to prove the opposite; and the shame of it at times makes her feel suicidal. In Ms. R's inner world, women are both blessed and cursed by their deep feelings, men are powerful and insensitive to their effects on women, sex is "suffocating and invasive," and yet the desire to feel loved dominates everything (see Rapid Reference 7.17).

What concerns me most are the extreme measures Ms. R takes to reassure herself that she can regain control of her passions in spite of how ugly, humiliated, and crazy they make her feel (see Rapid Reference 7.18). I think that we can interpret her eating disorder in this context. When Ms. R binges, she gives herself over to a completely unchecked desire for what she craves. When she purges, though, she forcibly regains control over and rejects her neediness.

Even more seriously, as she feels increasingly desperate, Ms. R begins to indulge how she feels crazy, as if by choosing to act outrageously she can reestablish herself as competent and intact. It is as if she wants to prove

≡ Rapid Reference 7.17

Confronting the Client's Weaknesses in Writing

Identifying when and how a patient does poorly in a document he or she will read is the most challenging aspect of writing a personality report. Even patients already in therapy, who have agreed to psychological testing, do not typically welcome confronting their "weaknesses" directly. The psychologist-consultant must balance sensitivity with honesty when writing about personality flaws for which patients often hate themselves.

≡ Rapid Reference 7.18

Presenting Ms. R's Weaknesses

For Ms. R, the love and passion she so desires also make her feel, and act, "crazy." She does desperate, self-denying things in an understandable yet dangerously misguided attempt to regain control. Over and over again the testing established the intensity of her self-loathing and the distance she will go to deny to herself needs she finds humiliating. In writing about her most dysfunctional self, I aimed to offer her a different, less judgmental, and more benign perspective. The testing revealed that she does not value herself much. Ms. R needs to hear and read repeatedly that her clinicians do.

In particular, Ms. R needs to hear that her clinicians feel concerned about her high risk for self-harm. Ms. Corcoran did not ask about this specifically, but psychologists' ethics dictated that I report it. Just as importantly, however, the report offered Ms. R a way to make at least provisional sense out of feelings and behaviors she had previously viewed as nonsensical. Yes, her suicidal tendencies alarmed me. Beneath them, though, I discerned and validated Ms. R's comprehensible wishes to feel less scared and out of control. By answering her self-condemnation with interest and caring, the report also anticipates recommending as a treatment goal that Ms. R "learn how to love and respect herself."

≡Rapid Reference 7.19

Are the referral questions answered? In some instances, one or more referral questions remain unanswerable, despite the examiner's best efforts. For example, some clients agree to testing but remain extremely guarded throughout. This certainly provides useful information, but rarely enough to ascertain the quality of their fantasy lives, whether they *have* active fantasy lives, their risk for suicide, or their representations of self and others. At best, psychologist-consultants can speculate, provided that sufficient data exist to do even that much. Sometimes examiners must state that the test data shed no light on what the referring clinician wants to understand. In this case, the consultant must respond to the clinician's query with a regretful "we still do not know."

More commonly, test data suggest more than one plausible answer to a referral question. A person's difficulty with concentration, for example, might stem from anxiety, a learning disability, or transient psychotic episodes. In these cases, the psychologist-consultant's task is to organize the findings into more and less likely interpretations, in view of the data as a whole.

What is most important is that examiners identify and discuss each and every referral question cited in the report's introduction. If they cannot answer a referral question definitively, it is their responsibility to say what they can while clearly acknowledging the limitations of their interpretations.

that passion does not overwhelm or defeat her, but rather that she *wants* to think and act in wild and scary ways. In the moment, Ms. R's giving herself over to passion does provide her some degree of relief. It also, of course, has the potential to endanger her life. Ms. R described her brother, whom she loves deeply and with whom she feels closely identified, as "a little time bomb of feeling." The same descriptor can be applied to Ms. R herself (see Rapid Reference 7.19).

≡Rapid Reference 7.20

Summary Paragraph

In the summary paragraph of Ms. R's report, I returned first to her strengths: intelligence and real-world accomplishments. This reinstates balance to my analysis of her personality following the immediately preceding discussion of her psychological liabilities and risk for self-harm. Especially for someone as sensitive to negative judgments as Ms. R, it reminds her that psychological experts credit her highest levels of functioning, not just her lowest.

Summary and Recommendations

Ms. R is an intelligent and accomplished woman whose anxieties about her adequacy within interpersonal relationships have created a painful and frequently destabilizing ambivalence at the core of her personality (see Rapid Reference 7.20).

The intensity of her desire for intimacy is matched only by her fears, and by the humiliation Ms. R believes she will suffer if her inner life is revealed. She alternates between a near manic level of activity and moments of excruciating despair. Her mantra is that in the end she will come out fine, but she really does not see how.

Ms. R's ambivalence about intimacy and commitment will inevitably dominate her participation in therapy as they did her engagement in psychological testing (see Rapid Reference 7.21). Unlike some individuals, however, who become very guarded and aloof in the face of perceived threats, Ms. R forces herself to keep going. Interactions become a highly demanding dance of self-revelation and retreat. The problem is that at a certain point Ms. R loses her hold on what she is doing. Her perceptions become distorted, her thinking self-referential, her emotions overwhelming, and her behavior potentially self-endangering.

Because of the counterintuitive defenses Ms. R has developed, what I earlier termed her counterphobic embrace of what scares her most, it is useless to tell her stop trying so hard (see Rapid Reference 7.22). She knows that already; she becomes so exhausted it makes her cry, and still she pushes on. What will help more, and what I understand from Ms. Corcoran has already begun in their sessions, is for Ms. R to learn ways to control better the pace and manner of her self-exploration. She needs to

Rapid Reference 7.21

How the Summary Leads to the Recommendations

I next reprise Ms. R's anxieties and ambivalence about interpersonal relationships. These are absolutely key to her relationship with Ms. Corcoran, about which most of the recommendations pertain. Anticipating the issue of medication, which I know Ms. Corcoran wants addressed, I then note the wide swings in Ms. R's moods from near mania to deep despair. The paragraph ends by recognizing Ms. R's strong wish to get better coupled with her inability to accomplish this on her own.

Rapid Reference 7.22

The summary poignantly emphasizes points and does not simply restate them. These interrelated themes segue naturally to a paragraph about how Ms. R's predominant personality style will affect her experience of and interactions with Ms. Corcoran. To some extent, this paragraph also summarizes material already presented, but with an emphasis on its ramifications for psychotherapy. In particular, it highlights her great difficulty pacing herself and her tendency to lose perspective on what she can reasonably achieve. I remind Ms. Corcoran and her patient that the consequences of this anxious and self-denying determination have serious implications for Ms. R's thinking, judgment, emotional balance, and ability to keep herself safe.

recognize and value her ability to slow herself down and take a deep breath—in effect, to take care of herself. Ms. R craves others' love and respect, but she needs to learn how to love and respect herself (see Rapid Reference 7.23).

Ms. R told me at a certain point that she has pursued a number of spiritual disciplines (see Rapid Reference 7.24). I did not take the time to ask her to elaborate. As I have worked on my interpretations of her test responses, though, I have thought that she might benefit from some practice of meditation. At present, Ms. R participates in highly disciplined exercise, certainly a healthful step away from her earlier eating disorder, but still an activity in which pushing herself to—and beyond—her limits is paramount. She would benefit more, I believe, from disciplines that aim toward "centering": accepting oneself where one is, staying in the moment, and seeking inner peace. In psychotherapy circles, dialectical behavior therapy is reputed to help individuals learn mindfulness and a range of self-soothing or self-regulating behaviors to counter self-damaging means of managing anxiety like binging and purging, for example. If such a therapeutic group is not available, though, various forms of yoga or Zen meditation could also provide some of these strategies.

I understand that Ms. R is considering Ms. Corcoran's recommendation of medication but is hesitant because of the possibility of gaining weight (see Rapid Reference 7.25). I

≡ Rapid Reference 7.23

The Primary Treatment Recommendation

The ground is now prepared for my primary treatment recommendation: "Ms. R [needs] to learn ways to control better the pace and manner of her self-exploration." The following paragraphs elaborate ways that she might get help achieving this. Prior to the evaluation, Ms. Corcoran had already told me about strategies she had begun to use to give Ms. R room to catch her psychological breath and become more mindful, and respectful, of her mounting anxiety. I allude to these, relating them to the longer-term goal of Ms. R's learning eventually to care lovingly for herself in this way.

≡ Rapid Reference 7.24

Work the client's strengths into the treatment recommendations. I then return again in this section to aspects of her personality that Ms. R likes: working independently and developing spiritual discipline. I suggest that meditation could serve as an adjunct to psychotherapy, sharing the goal of reasonably paced and self-respectful psychological exploration, but without the burdens of face-to-face interacting. Alternately, I mention dialectical behavior therapy skills groups: a wonderful program, but one that I know is hard to find in our community.

do not dispute this possible side effect, especially for the mood stabilizers that might most smooth out Ms. R's swings from anxious hyperactivity to periods of dark despair. I suspect that Ms. R also fears that taking medication will somehow further undermine her feeling of being in control, something that she clings to tenaciously. This is not their purpose. I believe that if she could find a medication that would decrease her anxiety, her self-control would improve and with it her sense of confidence and self-worth. For women especially this is a sometimes agonizing decision, but many find that 5 or even 10 pounds is a small price to pay for the greater stability and satisfaction medications allow them to achieve.

> ≡ *Rapid Reference 7.25*
>
> *Make a strong case for recommendations that may be challenged.* Last but not least, I address the issue of medications very directly and personally, something I later repeated in the feedback session. I acknowledge her terror of losing control over her emotions, her actions, and her weight. I make a case for how medication might help her gain greater self-control, but I do not minimize the possibility of moderate weight gain. I invite this troubled, but intelligent and accomplished, woman to make her own decision, with my help.

Rita W. McCleary, Psy.D. [Signed]
Examiner

Rapid References 7.26 and 7.27 explain why I chose to include Ms. R's WAIS-III results in an appendix at the end of the report.

Appendix to Elizabeth R's Report: WAIS-III-III Results

On the WAIS-III, Ms. R obtained a Full Scale IQ of 105, placing her in the Average range, at the 63rd percentile, for individuals her age. Her Verbal and Performance IQs, measuring verbal and nonverbal comprehension and reasoning abilities, also placed her at the 63rd percentile. The evenness of her scores across both verbal and performance factors suggests that Ms. R's Full Scale IQ is an accurate measure of her overall intellectual abilities at the present time. Her subtest scores, analyzed into four indexes, however, demonstrate her relative strengths in the areas of verbal comprehension and processing speed. High scores on the Processing Speed Index are correlated with high levels of motivation, something Ms. R demonstrated throughout the evaluation.

Each subtest score has a mean of 10 (marking the 50th percentile) and a stan-

Intellect is integral to personality. The common division of psychological test reports into intellectual and emotional or personality findings suggests that patients' planning abilities, verbal facility, concentration, and abstract reasoning abilities are somehow separate from their passions and desires. Making matters worse, the implicit assumption behind this separation is that the WAIS-III and other educational tests exclusively measure intellectual functioning, while the projective tests exclusively assess emotional well-being.

A more comprehensive view posits that people pay attention, think, solve problems, and act in characteristic ways, across a wide variety of circumstances. Their cognitive abilities shape every aspect of their lives, as much as their capacities for affect regulation, interpersonal relatedness, and self-directed behavior do. Thus, evaluating an individual's thought processes, judgment, and/or susceptibility to distraction *of necessity* includes determining his or her intellectual abilities and what impedes his or her optimal use of them.

At the same time, however, the Rorschach also identifies individuals' problem-solving styles, more broadly conceived, and the TAT demands that they draw upon cognitive skills to organize a narrative with a beginning, middle, and end. Integrating all of these intellectual findings into a comprehensive and dynamic assessment of personality places them in the broader context of an individual's motivations, fears, passions, relationships, and values.

The strong arguments for integration and against presenting test data test by test in personality reports does not stop most psychologists from including Wechsler intelligence scores in their reports. The Wechsler subtest profile and indexes provide a remarkably valid and reliable measure of a certain type of intelligence that has great utility for tracking the course of a person's illness. Not only do the Wechsler tests help schools to determine learning disabilities and educational placements, but they also help to rule out (or in) the onset of Dementia, a major affective disorder, a psychotic illness, or an Anxiety Disorder. Frequently diagnosticians can infer a previously higher level of functioning from the pattern of an individual's Wechsler scores. Other psychologists in particular appreciate having direct access to this pattern, even as they acknowledge the inconsistency of including these indexes, not Rorschach ratios, in testing reports.

Placement of Ms. R's Cognitive Assessment Results

In Ms. R's case, I placed her WAIS-III scores at the end of the report. As noted there, her index scores were even, with the exception of her superior processing speed, interpreted as another confirmation of her strong motivation to do well. For other individuals, for whom the referral questions more directly pertain to reasoning abilities or difficulties with concentration, for instance, psychologist-consultants might create a subsection within Diagnostic Understanding to discuss intellectual functioning. Even in these cases, however, they would make every attempt to consider all aspects of the test data relevant to information processing, ideation, problem solving, and judgment before drawing any conclusions.

dard deviation of 3. The index scores, like the IQ scores, have a mean of 100 and a standard deviation of 15. Ms. R obtained the following scores:

Verbal		Performance	
Vocabulary	14	Picture Arrangement	10
Similarities	12	Picture Completion	12
Information	10	Block Design	10
Comprehension	10	Matrix Reasoning	09
Arithmetic	11	**Coding**	**14**
Digit Span	09	**Symbol Search**	**14**
Letter-Number Sequence	**14**		

Verbal Comprehension Index	**110**	**High Average**	**75th percentile**
Perceptual Organization Index	101	Average	53rd percentile
Working Memory Index	106	Average	66th percentile
Processing Speed Index	**122**	**Superior**	**93rd percentile**

Note: Ms. R's relative strengths are highlighted in bold print.

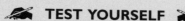 **TEST YOURSELF**

1. **Personality tests are essentially subjective because they assess an individual's unconscious.** True or False?

2. **To say that the diagnostic understanding of personality is dynamic means that it provides**

    (a) a description of how the individual's personality has changed over time.

    (b) a measure of the distance between a person's fantasies and their reality testing.

    (c) an interpretation of the underlying conflicts and motivations that organize an individual's manifest behaviors.

    (d) a far more cogent understanding of personality than does a *DSM-IV* diagnosis.

3. **Frequently a dynamic understanding of personality functioning complements and enriches a *DSM-IV* diagnosis.** True or False?

4. **In writing a personality report it is important to choose one theoretical viewpoint to ensure that you interpret the test data consistently.** True or False?

(continued)

5. Personality reports should always identify a person's strengths because

(a) this will make the individual feel better about him- or herself.

(b) a person's strengths provide a basis for treatment planning.

(c) understanding a person's strengths gives hope for positive change.

(d) all of the above

6. Psychologist-consultants should always discourage parents from reading their adolescent's personality assessment. True or False?

7. A borderline level of personality functioning means

(a) the individual may evidence psychotic thinking in certain circumstances.

(b) the individual meets criteria for a Borderline Personality Disorder.

(c) the individual probably suffers significant cognitive deficits.

(d) the individual has an hysterical personality structure.

8. Individuals who pay out of pocket for their test reports almost always expect to receive a copy. Therefore psychologist-consultants should carefully edit their findings to minimize the person's weaknesses, discussing these off the record with the referring clinician. True or False?

9. Good personality reports are not written using technical terminology because

(a) many psychological terms are protected and require at least a master's-level degree to use properly.

(b) frequently these terms sound off-putting and pejorative to the individuals tested.

(c) the theories behind most psychological terms are not scientifically proven.

(d) none of the above

10. Writing an Observations section in a personality report is optional because

(a) personality reports aim to get beneath manifest appearance to what makes a person tick.

(b) the referring clinician usually knows already how the person dresses, talks, and interacts.

(c) what the examiner notices is not controlled by standardized procedures.

(d) examiners often consider their observations as data and interpret them together with the individual's test results.

Answers: 1. False; 2. c; 3. True; 4. False; 5. d; 6. False; 7. a; 8. False; 9. b; 10. d

Eight

RECOMMENDATIONS

The Recommendation section of the report contains specific ways to resolve the referral questions by addressing the evaluation's key findings. In this section, evaluators suggest strategies and interventions that are designed to facilitate change and result in improved outcomes for the individual. Because evaluations are requested for a variety of reasons, different types of assessments will require different types of recommendations. Additionally, the setting in which the evaluation takes place, such as a school, hospital, private clinic, postsecondary setting, or vocational training center, will influence the types and number of recommendations.

Historically, in many school settings, the focus of certain types of assessments was on eligibility for special services rather than on early intervention and educational planning. The assessment was centered on single test scores and mechanistic procedures rather than on the student's educational needs and programming. Scores were derived to establish eligibility and not to determine meaningful goals and interventions.

Clearly, this type of practice minimizes the value of assessment. Even though a student may be deemed ineligible for certain services, all evaluations need to address the referral concerns and propose solutions. As Cruickshank (1977) noted several decades ago, "Diagnosis must take second place to instruction, and must be made a tool of instruction, not an end in itself." We begin this chapter with general principles to observe when writing recommendations, and then in subsections we discuss and provide examples of specific types of recommendations to be written.

GENERAL PRINCIPLES

As with other sections of the report, before writing the recommendation section, consider all prior information, including the referral question, any important background information, all behaviors observed, and the results of diagnostic testing. Become informed about the individual and the setting in which the recommendations will be implemented (e.g., the teacher's familiarity with a methodology, the available resources and materials, the opportunities for one-to-one instruction; Connolly, 1988). When writing recommendations, consider the following general principles: (1) the focus, (2) the placement, (3) the complexity, (4) the number, (5) the specificity, (6) the prescriptive nature, (7) implementation, and (8) the organization and introduction. Each of these factors will be briefly discussed.

Focus of the Recommendations

In many cases, a person is referred because he or she is struggling and needs specific psychological, educational, or behavioral interventions to profit more fully from experiences. In these cases, the majority of recommendations address the specific areas of concern. The goal is to select specific modifications and interventions that will enhance an individual's opportunities for success and lead to the resolution of the concerns.

In addition to addressing concerns regarding behavior, personality, or academic functioning, recommendations should also address an individual's strengths. Placing sole emphasis on difficulties can increase a person's negative perceptions of the evaluation process as well as perceptions of self and present circumstances. Even in cases of individuals with generalized low cognitive functioning, the recommendations may address areas of relative competence. Recommendations about strengths can address how the individual can use well-developed abilities or skills to enhance personal, academic, or vocational successes. Rapid Reference 8.1 presents a sample case and some of the recommendations that focus on the client's strengths.

Recommendations can also begin by indicating what the person can presently do, followed by an appropriate instructional recommendation. For example, the evaluator may write, "Presently, Zeb can subtract two-digit numbers when regrouping is not required. He is now ready to learn to subtract two-digit numbers involving regrouping."

Placement of the Recommendations

Recommendations typically follow the Test Results and Interpretation or the Diagnostic Impressions and Summary sections. As a general rule, the recommendations only belong in the Recommendations section. Although this sounds like an easy principle to follow, when writing a report it is often tempting to embed

≋Rapid Reference 8.1

Sample Case Utilizing Client's Strengths in Recommendations

Case Information	Recommendations
Jen, a middle-school student, was referred for an evaluation because of difficulties in math class. Results from the evaluation indicated that although Jen was struggling with concepts related to mathematics and science, her performance on reading and writing tasks was very advanced. During the evaluation, Jen commented that she did not feel challenged in her language arts class, and she discussed her interest in using the computer to conduct in-depth research on topics.	1. In language arts and history classes, use a contract learning approach to allow Jen to engage actively in the decision-making process and to participate in designing her course of study. As an alternative to having her complete all of the regular class assignments, give her the option of designing some in-depth projects requiring more advanced research skills than might be expected of her classmates. 2. Provide enrichment activities for Jen. For example, have Jen research information on the computer. Examples of activities include (1) finding URLs to complete a project, (2) determining the accuracy of the information that various web sites provide, and (3) creating a personal or school web site.

recommendations into the Interpretation section. For example, after stating that Marco made numerous errors on vowel sounds and consonant blends when attempting to pronounce words, you may be tempted to write that this finding suggests that he needs a structured phonics approach to improve his basic reading skills. Although this recommendation for a specific instructional approach may be appropriate, the suggestion belongs in the Recommendations section, not the Interpretation section.

Similarly, you may observe that a client is having trouble meeting certain work demands. Wait until the Recommendations section to suggest that the person would benefit from a shorter work day or would profit from being able to complete certain work tasks at home. Keep your observations and

DON'T FORGET

Keep all recommendations in the Recommendations section of the report.

interpretations in the appropriate sections and your suggestions for addressing and resolving the problem in the Recommendations section. The Don't Forget box provides a reminder of where to place recommendations.

Complexity of Recommendations

As with the other sections of the report, the recommendations must be easy to understand and should use terminology that will be familiar and simple for the reader to comprehend. Recommendations that are not clear will be ignored. For example, a report contained the following recommendation: "Use exaggerated auditory reformulations, particularly for spelling." Although the evaluator most likely knows exactly what this means, few parents or teachers would have any idea of how to implement this suggestion. Also, too many suggestions within one recommendation can render it useless. One case report provided the following recommendation: "Due to evidence of language-based learning difficulties, help Austin to process complex and/or lengthy auditory information and oral directions, improve verbal organization and verbal formulation skills, build word and label retrieval skills, ability to interpret questions, descriptive and persuasive skills, ability to paraphrase information concisely and sequentially, ability to organize information, ability to answer questions, and apply her higher-level metalinguistic skills to classroom materials." Although the grammar is also problematic, this recommendation contains so many ideas that it is totally useless. It would be far more effective to take one of these ideas and then to describe exactly how the idea should be implemented.

Number of Recommendations

No hard and fast rules exist about how many recommendations are needed or appropriate. Before writing the recommendations, most evaluators have a sense of about how many recommendations they will write. Too many recommendations can overwhelm a teacher, parent, or client, whereas too few can render the report useless because not enough substantive guidance is provided to carry out the recommendation. The number of recommendations will also vary based upon the complexity of the case. In a case where multiple issues exist, the final report may contain several pages of recommendations. In a case that is more straightforward in nature, only a few specific recommendations may be necessary.

The scope of the evaluation will also influence the number of recommendations. For a child or adult who has never been evaluated, a full battery of tests may be administered that may include language, academic, social, vocational, personality, medical, and psychological tests. In some reports, whether clinical or school based, recommendations are written to cover all aspects of performance and to create comprehensive treatment programs. In other reports, recommendations only address the areas of functioning that are seen as critical. In a school setting, where continued eligibility for special education services may be an issue, administration of selected cognitive and academic tests supplemented by informal testing and classroom work samples may be sufficient. In this situation, few recommendations may be needed, as an effective treatment plan is already in place.

Some reports do not include any recommendations. For example, in a school setting, the evaluator may note that recommendations will be created and written by the educational team once all of the findings have been integrated and reviewed. In this case, the school psychologist may write, "The results from this psychological evaluation will be combined with the results from the educational and speech/language evaluations to determine how best to meet Ferdinand's educational needs." In other cases, the evaluator may specify that recommendations will be written by a more knowledgeable other (e.g., "Specific recommendations for language therapy will be developed by the speech/language pathologist"). If you plan to have an ongoing relationship with the person, you may write that he or she should contact you when further therapeutic, psychological, or educational recommendations are needed. In this way, you can keep track of the progress the individual has made toward the recommended goals and objectives and revise the plan as needed.

Specificity of Recommendations

Reports will also differ in the specificity of recommendations. Some reports may refer to general interventions, whereas others will include suggestions for specific techniques and materials. We distinguish three levels of specificity in recommendations: (1) general, (2) specific, and (3) very specific. Envision the specificity of recommendations as the steps on a ladder. The bottom step is the broadest recommendation, and with each step up the steps become increasingly narrow. Rapid Reference 8.2 exemplifies these levels of specificity.

How high up the ladder do you need to go to provide appropriate solutions to a referral question? It depends. Examples of the factors that drive specificity are the evaluator's background and training in the types of interventions needed, the setting where the recommendations will be implemented, the availability of services and resources, and other pragmatic considerations, such as:

- Is a specific program or treatment offered locally?
- What is the cost of that program?

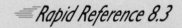

Rapid Reference 8.2

Levels of Recommendation Specificity

Level of Specificity	Example Recommendation
General	Help Alicia improve her basic reading skills.
More specific	Teach Alicia phonics skills. *or* Teach Alicia initial phonics skills using a multisensory approach.
Very specific	Teach Alicia phonics skills, using a specific multisensory phonics approach, such as the Slingerland method or the Wilson Reading System.

Rapid Reference 8.3

Factors That May Influence the Specificity of the Recommendations

- Evaluator's training and background
- Individual's needs, goals, motivation, and desires
- Parent's or caregiver's needs and goals for the individual
- Prior treatments and interventions
- Setting
- Availability of resources and services
- Cost of services
- Availability of personnel to implement services
- Intensity and duration of services
- Severity of the problem

- How long will the person need to be in the program?
- Is there someone in the environment who will follow through and carry out the recommendations?
- Will the person be willing to undergo the treatment?

Rapid Reference 8.3 reviews several factors that influence the level of specificity.

As a general guideline, only make specific recommendations for certain programs or instructional practices when you have a solid background in that area, have knowledge of the program's or treatment's efficacy, and are familiar with the scope of available services and resources. If you do not have sufficient background in an area, refer the individual to a more knowledgeable other who will be able to prepare specific recommendations (e.g., psychiatrist, speech/language therapist, reading specialist, mental health professional, pediatrician, vocational counselor). General recommendations allow the person implementing the recommendation to choose the appropriate strategies and materials. Specific recommendations are written so that they can be carried out precisely without question about the procedure or procedures to use. If you are highly familiar with the scope and types of interventions in an area, your recommendations will be even more precise and prescriptive and have sufficient specificity that they can be carried out by another without further explanation. Three examples of general and specific recommendation are presented in Rapid Reference 8.4.

As noted in Rapid Reference 8.4, at times, evaluators write a short recommendation but then attach descriptions of methodologies or specific services as an addendum or appendix to the report. For example, you may include a one-

≡Rapid Reference 8.4

Examples of General and Specific Recommendations

General	Specific
To increase phonological awareness, engage Sandra in a variety of activities that focus on the sounds of words.	To improve sound blending abilities, provide Sandra with direct instruction in sound blending using the following steps: (1) have the student say the word, (2) present the word with prolonged sounds but no break between the sounds and ask the student to say the word, (3) present the sounds with a short break between them and ask the student to say the word, (4) present the word with a quarter-second, then half-second, then 1-second break between the sounds, with the student saying the word after each presentation (Kirk, Kirk, & Minskoff, 1985).
When teaching Julio vocabulary, use a variety of activities that involve active learning.	When teaching Julio vocabulary, use a directed vocabulary thinking activity (Cunningham, 1979). Follow these steps: Write the word on the board and ask Julio to guess the meaning. Record his guesses. Write the word used correctly in several sentences and have him guess again and record his responses. Look up the word in a dictionary and compare his guesses with the dictionary definition.
Set up a behavioral intervention program for Jonas that provides both positive reinforcements and negative consequences.	Set up a behavioral intervention program for Jonas that is based on a token reinforcement system. This procedure is fully explained in Appendix 1, which is attached to the end of this report.

page handout for a teacher that explains the steps in a various procedure for teaching spelling. Or you may provide parents with a handout that further clarifies available local services for children with ADHD or explains the benefits and risks associated with various medications. You can also write recommendations to direct clients, parents, or teachers to specific resources, such as books, organizations, or web sites that will provide additional information or materials. The following are examples of this type of recommendation:

- To obtain more information about management of ADHD, consider joining Children and Adults with Attention-Deficit/Hyperactivity Disorder (CHADD). (800-233-4050, *www.chadd.org*). This organization provides valuable resources for both children and adults.
- Because Carmen has been identified as having a reading disability or dyslexia, help her register with Recordings for the Blind & Dyslexic (RFB&D) and secure textbooks on audiotape or CD-ROM. Contact Recordings for the Blind and Dyslexic, The Anne T. Macdonald Center, 20 Roszel Road, Princeton, NJ 08540 (phone (800) 221-4792, web site *www.rfbd.org*).

Rapid Reference 8.5 provides examples of several websites of organizations that provide information about learning, behavioral, and psychological issues.

≡Rapid Reference 8.5

Examples of Organizations and Web Sites

Anxiety Disorder Association of America: www.adaa.org

Association on Higher Education and Disability: www.ahead.org

Children and Adults with Attention-Deficit/Hyperactivity Disorder (CHADD): www.chadd.org

Council for Exceptional Children (CEC): www.cec.sped.org

International Dyslexia Association (IDA): www.interdys.org

Internet Mental Health: www.mentalhealth.com

Learning Disabilities Association of America (LDA): www.ldanatl.org

National Association for School Psychologists (NASP): www.nasponline.org/

National Center for Learning Disabilities: www.ncld.org

National Depressive and Manic-Depressive Association: www.ndmda.org

Obsessive-Compulsive Foundation: www.ocfoundation.org

Prescriptive Nature of Recommendations

The focus of the recommendations is on the specific person evaluated. These recommendations are developed on an individualized basis and guided by the specific referral questions. Because recommendations are as varied as the people whom you evaluate, formulate them with great care and concern. On occasion, we have seen reports in which the evaluator has adopted a one-size-fits-all approach to writing recommendations. The recommendations seem to be generated by a computer rather than a skilled clinician: For each evaluation, the same or very similar recommendations are proposed (even though the referral questions may differ).

We have also encountered reports in which the evaluator shows a clear bias toward one particular type of program or one particular type of treatment and recommends this procedure for the majority of students or clients who are referred. Many excellent techniques, strategies, and programs are available for teaching and helping individuals with attentional, language, learning, psychological, emotional, behavioral, and/or social difficulties. Depending upon an individual's characteristics and the severity of the concerns, different strategies, interventions, and techniques will be more effective than others.

For all types of interventions, recommendations may be written to address the intensity and duration of the services. Examples include the following:

- Over the next 9-week period, provide Jonas with daily individual tutoring of 50-minute sessions each day.
- Provide Sandra with 30 minutes daily of individual tutoring for 15 weeks.
- Provide Jake with psychological counseling for 1 year.
- Because of his continued suicidal ideations and delusions, consider sending Ruben to a therapeutic treatment program for 18 months.

Alternatively, the recommendation may contain a timeline for the completion of the goal.

Implementation of Recommendations

When evaluators write recommendations, the assumption is that someone will follow through and implement them. Unfortunately, this assumption is not always true. Carefully constructed recommendations can wind up in a folder or filing cabinet with little consideration, as suggested in the Caution. Furthermore, they may not even read the recommendations if they have already decided

CAUTION

People will not carry out recommendations if they do not

- understand the recommendation
- know how to implement the strategy or intervention
- have the resources to implement it
- think that the recommendation is feasible in the setting
- believe that the recommendation is necessary or appropriate

that a particular evaluator's reports are not helpful. This can occur when a person writes reports for the same school or agency. After becoming discouraged with the poor quality of psychological reports in a school setting, a teacher remarked: "I don't even bother to look at the report or the recommendations. I just want to know if he or she qualifies for help." This lack of connection between assessment and interventions occurs because teachers do not see the value in the assessment when the reports do not provide practical, effective recommendations. Similarly, parents may find it impossible to alter their child's environment in the ways that you suggest, or a client may not be able to or willing to change his or her circumstances. Rapid Reference 8.6 reviews common reasons why recommendations are not followed or ignored. As you write recommendations, remember to keep the background of your readers in mind (Bradley-Johnson & Johnson, 1998). To ensure that your recommendations are considered, make them prescriptive, positive, practical, and possible to implement (see Don't Forget).

Prior to writing a recommendation, ascertain whether the person involved is

≡Rapid Reference 8.6

Reasons Why Recommendations Are Not Followed

The recommendations are
- Too vague
- Not shared with appropriate personnel
- Too complex
- Too lengthy
- Inappropriate for the person's age or ability levels
- Not understood by the person responsible for implementation
- Impossible to implement in the setting
- Too time-consuming
- Rejected by the client or student

willing to and able to carry out the recommendation. For example, ask a general education teacher if she is willing to provide extra assistance to a student before or after class, or check with the employer to verify that an office in a new location is a possibility. If you would like to recommend some type of private therapy or inter-

> **DON'T FORGET**
>
> Keep recommendations
> * Prescriptive
> * Positive
> * Practical
> * Possible to implement

vention, check with the parents or your client to see if they are willing to go to and pay for the treatment.

Organization and Introduction of the Recommendations

For some reports, you may organize the Recommendations section by the person responsible for implementation and then adapt the wording accordingly. For example, make recommendations directly to a student or client, such as "You should arrange appointments with each of your teachers at the beginning of each semester" or "Discuss a change in work schedule with your employer." You may also make a recommendation to the student's teacher, parents, or counselor, such as "Help Andrew arrange appointments with his teachers at the beginning of each semester" or "Andrea will benefit from placement at a small college that has a learning disability coordinator as well as tutorial services that address study skills, coaching, and specific subject area tutoring."

You may also organize recommendations by the major areas of performance that are addressed (e.g., counseling, reading, math, oral language, behavior, self-advocacy). As a general rule, group the recommendations under a category, place a heading or subheading to indicate the content of the category, and number each recommendation, beginning each subsection with number 1. In some instances, place the most important recommendations first. In other instances, arrange the recommendations in a hierarchical order based upon a developmental sequence.

As with other sections of the report, describe each recommendation from its most general points to its most specific. For example, if your first recommendation is to provide Maria with a math tutor, then follow it with more specific recommendations that suggest providing instruction in concepts involving money, fractions, decimals, and percentages. Or suggest that Maria's parents provide additional nightly assistance with homework, and then propose specific strategies for increasing assistance.

In some reports, the Recommendations section is introduced with a simple

≡ Rapid Reference 8.7

Examples of Transitions into the Recommendations Section

- Because of the underlying difficulties with (problem), (name) will benefit from the following classroom accommodations and interventions:
- Several accommodations and interventions will be helpful to (name). They include, but are not limited to, the following:
- In light of the assessment findings and observations of Lynne's educational team, the following recommendations are made to address the referral question:
- In order to address (name's) particular learning and behavioral needs, the following recommendations are offered:
- Based on the results of this evaluation, the examiner believes that (name) has the abilities and skills to succeed in school.
- In an effort to facilitate her success, the following recommendations are suggested:
- The following recommendations are based not only on the results of the norm-referenced tests but also on results from interviews, observations, and informal assessments.

heading. In others, a statement or two is used to provide a transition. Rapid Reference 8.7 provides example transitions into the Recommendations section.

SUBSECTIONS

Typically, the Recommendation section is ordered by recommendations for further assessment, accommodations, and specific interventions to address behavioral, social, linguistic, psychological, academic, or vocational concerns. Although it is beyond the scope of this book to provide substantive lists of recommendations for any one area, we will discuss and provide examples of the types of recommendations that are often included in these subsections.

Further Assessment or Evaluation

Some reports have recommendations for further assessment or evaluation. Recommendations are made for further assessment when the results of the evaluation do not fully answer the referral questions or when new questions and concerns emerge. For example, Mr. and Mrs. Gerner referred their son Michael for a private evaluation to assess his intellectual abilities and determine if he should be eligible for the school's talented and gifted program (TAG). Michael missed the cutoff by 1 point on group school testing. In addition, the Gerners' two other children, Ana and Ben, were performing successfully in the school's TAG program.

On the Stanford-Binet Intelligence Test–Fifth Edition (SB5) Michael obtained a Verbal IQ score of 136 (99th percentile), which falls in the Very Superior range, and a Nonverbal IQ score of 121 (92nd percentile), which falls in the Superior range. His Full Scale IQ score of 130 (98th percentile) falls in the Very Superior range. From the obtained scores, the evaluator concluded that Michael possesses gifted intellectual abilities.

When discussing these results with Michael's teachers, additional concerns were raised about his writing abilities. His teacher felt that Michael would become extremely frustrated with the amount and type of writing assignments required in the TAG program. Therefore, the psychologist recommended further evaluation in the area of written language to determine possible accommodations for writing in the TAG program, as well as specific interventions for improving Michael's writing skills.

At other times you will recognize that further evaluation is needed by another type of professional. As part of your evaluation, for example, you may note weakness in aspects of oral language and feel that a speech/language pathologist would provide a more comprehensive language evaluation. An appropriate recommendation in such a situation is "Martha needs a comprehensive language evaluation by a speech/language pathologist that will include the assessment of receptive and expressive language skills, as well as analyses of several oral language samples." In another case, you may be concerned about a child's visual-motor functioning and poor handwriting and recommend that he be seen by the clinic's occupational therapist. An appropriate recommendation is "Based upon the severity of Dan's fine-motor problems, refer him to Dr. Thompson, who will evaluate hand skills, muscle tone, flexibility, and general coordination." In still another case, you may note that your client has superior visual-spatial abilities and, as a result, refer him to a vocational counselor to assist in developing appropriate career goals.

In addition, the qualifications of specific professionals are needed for certain types of recommendations. If you are not a medical doctor, you would not recommend that a child be prescribed a certain drug for treatment for inattention. Physicians or psychiatrists make recommendations for medical treatments. Instead, you may write, "Because the student has noticeable difficulty staying on task, working carefully on mildly challenging tasks, and sitting reasonably still, consult with a behavioral pediatrician or psychiatrist about the benefit of medical therapy for the treatment of Attention-Deficit/Hyperactivity Disorder (ADHD) and the benefits of medical therapy."

In addition to more in-depth assessments and referrals to other professionals, you may write a recommendation for a reevaluation of certain abilities after a certain amount of time. Take the case of Joe, for example, a college freshman who sustained a head injury from a motorcycle accident. Although he had been an honors student prior to the accident, results of the evaluation indicated severe word-finding difficulties. Joe understood the concepts and functions of words, but he had trouble providing specific, clear definitions. For example, when shown a picture of door hinges, Joe responded that they were the things that let the door swing back and forth, but he could not remember what they were called. When shown a picture of a toga, he remarked that it was what the Romans wore and that he used to know the word but not any more. To help determine rate of recovery, the evaluator recommended that Joe's vocabulary knowledge be reevaluated in 6 months after completion of language therapy. As another example, when a student is transitioning from one setting to another (e.g., high school to college), you may write a recommendation to update the person's file, such as "Re-evaluate Carlos in 2 to 3 years to assess his progress and to make educational plans for college."

You can also write recommendations for further evaluation that address a need for more frequent measurements to assess growth and progress. Examples include the following:

- In order to monitor Scott's reading development, conduct weekly curriculum-based measurements by counting and charting the number of words read aloud in 1 minute from the first reader in the classroom reading series.
- Conduct daily drills on multiplication math facts and count and record the number of problems completed correctly in 1 minute.
- As part of an assessment, the evaluator may establish a person's present performance levels and then set a benchmark based on weekly data points.

Accommodations

The need for accommodations is often established by actual performance within a setting, as well as the results from cognitive and academic testing. Results from intelligence and achievement tests can help the evaluator develop a hypothesis that will lead to the selection of appropriate accommodations. This information can also help create a stronger rationale for why the person needs and is entitled to specific accommodations.

For example, low scores on timed measures, such as processing speed tests, suggest that the person may need more time on tests that involve lengthy reading. Before drawing this conclusion, however, you need additional supportive data (e.g., reports from classroom teachers, measures of reading rate). The low processing speed score, confirmation from the teacher that reading rate is a concern, and a score indicating a compromised reading rate all support the conclusion that additional time is warranted and necessary.

The central purpose of accommodations is to provide equal access to academic and vocational opportunities, not unfair or preferential access. If an accommodation would give the person an unfair advantage (e.g., a waiver of a foreign language test when the person could complete the requirement), then the accommodation is not appropriate. Accommodations are adaptations in the school, home, or vocational settings that allow the person to succeed. They typically provide adjustments to a task so that the person is able to perform the task or some portion of the task. The task itself may not change but instead may become more accessible because the format is adapted (e.g., by use of a reader, an oral exam, or a version of a test in braille).

Although sometimes the words *accommodations, modifications,* and *compensations* are used interchangeably, modifications most often involve a change in the task. For example, a student may be allowed to take a computer course as a substitution for the foreign language requirement, or the amount of homework may be modified to 1 hour nightly rather than the 4 hours nightly the student is currently spending. Compensations often involve use of some type of assistance, such as technology, to make material accessible. For example, a student may tape record lectures to compensate for a poor memory or slow handwriting speed.

Because accommodations, modifications, and compensations involve adjustments and changes of the demands of a task, it is important to discuss them with the student or client. In general, most people do not want to stand out as being different. Thus, the student (or teacher) may view an appropriate accommodation, such as taped books, as embarrassing or not feasible. Often, a few questions can help clarify which accommodations will be most acceptable and useful for the individual as well as for the person implementing the accommodation. Rapid Reference 8.8 provides sample questions to ask in determining the usefulness of an accommodation.

As with other recommendations, base the suggested accommodations and modifications upon the unique characteristics and needs of the person. At times the necessary adjustments are easy to determine. The types of accommodations that are necessary and appropriate are often obvious for individuals with physical or sensory impairments. It is immediately apparent that a person confined to a

≋ *Rapid Reference 8.8*

Sample Questions to Ask in Determining the Usefulness of an Accommodation

- Would it help for you to sit near the teacher?
- Would you listen to books on tape in the classroom?
- Would you use the Alphasmart in class for writing?
- Would you mind if the supervisor recorded your tasks on tape?
- Would it help you to sit in a quiet room when you take your tests?
- Would it help if your teacher read you your tests?
- Would it be easier to pay attention if you did not sit next to Mary?
- Would you be able to arrange time so that Tom could dictate his test answers to you?
- Would it help you if you could work part of the day at home?

wheelchair will need facilities that have physical accessibility or that extra time will be needed to get to class. A person with cerebral palsy may need assistive technology devices to communicate. A student with a visual impairment may require that reading materials be enlarged or need a special type of lighting on the desk.

In contrast, accommodations for students with less visible disabilities, such as learning disabilities or ADHD, are more difficult to justify. Therefore, you must develop a justification or rationale that explains why the accommodation or modification is necessary and appropriate.

Provide a Clear Rationale

In all instances, provide a clear rationale for why a specific accommodation is justified. Before you write an accommodation, revisit what information, both qualitative and quantitative, supports the need for accommodation. Often, a prior history of receiving the accommodation in the classroom or workplace will help strengthen the statement of need. The rationale must provide a detailed explanation of why each accommodation is recommended and how the person's current functional limitations can be addressed by provision of the accommodation. It is insufficient to say that because a student has a certain condition, such as ADHD, he needs extended time for testing. Do not make statements such as "Given the formal ADHD diagnosis, Mark is entitled to receive accommodations when taking standardized tests, such as the SAT." Diagnosis of a disability, in and of itself, does not entitle one to specific accommodations. For some students with ADHD the provision of additional time only creates additional anxiety, and they would be better served with extra test breaks, not more time. A more appropriate, compelling recommendation would be "Because of his attentional difficulties, Mark is easily distracted in group testing situations. He looks up any time there is movement in the room and is distracted by all extraneous noises. Moreover, his classroom teachers report that Mark has to redirect his attention continually to the tasks at hand. His difficulty focusing necessitates increased time to complete assignments and tests. Furthermore, all of Mark's classroom teachers report that they provide him with extended time on all in-class exams."

When creating recommendations, provide a clear link between the concern and the recommended solution.

> **DON'T FORGET**
> ....
>
> ### How to Begin Recommendations That Suggest Accommodations
>
> - Given Sally's difficulty with ...
> - In view of Magda's difficulties with ...
> - Because Mary has had trouble getting along with peers ...
> - As Rudy has been diagnosed with ADHD as well as learning disabilities,
> - Due to problems in handwriting and spelling, Edward will require ...
> - Because of Ethan's advanced competencies in mathematics, he will benefit from ...
> - To address Myrna's low self-esteem, ...
> - To decrease Alicia's anxiety, ...

The first part of the sentence can remind the reader of the problem or specific finding that suggests the need for an accommodation or intervention. The Don't Forget box provides examples of how to begin recommendations that suggest accommodations.

The following examples demonstrate how to link the problem with the suggested recommendation:

- Based upon his severe fine-motor difficulties and extremely compromised writing rate, Dan will need to take all written exams using a computer.
- Given Amanda's difficulties with note taking, she should have a note taker assigned to her in each class who will then provide her with a copy of these notes. However, Amanda should still take her own notes to help improve her note-taking skills and help her maintain focus on the instruction.

Address each problem with a recommendation that explains (1) why the recommendation is needed, (2) how the recommendation relates to the findings, and (3) how the recommendation will be carried out (Bradley-Johnson & Johnson, 1998). The next Don't Forget provides a reminder that all accommodations re-

DON'T FORGET

Provide a clear rationale for why a person is entitled to a specific accommodation.

quire a clear, specific rationale that is derived from and supported by both quantitative and qualitative data.

On some occasions, a person's circumstances change, necessitating adjustments in the environment or curriculum that were unnecessary in the past. This may occur when a student transitions into a new setting (e.g., moving from high school to a postsecondary setting or from one workplace to another) or when the demands of a job suddenly change. For example, George, a 35-year-old man with a childhood diagnosis of dyslexia, had been employed with a company as a reference writer for 10 years. In this capacity, he interviewed past employers to ascertain the qualifications of people who were applying for new jobs in this company. George would then turn over his written reports to his secretary, who would correct any errors in spelling and grammar. With budget cuts, the secretary was replaced and George was given a laptop computer to use for all writing. Suddenly, his ability to produce error-free reports was compromised. To maintain his job, George had to be permitted to have secretarial and editorial assistance for his final reports. This meant that he had to be diagnosed as having a specific writing disability with a clear explanation of how this disability affected his vocational performance. In this way, the evaluator was able to justify the specific request for editorial assistance on the final drafts of his reports, and George was able to keep his job.

Test Accommodations

The most common type of accommodation in psychological and educational reports is a recommendation for adjustments in the conditions of standardized group assessments. Test accommodations may be grouped into the following four basic categories: (1) presentation format, (2) response format, (3) test setting, and (4) timing of the test (Thurlow, House, Scott, & Ysseldyke, 2000). The presentation format involves a change in the appearance of the test, such as a version in braille or large-print text. The response format refers to how the person will answer (e.g., through writing, speaking, pointing, or clicking a button). The setting is where the person will take the test (e.g., in the classroom or a private room), and the timing refers to the amount of extra time the person will receive, the time of day the test is administered, or the number of breaks that will be provided. Rapid Reference 8.9 provides a list of commonly recommended test accommodations.

If you are requesting an accommodation in the form of increased time for someone on a timed standardized test, then specify the amount of extra time. Do not write "Provide Samantha with untimed accommodations on all standardized

≡ *Rapid Reference 8.9*

Sample Accommodations for Testing

- Allow Sara extra time to complete tests.
- Allow Jesse to mark responses directly in his test book, rather than on a separate answer sheet.
- Provide testing in a quiet room.
- Read tests out loud to Ernie.
- Enlarge test materials so that they are easier for Karyn to see.
- Provide Jonathan with breaks between the sections of all group-administered standardized tests.
- Keep track of the amount of typical time for a test and the actual amount of time that Sonia needed. Use this information to help determine the amount of extra time she requires.
- Test Tucker on small amounts of information at one time.
- Provide partial credit for corrections Tyler makes on test and quizzes.
- Permit Sheldon to take oral exams rather than written tests.
- Have Kristen take multiple-choice tests rather than fill-in-the-blank.

testing." Decide if Samantha needs twice as much time as normally allotted, one third more time than is typically allotted, or another degree of increase. How do you make this determination? If the student has a reading disability, document the severity of the problem, the need for extended time on classroom exams, and his or her present levels of reading accuracy and rate. Also consider how much extra time the student needs on typical classroom tests. If the person has a disability in only one area of functioning, such as mathematics, request an accommodation for exams involving math content but not for reading exams.

Some clients cannot handle a task even if accommodations or modifications are provided. The task is just too far beyond the individual's present performance levels. For example, students with severe cognitive impairments will require alternative examinations. These may include observations, portfolios, and direct assessments of functional performance. The specific policies for types of acceptable assessments vary from school district to district.

Interventions

The majority of referrals in school settings result from behavioral, emotional, or social concerns and/or concerns regarding poor academic performance. The referral sources, most often teachers, are in search of ways to increase and improve the student's performance. Referrals related to concerns regarding linguistic competence, behavior, or academic development are also frequent in clinical settings. In some cases, a special education teacher, a speech/language therapist, a case manager, a school psychologist, or a classroom teacher develops the specific goals and objectives for instruction. When preparing recommendations, consider what skills and concepts the student has mastered and what ones need to be taught. Several resources provide many sample recommendations that can be incorporated into reports (e.g., Mather & Jaffe, 2002; McCarney & Bauer, 1995; McCarney, Wanderlich, & Bauer, 1993).

Although recommendations may address any aspect of school performance (e.g., science, history, physical education), the majority of recommendations center upon the core curricular areas of oral language, reading, writing, and mathematics. These curricular areas are covered in comprehensive achievement tests, such as the KTEA-II, WIAT-II, and WJ III ACH. In addition, recommendations are often written to address psychological and social, behavioral, or emotional concerns, as well as vocational issues.

Recommendations for Oral Language Difficulties

Although speech/language pathologists most often perform comprehensive oral language evaluations, many aspects of linguistic performance are also revealed in psychological and educational assessments. In addition, an evaluator will often recognize problems in language processing that must be addressed (e.g., the examinee had trouble understanding and following directions, or the examinee asked for directions to be repeated). Rapid Reference 8.10 provides examples of

≡ Rapid Reference 8.10

Sample Accommodations for Oral Language

- Keep oral directions short and simple.
- Seat the student away from environmental noises.
- When speaking to Bruce, clarify and simplify the instructions.
- Prior to a class discussion, let Barbara know that you will be calling on her and asking her a particular question.
- Ask Karla to repeat and paraphrase oral instructions, as needed.
- Provide rephrasings of directions for Clarissa rather than repetitions.
- Modify all class assignments to accommodate Alicia's difficulties with aspects of language, including vocabulary, sentence formulation, and ideation.
- Provide Alicia with a copy of the lecture notes prior to class.
- Provide Noel with a course substitution for the foreign language requirement.

the types of interventions that are commonly written in psychological and psychoeducational reports for individuals with low oral language abilities.

Oral language abilities are often broken into receptive language (the ability to comprehend spoken language) and expressive language (the ability to speak and express ideas). Because language provides the basis for many academic and social pursuits, individuals with advanced oral language competence are often highly successful in school and in life, whereas individuals with limited linguistic competence often experience difficulties in many aspects of daily living. Recommendations under the subsection of oral language may address: (1) phonological awareness, the ability to detect and manipulate speech sounds (phonemes); (2) oral syntax, the ability to order words correctly in sentences; (3) receptive and expressive vocabulary, the abilities to understand and use words; (4) listening comprehension, the ability to understand spoken language, or (5) pragmatics, the use of language for social purposes.

Recommendations for Reading Difficulties

Several aspects of reading performance may be addressed in an evaluation and, subsequently, in the Recommendations section. The findings may indicate that the person has poor reading skills relative to peers and thus will need accommodations on tasks requiring reading. Rapid Reference 8.11 provides examples of the types of accommodations that are commonly written in psychological and psychoeducational reports for individuals with compromised reading performance.

Instructional recommendations under reading may address: (1) beginning knowledge of phoneme-grapheme (sound-letter) correspondences; (2) phonics knowledge, the ability to apply phonics skills to word pronunciation; (3) sight-

---

≡Rapid Reference 8.11

Sample Accommodations for Reading

- Shorten the amount of required reading.
- Provide Charles with books on tape.
- Do not require oral reading in front of classmates.
- Ensure that texts are at Emily's instructional level.
- Have Stephen listen to tape-recorded books and follow along with the print version.
- Provide Kevin with textbooks in which the most important information is highlighted.
- Provide information to Esther about what will be covered next. Encourage her to preview the chapter and review new vocabulary prior to the lecture.

word vocabulary, the number of words recognized instantly without phonic analysis; (4) reading fluency and rate, the ease and speed of reading; (5) reading comprehension, or understanding of what is read; and (6) reading strategies, the use and active application of procedures to improve reading performance (e.g., self-monitoring, rereading). The clinical observations of the evaluator coupled with the findings of the evaluation will suggest which aspects of reading performance should be addressed. Many of the instructional strategies and interventions that focus on basic reading skills suggest programs and techniques for direct instruction in the missing skills. An example is "Use a synthetic phonics approach to teach Trisha how to recognize and pronounce words. Explicitly teach her the relationships between letters and sounds and then how to blend letter sounds together to pronounce words." The evaluator may or may not recommend use of a specific instructional program. Strategies for development of a sight-word vocabulary often focus on repeated exposures with practice and review of specific words. For fluency, many of the strategies are based on timed repeated readings of words or text with graphs to illustrate progress.

Many of the interventions and strategies that focus on reading comprehension are designed to help the reader become a more active participant in the reading process. An example is "To enhance reading comprehension, teach Amelia how to preview the chapter before it is introduced in class. Show her how to read the bold headings throughout the chapter, note all new vocabulary words, and review the questions at the end of the chapter." For older students, more attention is directed toward the goal of becoming strategic readers so that they self-monitor their comprehension; retell, paraphrase, and summarize what they read; make inferences and predictions based on reading; and ask and answer questions. A variety of strategies can be used prior to reading, during reading, and after reading to enhance reading comprehension.

Recommendations for Writing Difficulties

Written language is often separated into (1) handwriting, (2) basic writing skills, and (3) written expression. Depending upon the age and educational experience of the individual, one of these areas may be of greater concern than the others. Fortunately, many individuals who struggle with the development of written language have relatively intact oral language and can therefore be successful when provided with accommodations. Rapid Reference 8.12 provides examples of the types of accommodations that are commonly written in psychological and psychoeducational reports for individuals who struggle with written language.

As with reading, there are many specific interventions and programs designed to increase writing competence. In some cases, the recommendations will be written to address performance in basic writing skills, including spelling, as well

≡Rapid Reference 8.12

Sample Accommodations for Writing

- Do not penalize Janice for spelling errors on in-class assignments.
- Provide a peer to assist Ralph with note taking.
- Provide Nicole with a copy of all class notes.
- Have Anna use spelling and grammar checkers on all written assignments.
- Permit Sandy to dictate all lengthy writing assignments.
- Encourage John to use a computer for in-class essays.
- Have Jeff use word prediction software that will provide suggestions of words and their spellings based upon the first few letters.
- Provide Serena with a separate grade for content on all written assignments.
- Have Andrea use voice recognition software to facilitate writing.

as knowledge of punctuation and capitalization rules. The evaluator may write recommendations that focus on one aspect of writing mechanics, such as how to select words for spelling tests or how to use a specific strategy for improving proofreading and editing skill, or on several aspects of basic writing skill.

To improve written expression, emphasis is often initially placed on prewriting strategies that involve brainstorming and organizing ideas prior to writing. Organization can then be facilitated through the use of graphic organizers and outlines. Specific strategies then exist to help the writer improve paragraph organization, including writing clear topic sentences, providing clear details to support the topic, and summarizing the information in a concluding sentence. For essay writing, individuals may benefit from direct instruction in how to use effective transitions between paragraphs to improve clarity and organization of writing. As with other areas of academic performance, the goals of the evaluation are to determine strengths and weaknesses within written language abilities and then to develop specific recommendations to improve the person's writing skills.

Recommendations for Math Difficulties

Mathematics is often separated into basic math skills, which include operations, and math problem solving, which includes concepts and applications. Rapid Reference 8.13 provides examples of the types of accommodations that are commonly written in psychological and psychoeducational reports for individuals who struggle with the acquisition of math.

Unlike reading comprehension and written expression, mathematics is based on a hierarchical structure, so failure to understand and master one basic math

⟨Rapid Reference 8.13⟩

Sample Accommodations for Math

- Provide Nico with graph paper for all numerical calculations.
- Divide Helen's paper into sections for each math problem.
- Allow Jonathan to use fact charts or a calculator with unknown math facts.
- Have Jeanne check problems with a calculator and then rework any incorrect solutions.
- Do not have Tanya copy problems from books or the board. Instead, provide her with problems already written.
- Make sure Janice's worksheets are visually clear by placing only a few problems on each page.
- Spread practice time over short periods. Have Arnold complete six to eight problems rather than an entire page.
- Rephrase or rewrite word problems for Jessica to reduce the linguistic complexity.
- Have Myrna jot down the steps when doing multistep math problems.
- Provide Ted with scratch paper and a calculator for all assigned problems.
- Give partial credit for parts of problems that Jonas solves correctly.

concept can contribute to difficulty with later concepts. For example, to engage in meaningful counting, a child must first understand one-to-one correspondence. This knowledge then contributes to an understanding of the properties of addition. The concept of repeated additions is then critical to understanding multiplication. Also, similar to the effect that a slow reading rate has on comprehension, slow performance or poor fact retrieval can interfere with higher-level problem solving. Therefore, prior to writing recommendations for mathematics, consider the prerequisite skills that are needed for performing the task, as well as the person's age and setting.

Many of the methods and strategies that focus on basic math skills have common elements. Teachers are encouraged to review prerequisite information and previously learned skills, provide practice distributed over time, and introduce new skills systematically. After reviewing 30 studies, Mastropieri, Scruggs, and Shiah (1991) concluded that validated instructional techniques to improve math performance include (1) providing immediate feedback through demonstration and modeling of the correct computational procedure, (2) setting goals, (3) using peers and computers, (4) providing practice to promote fluency with facts, (5) using "talk alouds" while solving problems, (6) teaching specific strategies for computation and problem solving, and (7) using a concrete-to-abstract teaching sequence. The concrete level involves the use of objects or manipulative devices, the semiconcrete level involves representations such as tallies, and the abstract level involves actual numbers.

Direct and systematic instruction through this sequence helps students to transform their concrete understandings into the abstract level of numbers. Students may also benefit from the use of mnemonic strategies as an aid to remembering the steps in math operations. For example, to help Joshua remember the steps in long division, he could memorize a list of family members in this order (Dad, Mom, Sister, Cousin, Brother) to recall the steps divide, multiply, subtract, check, and bring down.

Methods for math problem solving often focus on strategies that provide the person with a series of steps to follow when solving problems. These steps may include reading the problem, rereading the problems, selecting an operation, writing a math equation, checking the operation, computing the answer, and checking to see if the answer is reasonable. As with methods for reading comprehension and written expression, strategies also include steps to help the person become more involved in problem solving, such as using objects to show the problem, drawing the problem, or visualizing the problem. The most critical components of these strategies seem to be (1) representing the problem through a diagram or drawing, (2) determining an operation and equation, and (3) solving and checking the problem. In addition to providing recommendations for school-age children, recommendations for math instruction are also written to address life skills mathematics to help individuals function independently after leaving school.

Recommendations for Difficulties with Attention, Organization, and Homework

In addition to academic areas, referrals for aspects of behavior and social functioning are also common. Some of the most common are characterized by concerns regarding attention, impulse control, and hyperactivity, the problems related to ADHD. For the majority of individuals with ADHD, the core impairment is impulsivity that results in poor self-control (Barkley, 1998; Goldstein & Goldstein, 1998). Because of difficulty sustaining attention to repetitive tasks, individuals with ADHD often experience inordinate problems with homework and organization, and subsequently, they require adjustments in the classroom or workplace. Rapid References 8.14 and 8.15 provide examples of the types of accommodations and suggestions that are commonly written in psychological and psychoeducational reports for individuals who struggle with attention, organization, and homework.

Sample Accommodations for Attentional/Organizational Problems

- Seat George in a quiet location that is free from distractions.
- Provide Emily with a seat in the front of the classroom, away from the hall or other sources of distraction.
- Avoid unnecessary changes in the schedule.
- Stand near Mr. Wolfe when giving him directions.
- Provide Jennifer with a small, structured setting that has clear and consistent expectations.
- Break longer assignments into shorter parts.
- Give Mark only one assignment to be completed at a time.
- Use color-coded materials to help draw attention to important features.
- Use a private signal to remind Barbara to return to the task.
- Permit Holly to have time out of her seat to run errands and so on.
- Provide Matthew with lists that help him organize tasks. Have him check off steps as each is completed.
- Help Jeremy create a plan for long-term assignments.
- Provide Rachel with copies of her class books to keep at home.

Sample Accommodations for Homework

- Provide Ralph with written lists of assignments so that he can check off completed steps or tasks.
- Adjust the amount of time needed to complete homework assignments.
- Provide June with an assignment book to be checked (daily, weekly) by the parent and teacher.
- Before Ben takes home assignments, make sure that he understands the directions and process for completing the work independently.
- Reduce the amount of John's homework so that he can complete assignments in the same amount of time as typical peers.
- Place a limit on the amount of time Tyrone is to work nightly on homework.
- Make sure that Jamie has one or two review problems on each homework assignment.
- Do not assign Martina homework. Instead, provide a time when she can complete all homework during school.
- Ensure that Melissa has written down her homework assignments each day before she leaves school.
- Assign Katrina a study buddy whom she can call for questions about homework after school.

Combinations of medical, behavioral, and counseling interventions are often recommended to help manage problems associated with impulsivity and inattention. A recommendation may be written to a school team, such as "Develop a multimodal treatment approach for Lynne. This treatment should include three components: (1) parent training to help understand and manage her behaviors, (2) a systematic behavioral intervention that is implemented consistently in both the home and the school, and (3) a trial of medication closely monitored by the school staff with frequent feedback to the parents and Dr. Goodman." Or the recommendation may describe an appropriate setting for the person:

Lynne requires a class placement incorporating the following components:
- a highly organized teacher who has a structured and systematic teaching style and calm, respectful manner of interacting with students;
- a behavioral program with clear rules, frequent and immediate positive reinforcement for target behaviors, and immediate consequences for specified negative behaviors;
- a consistent daily schedule so that areas of academic instruction, recess, and routines (e.g., passing out daily work, assigning homework) are done in the same manner and order daily;
- a morning review of each day's schedule (with the student given a copy of [her] schedule for that day);
- a minimum of classroom noise and confusion (visual and auditory);
- a system in which students are aware that a transition is coming, when the current activity will end, what will happen next, and what they are expected to do to be ready; and
- an emphasis on interactive and participatory instructional activities in which students have little or no wait time. (Mather & Jaffe, 2002)

In addition to classroom adaptations, most individuals with ADHD require behavior management techniques—often the same techniques as those recommended for a broader range of students with behavior disorders unrelated to or comorbid with ADHD (e.g., Oppositional Defiant Disorder, Conduct Disorder, Antisocial Personality Disorder, depression, Tourette Syndrome). When choosing recommendations for an individual with ADHD, differentiate between a skill deficit (not knowing the skill) and a performance deficit (not using a known skill) and between problem behaviors that are intentional and within the person's control and those that result from weak self-regulation and poor impulse control (Mather & Jaffe, 2002). As with other areas of functioning, use specific information about the person's unique characteristics and needs to determine the specific recommendations that are the most appropriate and effective.

Recommendations for Behavioral, Emotional, or Social Difficulties

In addition to ADHD, referrals are often concerned with questions regarding behavioral, emotional, or social development. In some instances the concerns center upon disruptive behaviors, whereas in others the behaviors are nondisruptive in nature, such as those caused by depression or anxiety. Individuals with behavioral difficulties often require adaptations in order to be successful. Rapid Reference 8.16 provides examples of the types of accommodations that are commonly written in psychological and psychoeducational reports for individuals who require adjustments in the environment because of behavioral, emotional, or social concerns.

A variety of interventions and techniques may be recommended to manage and change behavior. Once you have defined the behaviors of concern, then select procedures to model and reinforce newly defined behaviors. Common interventions for managing behavior focus upon altering the setting demands and increasing the person's ability to comply. These interventions may involve behavior therapy, behavior modification, or cognitive interventions that focus upon changing how people think about and view themselves. Examples of interventions include: (1) setting expectations that adjust for behavioral difficulties, (2) implementing a classroom or home behavior management system, (3) increasing the immediacy and frequency of rewards, (4) teaching the person self-monitoring strategies, and (5) establishing goals with the person, identifying reinforcements,

≡ Rapid Reference 8.16

Sample Accommodations for Behavioral/Social/ Emotional Difficulties

- Ignore Steve's minor, inappropriate behaviors.
- Supervise Rosa closely during transition times.
- Seat Rachel near the teacher or next to a good role model.
- Send notes home with positive comments about Jacob's behavior.
- Mark Colin's correct responses and do not penalize him for mistakes.
- Send (daily, weekly) progress reports home.
- Recognize and reinforce Nick's efforts as well as his improvements.
- Call on Emily when you know she will be successful.
- Watch for situations where Tim is behaving appropriately and make a positive comment.
- Recognize and comment on Joanna's unique talents.

and implementing a reinforcement system. With more severe behaviors, such as conduct problems and oppositional disorders, counseling and family therapy are also recommended.

Recommendations may also address specific aspects of social functioning. Take the case of Bryan, who, despite years of social difficulties, had only been diagnosed as having nonverbal learning disabilities as a senior in high school. The following recommendation, adapted from Mather and Jaffe (2002), was written to address Bryan's difficulties in social interactions:

> Due to Bryan's nonverbal learning disabilities and resultant difficulties in social interactions, he may experience difficulties in either the workplace or in postsecondary education. Prior to transition from high school, he needs to receive a program of social skills training that directly addresses his abilities to: recognize and interpret nonverbal communications (such as facial expressions, body postures, and gestures); recognize and respect personal space; and interpret subtle language cues, such as changes in voice, pitch, tone, or volume.

Vocational Recommendations

In addition to problems in school or home, some clients are referred or refer themselves because of problems or challenges in the vocational setting. These types of evaluations typically focus upon assessing the person's ability to function independently and age-appropriately in the following areas: current vocational skills, vocational training, independent living or residential placement, transportation, finances, recreation/leisure, social relationships, and sexual awareness. After a functional vocational evaluation, the evaluator may make recommendations that address the person's interests, preferences, and abilities. Based upon the person's aptitudes, the recommendations may address provision of relevant work experience, skills needed for independent living, vocational training, career and technology courses, or the need for related services, such as rehabilitation counseling. School districts are required to develop specific goals and objectives for transition planning that are to be written in Individual Transition Plans (ITPs). Thus, recommendations for vocational training, the transition from school to independent living, or the transition from secondary to postsecondary education are often included as part of a comprehensive evaluation.

CONCLUSION

Preparing a report with meaningful and useful recommendations takes time, but this time investment is returned by the development of appropriate goals and interventions tailored to the needs of the specific individual (Connolly, 1998). Identify an individual's specific strengths and weaknesses, and then use this information to create specific recommendations to enhance his or her performance. These suggestions for accommodations, interventions, and treatments are the solutions to the referral questions, and they provide the involved participants with a road map to follow.

🔎 TEST YOURSELF 🔎

1. **An appropriate accommodation for Juanita, a student with a slow reading rate due to her learning disability, is**
   (a) Give Juanita an unlimited amount of time to take the SAT.
   (b) Give Juanita one extra hour to complete the SAT.
   (c) Juanita should not have to take the SAT because of her slow reading rate.
   (d) Allow Juanita to take the SAT multiple times with no penalty because of her slow reading rate.

2. **To make sure that recommendations are followed, you should write them in the Test Results and Interpretation section and then review them again in the Recommendations section.** True or False?

3. **An accommodation often involves an adjustment of a task so that a person can perform the task or portion of the task.** True or False

4. **The use of subsections and subheadings in the Recommendations section does not improve the organization.** True or False?

5. **The specificity of the recommendations may depend upon**
   (a) availability of resources.
   (b) background and training of the evaluator.
   (c) cost of treatments.
   (d) motivation and desires of the individual.
   (e) any of the above

6. **As a rule of thumb, you should**
   (a) always include at least two recommendations.
   (b) never write more than ten recommendations.
   (c) have as many recommendations as you have pages in your report.
   (d) not have a hard and fast rule about how many recommendations to write in each report, and let the number of issues in the report dictate the number of recommendations.

7. **Some case reports will have few recommendations and instead will refer the person for further evaluation or to another professional with special expertise in the area of concern (e.g., an occupational therapist).** True or False?

Answers: 1. b; 2. False; 3. True; 4. False; 5. e; 6. d; 7. True

Nine

SPECIAL ISSUES IN REPORT WRITING

This chapter covers several issues related to report writing, including presenting feedback to the examinee and referring persons, using computers to facilitate assessments, and adhering to ethical standards in assessment.

FEEDBACK

After the evaluation has been completed and the assessment report written, you will usually conduct a conference with parents, teachers, other professionals, or the person whom you evaluated. (Or whoever requested the evaluation in the first place, if another party.) The central purpose of this conference is to address and resolve the referral questions and ensure that the findings of the evaluation are understood.

Providing accurate and clear feedback to people about assessment results requires considerable clinical skill. Not only do you need to communicate clearly, but you also need to observe how people are responding to the information so that you can modify your approach, if necessary.

Additional factors need to be considered when you are working with people or families for whom English is a second language. Prior to the conference, think about whether a translator is necessary. Be aware that both parents and children may have different levels of English language ability. Thus, a translator would be beneficial even if just one family member needs the service. In such situations, more visual ways of communicating (such as graphs to indicate test results) can also facilitate the feedback session.

Conference Participants

In preparing for the conference, you will want to consider these points:

- Who will be attending the conference? (e.g., child, parents, an adult client, teacher, social worker, counselor, multiple participants)
- How are they likely to respond to your findings and conclusions?

Parents

When meeting with parents, first and foremost, make sure that they feel at ease. Keep in mind that in some cases parents may be feeling frightened, emotional, and concerned about your findings. At the beginning of the conference, it may be wise to ask for an update on how the child is doing at present, since you first met with the parents. This way you may learn about new circumstances that could have been forgotten once the conference proceeds. It also allows the parents to begin their role in the conference as active participants. After the parents have given their update, spend at least the first 5 minutes discussing the relative strengths that you gleaned from the background information, teacher reports, and observations during the process of the evaluation. Summarize competent behaviors related to all aspects of functioning, including behavioral, emotional, social, cognitive, linguistic, academic, and vocational domains. To encourage parent participation and elicit their perceptions, stop and ask them if they agree with your observations and if there are other areas of strength or competence that they have observed at school or at home.

Next, you will want to address any concerns or relative weaknesses that have emerged from your review of all the qualitative and quantitative data. You may transition into this part of the discussion with statements like "Although Rosalda is an excellent reader, her math skills are not as advanced" or "Although Tom has advanced verbal reasoning ability, he struggles on tasks that require listening to and repeating back information." It is best to discuss these weaknesses in general terms, rather than relying on or discussing specific test scores. The final stage of the conference then focuses on the solutions and recommendations, including what changes need to be made in the environment or setting. Although the parents of children you assess comprise a heterogeneous group with differing levels of education and income, they share one experience: You evaluated their child. In most instances, they will respond positively to your presentation of results when they recognize that you understand and are an advocate for their child.

You will also want to consider the dynamics between the parents as well as the parents' relationships with their child. Do the parents have the same view of the presenting problem? If they do not, make sure that the differing views are addressed. Ensure that you acknowledge the views of both parents. Furthermore, the parents may differ in their feelings toward the evaluation. Were both parents in favor of having their child assessed? If one parent was less supportive, then you may need to work harder to convince that parent of the benefits of following through with the recommendations. Is one parent more protective of the child than the other? An overly protective parent may not be as receptive to your feedback, especially if it contradicts his or her opinions. When differences are not easy to reconcile, explain to the parents that working as a team with similar goals and plans will more quickly resolve their child's difficulties.

To prepare for delivering feedback, review the dynamics that were present during the first session with the parents. If the mother asked multiple questions during the intake, she may behave similarly at the feedback session. If the mother and father disagreed about the severity of the presenting problem, they may also disagree about your conclusions. No matter how well you prepare for the conference, however, the parents' reactions may still surprise you.

In addition to preparing yourself for a particular audience, consider the background of the people attending the conference. Some parents will require a more careful explanation of the results. Other parents will more readily understand the assessment findings. As with a written assessment report, use clear, concise descriptions and avoid using technical terms.

In instances where you are providing a first diagnosis of a serious condition— for example, a diagnosis of autism for a 4-year-old—you may need to plan on presenting more documentation, creating steps for the parents to digest information before proceeding with the buildup of evidence, and showing how you eliminated other possible diagnostic categories.

Children

You may also discuss your assessment results with children, but the type of feedback given to children is quite different from that given to parents. Clearly, the information discussed with a child needs to be appropriate to the child's developmental level. An adolescent may receive feedback that is somewhat similar to a parent's, whereas the feedback to a young child would be much shorter and more simplistic. Children will not understand or particularly care about the details of an assessment, but by choosing developmentally appropriate language, you can communicate to them what the results mean and how the findings will be used to help them. Rapid Reference 9.1 provides several examples of how to share results with a young child.

Teachers

In addition to holding conferences for parents and children, you may meet individually with a teacher, particularly if the teacher was the one who made the referral. A face-to-face meeting with the child's teacher may help the teacher select or consider appropriate classroom interventions. Like parents, teachers often welcome the chance to ask questions about the assessment report so that they clearly understand the results and recommendations. In addition, you can often elicit suggestions from the teacher for additional ways to improve the child's social adjustment or academic performance.

≡ *Rapid Reference 9.1*

Samples of Feedback for Children

"Remember those different things that we did? It was easy for you to do all those math problems, but you had a harder time when I asked you to read words. Because of this, I told your parents about a good teacher who can help you with your reading after school."

"Some of the things we did today helped me to understand how you feel about going to school. When you told stories about some of the pictures I showed you, I learned that you feel pretty scared about going to school. Sometimes you feel so scared that you get sick, so you don't have to go to school. I told your parents that it would be good if you went to see a special person who can talk with you about your feelings and who will work with you and your parents to help you feel less scared about going to school."

"During the time that we spent together, I noticed that it was hard for you to sit still, even for things that were fun for you. Your teacher and parents told me that you have a hard time sitting still at school and at home too and that sometimes you can't get your work done, so you get in trouble. I'm going to talk to your parents about some ideas that will help you be able to sit and listen for a longer time."

When an evaluation has originated outside of the school and the teacher has been interviewed for background information concerning one of his or her pupils, providing feedback is a courtesy that the teacher may expect. But be sure to discuss with the parents the need for the teacher's learning of the evaluation's results, even if some detail is omitted to protect the family's privacy. Help parents who are concerned about sharing this information to develop enough trust and understanding of the need for their child's teacher's involvement in carrying out some of the recommendations.

Multiple Participants

Conferences, particularly those in schools, often involve multiple participants. In some situations, you may be the person who facilitates the conference. In school conferences where many people are attending, do not begin the conference with a discussion of test scores or test performance. Instead, begin the meeting by encouraging everyone to contribute to the discussion and share his or her perceptions of what the student does well. Once the parents, teachers, and others have shared their thoughts about areas of competence, encourage each member to discuss any areas of perceived challenges. As with your report, the last part of the conference will focus upon ways to address and resolve the referral questions.

Encourage conference members to ask questions or to interrupt you, if necessary. You may begin your discussion with a statement such as "Let me know if I am speaking too quickly" or "Feel free to stop me if you have questions or would like clarification." Be a keen observer, and if someone looks confused, stop and ask, "Do you have any questions up to this point?" After you have presented your summary of the results, encourage the participants to respond. You may ask, "What questions do you have for me?" or "What is your opinion of the results?"

Responses to Findings

If you begin the conference by discussing positive results and reminding participants that the main goal is to work together to come up with strategies that will help the person, most participants will respond favorably to your conclusions. Parents often feel an immense sense of relief when someone understands their child's situation and can help them plan an appropriate course of action. Your findings can also help a person develop a clearer understanding of strengths and weaknesses so that he or she can be a more effective advocate for him- or herself in the classroom or workplace.

On occasion, you may encounter some clients or parents who have personal issues (e.g., underlying feelings of insecurity, past history of being negatively labeled, previous negative experiences with a therapist, problems with prior evaluations) that may predispose them to respond in a defensive manner. In other cases the evaluation may be court ordered, and you may be viewed as an authority figure, not as an advocate. If you encounter negativity, one way to regain positive footing is to turn it into a team approach and ask the defensive person for interpretations and suggestions. Also, you may be able to reduce any tension that develops during the meeting by validating what the person is experiencing and then reminding him or her of the purpose of the assessment. For example, you may say, "All people have learning and behavioral differences, and by understanding Steve's unique abilities we are better prepared to help him in school." If someone appears uncomfortable with a diagnosis or your conclusions, remind him or her that an understanding of difficulties can be used effectively to select appropriate treatments.

If the primary person to hear the results at the conference has long-standing, severe emotional or psychological problems (e.g., severe depression or anxiety), you may suggest that he or she bring along another family member or trusted representative to hear the feedback. The presence of additional familiar people in the session can help lend support to the person. The next Don't Forget reviews several factors to consider for the feedback conference.

DON'T FORGET

Dos and Don'ts of Feedback Conferences

Do	Don't
• Prepare for the conference by anticipating questions that may be asked.	• Cover up important findings.
	• Discourage questions.
• Discuss strengths and areas of competence.	• Be caught off guard by an angry parent or client.
• Be honest, even about difficult information.	• Make unsupported long-term predictions, such as "Jaime will always struggle with math."
• Encourage the person to ask questions.	• Expect all conferences to run completely smoothly. (Some clients and parents may need time to accept the assessment results.)
• Elicit ideas from others about the results.	
• Bring visual aids (such as a picture of a bell curve to explain the meaning of percentile ranks).	• Try to provide professional services beyond your scope of expertise (e.g., when a parent asks you for specific information on biofeedback or on marital counseling and you do not have training in those areas).
• Practice giving the feedback.	
• Schedule adequate time for the feedback conference.	
• Keep the tone of the conference as positive as possible.	

The amount of time that a person takes to digest the information presented in an assessment report will also vary. During and after the face-to-face feedback session, some individuals will immediately have multiple questions for you. Others will first go home, read the written report, and reconsider the information that you presented in the session. Remind them that if they have questions later, you will be happy to answer them. They are likely to find the invitation for future professional contact reassuring.

It is not uncommon to receive a phone call from the person evaluated or his or her parents a few days or weeks after the feedback conference with a request for clarification on issues or with more specific questions. Some people will share their written report with other sources, such as the child's pediatrician or classroom teacher. Then, after you have discussed the information with the child's doctor or teacher, more questions will arise and they will contact you again.

You can handle post–feedback session questions in several ways. If the person's questions are few and straightforward, you may simply respond to the questions over the phone. In other situations, you may want to schedule a follow-up face-to-face consultation. We recommend such a consultation if the questions are complicated, if the person seems to have a high level of anxiety or concern about the particular issue, or if the person asks to see you again in person.

Occasionally, people whom you have evaluated or their parents may contact you several years after the initial evaluation. For example, a mother may call you a year after you evaluated her son for a learning disability because he has made good progress in school and she would like to document his progress. Or a father may call you months after an assessment and request that you update your report because he feels his daughter, who did not qualify for special services at the time of the report, is still struggling in school and may now be eligible for services. In such situations, a brief follow-up assessment or mini-assessment may be completed, and you can write a letter or brief report to document the changes. Do not modify a past report (it serves as a written record), but instead report new or different findings in a follow-up document.

You also may receive calls several years after the evaluation. This typically occurs when the person whom you evaluated is transitioning into a new setting and the results need to be reconfirmed or updated. For example, when Kevin began law school, a reevaluation was needed to document a continued need for the accommodation of extended time on examinations. Thus, it is important to keep evaluations for over a decade. Fortunately, computers can facilitate the storing and retrieving of written reports.

COMPUTERS IN THE ASSESSMENT PROCESS

Over the past couple of decades computers have changed the way many assessments proceed—from administration to scoring and report writing. Computers assist in the administration of some types of instruments, such as clinical interview, behavioral observation, and continuous performance measures (e.g., BASC, Structured Clinical Interview [SCID], and Conner's Continuous Performance Test–II [CPT-II]). Computers also help score tests and provide basic results in report form for various measures, including tests of intelligence (e.g., WAIS-III, WISC-IV, KABC-II, WJ III COG), achievement tests (e.g., WIAT-II, K-TEA-II, WJ III ACH), and personality tests (e.g., MMPI-II, MCMI-III). Figure 9.1 contains examples of a report generated by the WJ III Report Writer (Schrank & Woodcock, 2002). This report can be compared to the actual report written by a clinician in Chapter 10.

Name: Downing, Martha
Grade: 5.7
Age: 11 years, 10 months

School: Green Acres Country Day
Sex: Female

TESTS ADMINISTERED

WJ III Tests of Cognitive Abilities
WJ III Tests of Achievement

These tests provide measures of Martha's overall intellectual ability, specific cognitive abilities, academic achievement, and oral language abilities. Relative strengths and weaknesses among her cognitive and academic abilities are described in this report. A description of each ability is provided. Martha's performance in each broad category is compared to grade peers using a standard score range. Her proficiency is described categorically, ranging from very limited to very advanced; Martha's test performance can be generalized to similar, non-test, grade-level tasks. Additional interpretation of cognitive and academic task performance is provided.

INTELLECTUAL ABILITY

Martha's general intellectual ability, as measured by the WJ III GIA (Ext) score, is in the average range of others her grade. There is a 68% probability that her true GIA score would be included in the range of scores from 93 to 97.

COGNITIVE ABILITIES

Among her cognitive abilities, Martha has a relative strength in Phonemic Awareness. Phonemic Awareness includes the knowledge and skills related to analyzing and synthesizing speech sounds. Her phonemic awareness standard score is within the very superior range (percentile rank of >99; standard score range of 151 to 178) when compared to others in her grade. Her awareness of phonemes is very advanced; Martha will probably find grade-level tasks requiring the ability to apply phonemic information in immediate awareness extremely easy.

Auditory Processing is also a relative cognitive strength for Martha. Auditory Processing measures Martha's ability to analyze, synthesize, and discriminate auditory stimuli, including her ability to process and discriminate speech sounds presented under distorted conditions. Although her overall auditory processing standard score is within the very superior range, her performance varied on two different types of auditory processing tasks. Martha's performance is very advanced on tasks involving synthesis of speech. Her performance is average on tasks requiring discrimination of speech sounds.

Martha's cognitive abilities are in the average range in Comprehension-Knowledge (the breadth and depth of language-based knowledge, including the ability to communicate (especially verbally) one's verbal knowledge and comprehension), Visual-Spatial Thinking (the ability to perceive, analyze, synthesize, and think with visual patterns, including the ability to store and recall visual representations), and Fluid Reasoning (the ability to reason, form concepts, and solve problems using unfamiliar information or novel procedures).

Short-Term Memory is the ability to hold information in immediate awareness and use it within a few seconds. Martha's short-term memory standard score is within the low to low average range (percentile rank range of 8 to 23; standard score range of 79 to 89) for her grade. Her short-term memory capacity is limited; it is likely that she will find grade-level tasks such as remembering just-imparted instructions or information or mentally manipulating information in immediate awareness very difficult.

Figure 9.1 Example of Computer-Generated WJ III Report

Working Memory measures Martha's ability to hold information in immediate awareness while performing a mental operation on the information. Martha's working memory standard score is within the low to low average range (percentile rank range of 8 to 19; standard score range of 78 to 87) for her grade. Her working memory capacity is limited; this suggests that she will find grade-level tasks requiring complex processing of information in immediate memory very difficult.

Among her cognitive abilities, Martha has a relative weakness in Long-Term Retrieval. Long-Term Retrieval is the ability to store and retrieve information. Her long-term retrieval standard score is within the low to low average range (percentile rank range of 5 to 16; standard score range of 75 to 85) for her grade. Her long-term retrieval is average; it is predicted that Martha will find grade-level tasks requiring strategies to store, and fluency to retrieve, information manageable.

Processing Speed is also a relative cognitive weakness for Martha. Processing Speed measures Martha's ability to perform simple and automatic cognitive tasks rapidly, particularly when under pressure to maintain focused attention. Although her overall processing speed standard score is within the low range, she performed differently on two types of speeded tasks. Martha's performance is average on tasks requiring speed in correctly processing simple concepts. Her performance is very limited on tasks requiring visual perceptual speed.

Cognitive Fluency

Martha's speed in performing simple to complex cognitive tasks is limited. Specifically, her fluency of retrieval from stored knowledge and speed of forming simple concepts are average; her speed of direct recall of simple vocabulary is negligible.

ACHIEVEMENT

When compared to others in her grade, Martha's academic achievement is in the average range in Oral Expression (linguistic competency in spoken English language), Written Expression (fluency of production and quality of expression in writing), Academic Knowledge (science knowledge, social studies knowledge, and cultural knowledge), Oral Language (linguistic competency, listening ability, and oral comprehension), Listening Comprehension (listening ability and verbal comprehension), Broad Written Language (production of written text, including spelling ability, writing fluency, and quality of written expression), and Basic Reading Skills (sight vocabulary, phonics, and structural analysis skills).

Broad Reading includes reading decoding, reading speed, and the ability to comprehend connected discourse while reading. Although Martha's overall reading standard score is within the average range, her performance was different for two types of reading tasks. Martha's performance is average on tasks requiring reading decoding and the ability to identify words. Her performance is very limited on tasks requiring efficient operation of reading processes.

Mathematics Reasoning includes mathematical knowledge and reasoning. Martha's mathematics reasoning standard score is within the low average to average range (percentile rank range of 17 to 29; standard score range of 86 to 92) for her grade. Her mathematics reasoning ability is limited; math reasoning tasks above the grade 5.1 level will be quite difficult for her.

Broad Math includes mathematics reasoning and problem solving, number facility, and automaticity. Martha's mathematics standard score is within the low average range (per-

Figure 9.1 continued

centile rank range of 9 to 17; standard score range of 80 to 85) for her grade. Her overall mathematics ability is limited; math tasks above the grade 4.7 level will be quite difficult for her.

Math Calculation Skills measures Martha's computational skills and automaticity with basic math facts. Martha's mathematics calculation skills standard score is within the low range (percentile rank range of 2 to 7; standard score range of 70 to 78) for her grade. Her mathematics calculation skills are limited; math calculation tasks above the grade 4.1 level will be quite difficult for her.

Academic Processing

Academic Skills. Martha's sight reading ability is average. Her math calculation skill and spelling are limited.

Academic Fluency. Martha's writing fluency is average. Her fluency with mathematics problems is limited. Her fluency with reading tasks is very limited.

Martha's ability to apply her academic skills is average. For example, her passage comprehension ability and writing ability are average. Her quantitative reasoning is limited to average.

SUMMARY

Martha's overall intellectual ability, as measured by the WJ III GIA (Ext), is in the average range.

When compared to others at her grade level, Martha's performance is very superior in auditory processing and phonemic awareness; average in comprehension-knowledge, visual-spatial thinking, and fluid reasoning; low average in long-term retrieval, short-term memory, and working memory; and low in processing speed. When her cognitive abilities are compared, she demonstrated significant relative strengths in phonemic awareness and auditory processing. She demonstrated significant relative weaknesses in long-term retrieval and processing speed.

Martha's English oral language skills (oral expression and listening comprehension) are average when compared to others at her grade level. Her overall level of achievement is average. Her fluency with academic tasks is low average. Martha's knowledge, her academic skills, and her ability to apply academic skills, are all within the average range.

When compared to others at her grade level, Martha's performance is average in broad reading, basic reading skills, written language, and written expression; low average in math reasoning; and low in math calculation skills. No discrepancies were found among Martha's achievement areas.

When Martha's cognitive and achievement abilities are jointly compared, she demonstrated significant relative strengths in auditory processing and phonemic awareness. She demonstrated a significant relative weakness in processing speed.

To help determine if any ability/achievement discrepancies exist, comparisons were made among Martha's cognitive, oral language, and achievement scores. When compared to her overall intellectual ability, her achievement is significantly lower than predicted in the area of math calculation skills. Her math calculation skills are significantly lower than would be predicted by her English oral language ability. Based on a mix of cognitive tasks associated with performance in each area, Martha is performing at predicted levels in reading, mathematics, written language, knowledge, and oral language.

Figure 9.1   continued

TABLE OF SCORES: Woodcock-Johnson III Tests of Cognitive Abilities and Tests of Achievement

Report Writer for the WJ III, Version 1.1
Norms based on grade 5.7

CLUSTER/Test	Raw	GE	EASY to DIFF		RPI	PR	SS(68% BAND)	AE
GIA (Ext)	—	4.7	2.6	7.6	86/90	37	95 (93–97)	10–0
VERBAL ABILITY (Ext)	—	6.1	4.4	9.3	92/90	57	102 (98–107)	11–8
THINKING ABILITY (Ext)	—	9.1	3.4	16.0	93/90	71	108 (104–113)	13–6
COG EFFICIENCY (Ext)	—	2.9	2.0	3.9	41/90	5	75 (71–79)	8–3
COMP-KNOWLEDGE (Gc)	—	6.1	4.4	9.3	92/90	57	102 (98–107)	11–8
L-T RETRIEVAL (Glr)	—	2.3	K.6	10.8	82/90	9	80 (75–85)	7–11
VIS-SPATIAL THINK (Gv)	—	6.2	2.1	16.6	91/90	53	101 (97–106)	11–3
AUDITORY PROCESS (Ga)	—	>19.0	>19.0	>19.0	100/90	>99.9	151 (138–163)	>25
FLUID REASONING (Gf)	—	3.6	2.3	5.8	76/90	28	91 (88–94)	9–0
PROCESS SPEED (Gs)	—	3.0	2.3	3.9	31/90	6	77 (74–80)	8–6
SHORT-TERM MEM (Gsm)	—	2.6	1.6	3.9	53/90	14	84 (79–89)	7–9
PHONEMIC AWARE	—	>19.0	>19.0	>19.0	100/90	>99.9	165 (151–178)	>28
WORKING MEMORY	—	2.7	1.8	3.9	53/90	12	83 (78–87)	8–0
COGNITIVE FLUENCY	—	2.0	K.9	3.5	45/90	4	73 (70–75)	7–4
KNOWLEDGE	—	5.8	4.2	7.7	91/90	52	101 (96–105)	11–1
ORAL LANGUAGE (Ext)	—	6.6	3.8	11.1	92/90	61	104 (100–108)	11–11
ORAL EXPRESSION	—	9.3	4.7	13.4	95/90	75	110 (105–115)	13–8
LISTENING COMP	—	5.2	3.2	9.1	88/90	45	98 (94–102)	10–8
TOTAL ACHIEVEMENT	—	4.3	3.4	5.6	74/90	27	91 (89–92)	9–9
BROAD READING	—	4.5	3.7	5.6	73/90	31	92 (91–94)	9–10
BROAD MATH	—	3.6	2.7	4.7	57/90	12	83 (80–85)	9–1
BROAD WRITTEN LANG	—	5.2	3.8	7.2	87/90	42	97 (94–100)	10–5

Figure 9.1 continued

CLUSTER/Test	Raw	GE	EASY	to	DIFF	RPI	PR	SS(68% BAND)	AE
BASIC READING SKILLS	—	5.0	4.0		6.5	84/90	43	97 (95–99)	10–6
MATH CALC SKILLS	—	3.0	2.1		4.1	49/90	4	74 (70–78)	8–5
MATH REASONING	—	4.1	3.3		5.1	63/90	23	89 (86–92)	9–7
WRITTEN EXPRESSION	—	6.2	4.3		9.2	92/90	60	104 (98–109)	11–8
ACADEMIC SKILLS	—	4.4	3.7		5.5	72/90	28	91 (89–94)	9–9
ACADEMIC FLUENCY	—	3.9	3.0		5.0	61/90	18	86 (84–88)	9–3
ACADEMIC APPS	—	4.8	3.5		7.0	84/90	39	96 (93–98)	10–4
ACADEMIC KNOWLEDGE	—	5.9	4.3		7.6	91/90	53	101 (96–106)	11–0
Verbal Comprehension	—	6.5	4.6		9.9	93/90	61	104 (99–110)	12–1
Visual-Auditory Learning	22–E	2.1	K.8		6.4	77/90	13	83 (79–88)	7–9
Spatial Relations	64–D	5.1	1.6		14.5	89/90	47	99 (94–103)	10–0
Sound Blending	33	>19.0	>19.0		>19.0	100/90	>99.9	166 (149–182)	>26
Concept Formation	20–E	3.1	2.1		4.6	64/90	24	90 (86–93)	8–6
Visual Matching	27–2	2.2	1.7		2.7	4/90	1	65 (62–69)	7–9
Numbers Reversed	8	2.0	1.3		2.7	27/90	9	80 (75–85)	6–11
Incomplete Words	29	>19.0	11.6		>19.0	98/90	96	127 (119–135)	>33
Auditory Work Memory	16	4.0	2.6		6.0	78/90	30	92 (88–96)	9–7
General Information	–	5.8	4.2		7.9	90/90	51	100 (94–107)	11–2
Retrieval Fluency	48	3.0	K.1		>19.0	86/90	17	86 (80–92)	8–6
Picture Recognition	49–D	7.3	2.7		>19.0	92/90	59	103 (98–109)	12–8
Auditory Attention	39	9.4	2.0		13.0	93/90	65	106 (99–113)	13–6
Analysis-Synthesis	22–E	4.4	2.6		7.5	84/90	37	95 (89–101)	9–8
Decision Speed	28	4.9	3.6		6.5	84/90	38	95 (91–100)	10–4
Memory for Words	16	3.9	2.3		6.0	77/90	35	94 (88–100)	9–0
Rapid Picture Naming	64	<K.0	<K.0		K.6	2/90	1	65 (64–67)	5–4

Figure 9.1 continued

Form A of the following achievement tests was administered:

Letter-Word Identification	58	6.3	5.2	7.8	94/90	61	104 (100–108)	12–0
Reading Fluency	28	3.0	2.5	3.5	11/90	10	81 (79–83)	8–4
Story Recall	–	9.8	1.7	>19.0	92/90	66	106 (100–112)	13–7
Understanding Directions	–	4.2	2.3	9.3	84/90	36	95 (89–100)	9–7
Calculation	13	3.2	2.6	4.0	36/90	8	79 (73–84)	8–8
Math Fluency	32	2.4	K.6	4.5	63/90	4	73 (70–75)	7–10
Spelling	31	4.1	3.2	5.2	67/90	27	91 (87–94)	8–11
Writing Fluency	20	6.6	5.2	9.5	95/90	67	106 (101–112)	12–1
Passage Comprehension	32	5.8	3.9	9.1	90/90	51	100 (94–107)	10–11
Applied Problems	33	4.4	3.6	5.4	70/90	32	93 (89–96)	10–1
Writing Samples	10–D	4.8	2.3	11.6	88/90	39	96 (87–105)	10–3
Word Attack	17	3.3	2.4	4.8	64/90	30	92 (90–94)	8–8
Picture Vocabulary	29	9.2	6.0	11.1	97/90	74	110 (105–115)	13–8
Oral Comprehension	21	6.0	4.0	9.5	91/90	53	101 (96–106)	11–5
Quantitative Concepts	–	3.7	2.9	4.7	55/90	16	85 (81–90)	9–1
Academic Knowledge	–	5.9	4.3	7.6	91/90	53	101 (96–106)	11–0

	STANDARD SCORES			DISCREPANCY		Significant at
DISCREPANCIES	Actual	Predicted	Difference	PR	SD	+ or – 1.50 SD (SEE)
Intra-Cognitive						
COMP-KNOWLEDGE (Gc)	102	97	5	66	+0.42	No
L-T RETRIEVAL (Glr)	80	101	–21	5	–1.62	Yes
VIS-SPATIAL THINK (Gv)	101	99	2	58	+0.20	No
AUDITORY PROCESS (Ga)	151	92	59	>99.9	+4.46	Yes
FLUID REASONING (Gf)	91	99	–8	24	–0.72	No
PROCESS SPEED (Gs)	77	101	–24	4	–1.81	Yes
SHORT-TERM MEM (Gsm)	84	100	–16	10	–1.28	No

Figure 9.1 continued

DISCREPANCIES	STANDARD SCORES			DISCREPANCY		Significant at + or − 1.50 SD (SEE)
	Actual	Predicted	Difference	PR	SD	
PHONEMIC AWARE	165	92	73	>99.9	+5.78	Yes
WORKING MEMORY	83	100	−17	8	−1.38	No
Intra-Achievement						
BROAD READING	92	94	−2	46	−0.11	No
BROAD MATH	83	97	−14	10	−1.26	No
BROAD WRITTEN LANG	97	92	5	67	+0.45	No
ORAL LANGUAGE (Std)	98	94	4	63	+0.32	No
Intra-Individual						
COMP-KNOWLEDGE (Gc)	102	95	7	76	+0.70	No
L-T RETRIEVAL (Glr)	80	98	−18	9	−1.33	No
VIS-SPATIAL THINK (Gv)	101	97	4	61	+0.29	No
AUDITORY PROCESS (Ga)	151	93	58	>99.9	+4.40	Yes
FLUID REASONING (Gf)	91	97	−6	31	−0.50	No
PROCESS SPEED (Gs)	77	98	−21	5	−1.67	Yes
SHORT-TERM MEM (Gsm)	84	98	−14	13	−1.11	No
PHONEMIC AWARE	165	93	72	>99.9	+5.58	Yes
WORKING MEMORY	83	98	−15	9	−1.32	No
BROAD READING	92	97	−5	35	−0.38	No
BROAD MATH	83	98	−15	8	−1.39	No
BROAD WRITTEN LANG	97	96	1	53	+0.08	No
ORAL LANGUAGE (Std)	98	96	2	57	+0.18	No
Intellectual Ability/Achievement Discrepancies*						
BROAD READING	92	96	−4	35	−0.39	No
BASIC READING SKILLS	97	97	0	49	−0.02	No
BROAD MATH	83	97	−14	8	−1.38	No
MATH CALC SKILLS	74	98	−24	3	−1.83	Yes
MATH REASONING	89	97	−8	21	−0.80	No

Figure 9.1 continued

BROAD WRITTEN LANG	97	97	0	49	−0.04	No
WRITTEN EXPRESSION	104	97	7	72	+0.60	No
ORAL LANGUAGE (Ext)	104	97	7	75	+0.67	No
ORAL EXPRESSION	110	97	13	87	+1.15	No
LISTENING COMP	98	97	1	54	+0.09	No
ACADEMIC KNOWLEDGE	101	97	4	67	+0.43	No

*These discrepancies compare GIA (Ext) with Broad, Basic, and Applied ACH clusters.

Oral Language/Achievement Discrepancies*

BROAD READING	92	102	−10	23	−0.73	No
BASIC READING SKILLS	97	102	−5	37	−0.34	No
BROAD MATH	83	102	−19	7	−1.47	No
MATH CALC SKILLS	74	101	−27	3	−1.84	Yes
MATH REASONING	89	102	−13	13	−1.12	No
BROAD WRITTEN LANG	97	102	−5	34	−0.41	No
WRITTEN EXPRESSION	104	102	2	56	+0.15	No
ACADEMIC KNOWLEDGE	101	103	−2	44	−0.14	No

*These discrepancies compare Oral Language (Ext) with Broad, Basic, and Applied ACH clusters.

Predicted Achievement/Achievement Discrepancies*

BROAD READING	92	95	−3	42	−0.21	No
BASIC READING SKILLS	97	100	−3	42	−0.21	No
BROAD MATH	83	84	−1	43	−0.18	No
MATH CALC SKILLS	74	82	−8	25	−0.68	No
MATH REASONING	89	89	0	49	−0.04	No
BROAD WRITTEN LANG	97	93	4	65	+0.39	No
WRITTEN EXPRESSION	104	94	10	80	+0.85	No
ORAL LANGUAGE (Ext)	104	104	0	50	+0.01	No
ORAL EXPRESSION	110	108	2	57	+0.17	No
LISTENING COMP	98	100	−2	42	−0.19	No
ACADEMIC KNOWLEDGE	101	103	−2	41	−0.23	No

*These discrepancies compare predicted achievement scores with Broad, Basic, and Applied ACH clusters.

Figure 9.1 continued

Descriptions of WJ III Tests Administered

Verbal Comprehension measured aspects of Martha's language development in spoken English language, such as knowledge of vocabulary or the ability to reason using lexical (word) knowledge.

Visual-Auditory Learning required Martha to learn, store, and retrieve a series of visual-auditory associations. On this test of associative and meaningful memory, Martha was asked to learn and recall rebuses (pictographic representations of words).

Spatial Relations required Martha to identify the two or three pieces that form a complete target shape, a visualization-of-spatial-relationships task.

Sound Blending measured Martha's skill in synthesizing language sounds (phonemes). She was asked to listen to a series of syllables or phonemes and then to blend the sounds into a word.

Concept Formation measured Martha's categorical reasoning ability. This test also measured Martha's flexibility in thinking. Martha was presented with a complete stimulus set from which to derive the rule for each item. Immediate feedback was provided regarding the correctness of each response before a new item was presented.

Visual Matching measured an aspect of cognitive efficiency—the speed at which Martha can make visual symbol discriminations. Martha was asked to locate and circle the two identical numbers in a row of six numbers. This task proceeded in difficulty from single-digit numbers to triple-digit numbers and had a 3-minute time limit.

Numbers Reversed required Martha to hold a span of numbers in immediate awareness (memory) while performing a mental operation on it (reversing the sequence).

Incomplete Words measured auditory analysis and auditory closure, aspects of phonemic awareness and phonetic coding. After hearing, from an audio recording, a word that has one or more phonemes missing, Martha was asked to identify the complete word.

Auditory Working Memory measured Martha's short-term auditory memory span. She was asked to listen to a series that contains digits and words, such as "dog, 1, shoe, 8, 2, apple." She was then asked to reorder the information, repeating first the objects in sequential order and then the digits in sequential order. This task required Martha to hold information in immediate awareness, divide the information into two groups, and shift attentional resources to the two new ordered sequences.

General Information provided an index of Martha's general verbal knowledge. This test has two subtests. In the first subtest, Martha was asked, "Where would you find . . . (an object)?" In the second subtest, she was asked, "What would you do with . . . (an object)?" The initial items involved objects that appear commonly in the environment. The items became increasingly difficult as the selected objects become more unusual.

Retrieval Fluency measured Martha's fluency of retrieval from stored knowledge. She was asked to name as many examples as possible from a given category within a 1-minute time period. The task consisted of three different categories: things to eat or drink, first names of people, and animals.

Picture Recognition measured visual memory of objects or pictures. Martha's task was to recognize a subset of previously presented pictures within a field of distracting pictures.

Figure 9.1 continued

Auditory Attention measured an aspect of speech-sound discrimination—the ability to overcome the effects of auditory distortion or masking in understanding oral language. This is an auditory processing ability requiring selective attention: Martha's task was to listen to a word, while seeing four pictures, and then point to the correct picture for the word. As the test progressed, the task increased in difficulty in two ways: the sound discriminations became increasingly difficult and added background noise increased in intensity.

Analysis-Synthesis measured Martha's ability to reason and draw conclusions from given conditions (or deductive reasoning). She was given instructions on how to perform an increasingly complex procedure; she was also given immediate feedback regarding the correctness of each response before a new item was presented.

Decision Speed measured Martha's ability to make correct conceptual decisions quickly. In each row, her task was to locate quickly the two pictures that are most similar conceptually. This test had a 3-minute time limit.

Memory for Words measured Martha's short-term auditory memory span. In this test, she was asked to repeat lists of unrelated words in the correct sequence.

Rapid Picture Naming required naming facility, a form of cognitive fluency. This test measured Martha's speed of direct recall of information from her acquired knowledge. This test had a 2-minute time limit.

Letter-Word Identification measured Martha's ability to identify letters and words. She was not required to know the meaning of any word.

Reading Fluency measured Martha's ability to quickly read simple sentences, decide if the statement is true, and then circle Yes or No. She was asked to complete as many items as possible within a 3-minute time limit.

Story Recall measured aspects of Martha's oral language ability including language development and meaningful memory. The task required her to recall increasingly complex stories that were presented using an audio recording. After listening to a passage, Martha was asked to recall as many details of the story as she could remember.

Understanding Directions required Martha to listen to a sequence of audio-recorded instructions and then follow the directions by pointing to various objects in a picture.

Calculation measured Martha's ability to perform mathematical computations. The items required her to perform addition, subtraction, multiplication, and division operations.

Math Fluency measured Martha's ability to solve simple addition, subtraction, and multiplication facts quickly. She was presented with a series of simple arithmetic problems to complete in a 3-minute time limit.

Spelling measured Martha's ability to write orally presented words correctly.

Writing Fluency measured Martha's skill in formulating and writing simple sentences quickly. She was required to write sentences relating to a given stimulus picture that includes a set of three words. This test had a 7-minute time limit.

Passage Comprehension measured Martha's ability to understand what is being read during the process of reading. Test items required Martha to read a short passage and identify a missing key word that makes sense in the context of the passage.

Figure 9.1 continued

Applied Problems measured Martha's ability to analyze and solve math problems. To solve the problems, she was required to listen to the problem, recognize the procedure to be followed, and then perform relatively simple calculations. Because many of the problems included extraneous information, Martha needed to decide not only the appropriate mathematical operations to use but also what information to include in the calculation.

Writing Samples measured Martha's skill in writing responses to a variety of demands. She was asked to produce written sentences that were evaluated with respect to the quality of expression. Martha was not penalized for any errors in basic writing skills, such as spelling or punctuation.

Word Attack measured Martha's skill in applying phonic and structural analysis skills.

Picture Vocabulary measured Martha's oral language development and word knowledge. The task required her to identify pictured objects. This was primarily an expressive language task at the single-word level.

Oral Comprehension measured Martha's ability to comprehend a short audio-recorded passage and then supply the missing word using syntactic and semantic cues. This oral language cloze procedure required use of listening, reasoning, and vocabulary abilities.

Quantitative Concepts measured Martha's knowledge of mathematical concepts, symbols, and vocabulary. There were two subtests administered: Concepts and Number Series. In the first subtest, she was required to count, use numbers and concepts, and identify mathematical terms. In the second subtest, the task required Martha to look at a series of numbers, figure out the pattern, and then provide the missing number in the series.

Academic Knowledge sampled Martha's knowledge in the sciences, history, geography, government, economics, art, music, and literature.

Figure 9.1 continued

In addition to administering, scoring, and reporting data, computers can also be useful for storing test data and other assessment-related materials. For example, you can compile and save lists of recommendations, cut and paste them into reports, and then individualize them for particular cases. Furthermore, some people have assessment data from multiple instruments and also have test data from prior assessments. Computers easily store all this information, and some programs can integrate assessment data from different assessment instruments (e.g., WAIS-III—WMS-III—WIAT-II Writer) or integrate observed behaviors and background information with test data (e.g., Kaufman WISC-III Integrated Interpretive System [K-WIIS]). Thus, computers allow evaluators to save time and help in the process of storing and retrieving assessment data. Rapid Reference 9.2 lists some of the advantages of using computers in the assessment process.

In general, computers are accurate in converting scores and performing statistical analyses. In hand scoring, people have to scan numerous tables to determine standard scores, percentile ranks, and confidence intervals. Unfortunately, it is easy to accidentally record a score from the next row or to transpose numbers when recording values from a chart. Although computers are more accurate, some software programs do have errors in the scoring tables. Indeed, you should always review the output of every computer-generated scoring program to make sure that that the results appear logical. For instance, if an examinee has Above Average subtest scores but the printout indicates that the overall standard score is in the Below Average range, then something must be wrong. Also, remember that computer programs operate upon the raw scores that were entered. If you mistakenly enter a raw score of 9 when the examinee truly earned a 6, then the computer will calculate the standard score accordingly and yield a higher score than the examinee obtained.

≡*Rapid Reference 9.2*

Computers can facilitate the following:
- editing and rewriting reports
- collecting data on several behaviors at once
- proceeding through decision-tree choices in making diagnoses
- converting raw scores to various types of standard scores
- calculating which scores differ significantly from others
- generating percentile ranks, confidence intervals, and descriptive classifications
- producing interpretive hypotheses to consider in reports
- storing significant amounts of testing data

Besides incorrectly entered raw scores, other errors can also affect assessment reports. Most clinicians use their computers as word processing instruments to write and save reports. Professionals and students who conduct many assessments often use report templates to expedite the report writing process. When using such templates, errors can be created by the find-and-replace functions in Microsoft Word, Word Perfect, and other word processing programs.

For example, the last report that Dr. X wrote on an adult with adjustment issues was on Jane Reid. Because their symptoms were similar and he administered the same instruments, he used the same basic report as a template for John Duncan's report. To expedite writing Mr. Duncan's report, Dr. X had the computer find all instances of the word *Jane* and replace them with *John*, and he also replaced all *Reid* references with *Duncan*. However, errors occurred because Dr. X forgot that he referred to Jane by her nickname, Jannie, two times in the report. Because Dr. X did not carefully review his report, he mistakenly referred to John by the name Jannie twice. Similar problems arose when replacing *she* with *he* and *her* with him. Because Dr. X did not carefully proofread the final report, Mr. Duncan was described as reporting that he had "intimacy issues with *him* spouse." Thus, be careful when using the find-and-replace function that all words have been correctly replaced.

In addition to find-and-replace errors, other problems arise when one depends too heavily on a computer's spell-check and grammar-check functions. Although these are valuable tools, they will not detect all errors. If the misspelling is a real word, the spell-check function will not highlight it as an error. For example, "She went *threw* all of the items quickly," "He made *for* errors on multiplication problems," or "His hand was *to* small to grip the scissors." Errors of this nature can be caught by human eyes proofreading a report, but they will not be detected by a computer. Furthermore, computer grammar checks are useful for finding simple mechanical problems, such as missing punctuation marks, incomplete sentences, or passive voice, but they will not judge the meaningfulness of your writing. Therefore, remember to check the final drafts of your reports for accurate, consistent, and meaningful writing.

Use caution not only when writing your own reports on the computer, but also when using computer-generated reports as a basis for your own report. Interpretive software is available with many tests, and such computer programs may generate useful assessment reports. These computer-generated interpretive reports should never, however, simply be printed out and handed to your client. Indeed, this would be unethical. Proper interpretation integrates test data with background information, behavioral observations, and supplemental test data. Clinical judgment and insight (attributes that computers lack) must be used to integrate the entire range of data. Computer-generated reports will describe the quantitative findings accurately and may provide a variety of hypotheses that can then be cross-checked with history, behavioral observations, and other data. As Ownby (1997) clearly states, "Under no circumstance should a computer interpretation be included in a report unless it is clearly supported by assessment data or clearly labeled as speculation" (p. 148). We see no reason to include something in a final written report that is merely speculation. The Caution reviews some of the problems created when computers are used in assessments.

Computerized test administration, scoring, interpretation, and computer-generated reports have raised many ethical, clinical, and professional issues. To address some of these issues, professional organizations such as the APA and the National Association of School Psychologists (NASP) have guidelines focusing on the use of computers in assessments. For example, the NASP Professional Code of Conduct (NASP, 2000) states the following relevant points:

- School psychologists do not promote or encourage inappropriate use of computer-generated test analyses or reports. In accordance with this principle, a school psychologist would not offer an unedited computer report as his or her own writing or use a computer scoring system for a test in which he or she has no training. They select scoring and interpre-

CAUTION

Problems Created When Using Computers in Assessments

- Using computer scoring and interpretive programs without carefully checking the results
- Accepting all the hypotheses derived from computer-generated interpretive reports and not considering and integrating history, behavioral observations, and supplemental test data
- Using computerized interpretive programs and generating reports without understanding the report's implications and how to modify them appropriately
- Failing to properly back up files
- Not noticing mistakes in written reports that can be attributed to helpful computer functions, such as find and replace and cut and paste
- Depending too much on the computer's spell-check and grammar-check functions and not carefully proofreading reports

tation services on the basis of accuracy and professional alignment with the underlying decision rules.

- School psychologists maintain full responsibility for any technological services used. Responsibility for decisions applies to the school psychologist and cannot be transferred to equipment, software companies, or data-processing departments.

ETHICAL STANDARDS IN ASSESSMENT

In addition to ethical use of computers, several codes exist that guide psychologists and other professionals who conduct assessments. These guidelines for assessment professionals are found in the following publications:

- *Ethical Standards of the American Psychological Association* (APA, 2002)
- *Standards for Educational and Psychological Testing* (APA, 1999)
- *Code of Fair Testing Practices in Education* (Joint Committee on Testing Practices, 1988)
- *Specialty Guidelines for Forensic Psychologists* (APA, 1991)

Familiarize yourself with the standards relevant to your area of practice so that you understand the responsibilities associated with conducting assessments and related clinical activities. The standards are considered minimum requirements for psychologists and other professionals. Rapid Reference 9.3 lists the APA's ethical standards that are relevant to assessment, and Rapid Reference 9.4 highlights

≡Rapid Reference 9.3

APA Ethical Principles for Assessment

1. Bases for Assessments
   (a) Psychologists base the opinions contained in their recommendations, reports, and diagnostic or evaluative statements, including forensic testimony, on information and techniques sufficient to substantiate their findings.
   (b) Except as noted in 1c, psychologists provide opinions of the psychological characteristics of individuals only after they have conducted an examination of the individuals adequate to support their statements or conclusions. When, despite reasonable efforts, such an examination is not practical, psychologists document the efforts they made and the result of those efforts, clarify the probable impact of their limited information on the reliability and validity of their opinions, and appropriately limit the nature and extent of their conclusions or recommendations.
   (c) When psychologists conduct a record review or provide consultation or supervision and an individual examination is not warranted or necessary for the opinion, psychologists explain this and the sources of information on which they based their conclusions and recommendations.

2. Use of Assessments
   (a) Psychologists administer, adapt, score, interpret, or use assessment techniques, interviews, tests, or instruments in a manner and for purposes that are appropriate in light of the research on or evidence of the usefulness and proper application of the techniques.
   (b) Psychologists use assessment instruments whose validity and reliability have been established for use with members of the population tested. When such validity or reliability has not been established, psychologists describe the strengths and limitations of test results and interpretation.
   (c) Psychologists use assessment methods that are appropriate to an individual's language preference and competence, unless the use of an alternative language is relevant to the assessment issues.

3. Informed Consent in Assessments
   (a) Psychologists obtain informed consent for assessments, evaluations, or diagnostic services, as described in Standards on Informed Consent, except when (1) testing is mandated by law or governmental regulations; (2) informed consent is implied because testing is conducted as a routine educational, institutional, or organizational activity (e.g., when participants voluntarily agree to assessment when applying for a job); or (3) one purpose of the testing is to evaluate decisional capacity. Informed consent includes an explanation of the nature and purpose of the assessment, fees, involvement of third parties, and limits of confidentiality and sufficient opportunity for the client/patient to ask questions and receive answers.
   (b) Psychologists inform persons with questionable capacity to consent or for whom testing is mandated by law or governmental regulations about

the nature and purpose of the proposed assessment services, using language that is reasonably understandable to the person being assessed.

(c) Psychologists using the services of an interpreter obtain informed consent from the client/patient to use that interpreter, ensure that confidentiality of test results and test security are maintained, and include in their recommendations, reports, and diagnostic or evaluative statements, including forensic testimony, discussion of any limitations on the data obtained.

4. Release of Test Data

(a) The term *test data* refers to raw and scaled scores, client/patient responses to test questions or stimuli, and psychologists' notes and recordings concerning client/patient statements and behavior during an examination. Those portions of test materials that include client/patient responses are included in the definition of *test data*. Pursuant to a client/patient release, psychologists provide test data to the client/patient or other persons identified in the release. Psychologists may refrain from releasing test data to protect a client/patient or others from substantial harm or misuse or misrepresentation of the data or the test, recognizing that in many instances release of confidential information under these circumstances is regulated by law.

(b) In the absence of a client/patient release, psychologists provide test data only as required by law or court order.

5. Test Construction

Psychologists who develop tests and other assessment techniques use appropriate psychometric procedures and current scientific or professional knowledge for test design, standardization, validation, reduction or elimination of bias, and recommendations for use.

6. Interpreting Assessment Results

When interpreting assessment results, including automated interpretations, psychologists take into account the purpose of the assessment as well as the various test factors, test-taking abilities, and other characteristics of the person being assessed, such as situational, personal, linguistic, and cultural differences, that might affect psychologists' judgments or reduce the accuracy of their interpretations. They indicate any significant limitations of their interpretations.

7. Assessment by Unqualified Persons

Psychologists do not promote the use of psychological assessment techniques by unqualified persons, except when such use is conducted for training purposes with appropriate supervision.

8. Obsolete Tests and Outdated Test Results

(a) Psychologists do not base their assessment or intervention decisions or recommendations on data or test results that are outdated for the current purpose.

(b) Psychologists do not base such decisions or recommendations on tests and measures that are obsolete and not useful for the current purpose.

(continued)

9. Test Scoring and Interpretation Services
   (a) Psychologists who offer assessment or scoring services to other professionals accurately describe the purpose, norms, validity, reliability, and applications of the procedures and any special qualifications applicable to their use.
   (b) Psychologists select scoring and interpretation services (including automated services) on the basis of evidence of the validity of the program and procedures as well as on other appropriate considerations.
   (c) Psychologists retain responsibility for the appropriate application, interpretation, and use of assessment instruments, whether they score and interpret such tests themselves or use automated or other services.
10. Explaining Assessment Results
   Regardless of whether the scoring and interpretation are done by psychologists, by employees or assistants, or by automated or other outside services, psychologists take reasonable steps to ensure that explanations of results are given to the individual or designated representative unless the nature of the relationship precludes provision of an explanation of results (such as in some organizational consulting, preemployment or security screenings, and forensic evaluations), and this fact has been clearly explained to the person being assessed in advance.
11. Maintaining Test Security
   The term *test materials* refers to manuals, instruments, protocols, and test questions or stimuli and does not include test data as defined in Standards on Release of Test Data. Psychologists make reasonable efforts to maintain the integrity and security of test materials and other assessment techniques consistent with law and contractual obligations, and in a manner that permits adherence to this Ethics Code.

Source: APA (2002).

the guidelines developed for test users by the Joint Committee on Testing Practices.

Some of the key points from the guidelines for assessment professionals encourage clinicians to

- know federal and state laws concerning assessment
- obtain informed consent from clients or clients' parents
- protect the confidentiality of assessment information
- use multiple methods of data gathering
- interpret data cautiously and appropriately
- explain assessment findings clearly
- maintain assessment data
- understand the power of recommendations
- recognize your own competencies
- be aware of personal and societal biases

≡Rapid Reference 9.4

Excerpts from the Code of Fair Testing Practices in Education

A. Selecting Appropriate Tests
   1. First define the purpose for testing and the population to be tested. Then select a test for that purpose and that population based on a thorough review of the available information.
   2. Investigate potentially useful sources of information, in addition to test scores, to corroborate the information provided by tests.
   3. Read the materials provided by test developers and avoid using tests for which unclear or incomplete information is provided.
   4. Become familiar with how and when the test was developed and tried out.
   5. Read independent evaluations of a test and of possible alternative measures. Look for evidence required to support the claims of test developers.
   6. Examine specimen sets, disclosed tests or samples of questions, directions, answer sheets, manuals, and score reports before selecting a test.
   7. Ascertain whether the test content and norms group(s) or comparison group(s) are appropriate for the intended test takers.
   8. Select and use only those tests for which the skills needed to administer the test and interpret scores correctly are available.

B. Interpreting Scores
   1. Obtain information about the scale used for reporting scores, the characteristics of any norms or comparison group(s), and the limitations of the scores.
   2. Interpret scores taking into account any major differences between the norms or comparison groups and the actual test takers. Also take into account any differences in test administration practices or familiarity with the specific questions in the test.
   3. Avoid using tests for purposes not specifically recommended by the test developer unless evidence is obtained to support the intended use.
   4. Explain how any passing scores were set and gather evidence to support the appropriateness of the scores.
   5. Obtain evidence to help show that the test is meeting its intended purpose(s).

C. Striving for Fairness
   1. Evaluate the procedures used by test developers to avoid potentially insensitive content or language.
   2. Review the performance of test takers of different races, gender, and ethnic backgrounds when samples of sufficient size are available. Evaluate the extent to which performance differences may have been caused by inappropriate characteristics of the test.
   3. When necessary and feasible, use appropriately modified forms of tests or administration procedures for test takers with handicapping conditions. Interpret standard norms with care in the light of the modifications that were made.

(continued)

D. Informing Test Takers
   1. Provide test takers or their parents/guardians with information about rights test takers may have to obtain copies of tests and completed answer sheets, retake tests, have tests rescored, or cancel scores.
   2. Tell test takers or their parents/guardians how long scores will be kept on file and indicate to whom and under what circumstances test scores will or will not be released.
   3. Describe the procedures that test takers or their parents/guardians may use to register complaints and have problems resolved.

Note. The Code was developed in 1988 by the Joint Committee of Testing Practices, a cooperative effort of several professional organizations that has as its aim the advancement, in the public interest, of the quality of testing practices. The Joint Committee was initiated by the American Educational Research Association (AERA), the APA, and the National Council on Measurement in Education (NCME). In addition to these three groups, the American Association for Counseling and Development/Association for Measurement and Evaluation in Counseling and Development and the American Speech-Language-Hearing Association also now sponsor the Joint Committee.

CONFIDENTIALITY

All professional assessment guidelines stress the importance of protecting the confidentiality of the client. Rapid Reference 9.5 reviews the APA ethical standards on privacy and confidentiality. Some clinicians simply stamp the pages of their assessment reports "confidential" to alert readers that the pages contain private information. However, a "confidential" stamp is rather vague and insufficient to ensure confidentiality, so depending upon the nature of your practice, you may want to include a more specific confidentiality notice. Zuckerman (2000) provides examples of points that may be included in confidentiality notices:

1. The contents of this report are considered a legally protected medical document.
2. The information in this report is to be used for a stated/specific purpose.
3. The report is to be used only by the intended recipient.
4. The report is not to be disclosed to any other party (list any exceptions).
5. The report is to be destroyed after the specified use has been met.

You may place a confidentiality notice on the report's cover page (if you have one) and in the footer of your document. Rapid Reference 9.6 provides examples of confidentiality notices that may be included in an assessment report.

≡Rapid Reference 9.5

APA Ethical Standards On Privacy And Confidentiality

1. Maintaining Confidentiality
   Psychologists have a primary obligation and must take reasonable precautions to protect confidential information obtained through or stored in any medium, recognizing that the extent and limits of confidentiality may be regulated by law or established by institutional rules or professional or scientific relationship.

2. Discussing the Limits of Confidentiality
   (a) Psychologists discuss with persons (including, to the extent feasible, persons who are legally incapable of giving informed consent and their legal representatives) and organizations with whom they establish a scientific or professional relationship (1) the relevant limits of confidentiality and (2) the foreseeable uses of the information generated through their psychological activities.
   (b) Unless it is not feasible or is contraindicated, the discussion of confidentiality occurs at the outset of the relationship and thereafter as new circumstances may warrant.
   (c) Psychologists who offer services, products, or information via electronic transmission inform clients/patients of the risks to privacy and limits of confidentiality.

3. Recording
   Before recording the voices or images of individuals to whom they provide services, psychologists obtain permission from all such persons or their legal representatives.

4. Minimizing Intrusions on Privacy
   (a) Psychologists include in written and oral reports and consultations only information germane to the purpose for which the communication is made.
   (b) Psychologists discuss confidential information obtained in their work only for appropriate scientific or professional purposes and only with persons clearly concerned with such matters.

5. Disclosures
   (a) Psychologists may disclose confidential information with the appropriate consent of the organizational client, the individual client/patient, or another legally authorized person on behalf of the client/patient unless prohibited by law.
   (b) Psychologists disclose confidential information without the consent of the individual only as mandated by law, or where permitted by law for a valid purpose such as to (1) provide needed professional services; (2) obtain appropriate professional consultations; (3) protect the client/patient, psychologist, or others from harm; or (4) obtain payment for services from a client/patient, in which instance disclosure is limited to the minimum that is necessary to achieve the purpose.

(continued)

6. Consultations

   When consulting with colleagues, (1) psychologists do not disclose confidential information that reasonably could lead to the identification of a client/patient, research participant, or other person or organization with whom they have a confidential relationship unless they have obtained the prior consent of the person or organization or the disclosure cannot be avoided, and (2) they disclose information only to the extent necessary to achieve the purposes of the consultation.

7. Use of Confidential Information for Didactic or Other Purposes

   Psychologists do not disclose in their writings, lectures, or other public media, confidential, personally identifiable information concerning their clients/patients, students, research participants, organizational clients, or other recipients of their services that they obtained during the course of their work, unless (1) they take reasonable steps to disguise the person or organization, (2) the person or organization has consented in writing, or (3) there is legal authorization for doing so.

Source: APA (2002).

≋ *Rapid Reference 9.6*

Sample Confidentiality Notices

- This is privileged and confidential patient information. Any unauthorized disclosure is a federal offense. Not to be duplicated.

- This is strictly confidential material and is for the information of only the person to whom it is addressed. No responsibility can be accepted if it is made available to any other person, including the subject of this report. Any duplication, transmittal, redisclosure, or retransfer of these records is strictly prohibited.

- This report contains confidential client information. Release only to professionals capable of ethically and professionally interpreting and understanding the information.

- The information contained in this report is private, privileged, and confidential. It cannot be released outside the school system except by the examining psychologist upon receipt of written consent by the parent or guardian. Not to be duplicated or transmitted.

- The contents of this report have been shared with the child's parents or guardian. They may review this report with the evaluator or a specified designee. Copies of this report may be released only by the parents or in accord with the school district's policy.

Source: Adapted from Zuckerman (2000).

🐦 TEST YOURSELF 🐦

1. **To help determine how well a person understands your oral feedback, encourage him or her to ask questions with a statement such as**
   (a) "Let me know if I am speaking too quickly."
   (b) "Feel free to stop me if you have questions or would like clarification."
   (c) "Do you have any questions up to this point?"
   (d) "What is your opinion of the results?"
   (e) any of the above

2. **Comprehensive feedback sessions are useful for adolescents but not as useful for young children. Therefore, you should depend only on the parents to give their child feedback about the assessment.** True or False?

3. **Computer-generated reports are now so sophisticated that they require no modifications or additions from examiners before they are handed to people.** True or False?

4. **According to professional codes of conduct, psychologists can be held responsible if the computer scoring program they use generates inaccurate scores.** True or False?

5. **If people promise that they will not disseminate the information to anyone else, it is acceptable to give them a copy of the MMPI-II questions that they answered.** True or False?

6. **It is unethical to interpret scores without taking into account any major differences between the norms (or comparison groups) and the actual test taker.** True or False?

7. **If Mr. Thompson asks you for the results of his wife's assessment, it is acceptable for you to give him this information without Mrs. Thompson's written consent because they are married.** True or False?

8. **What two things can evaluators do more accurately than computers?**
   (a) derive standard scores from raw scores
   (b) integrate information from background information, behavioral observations, and test data to support or refute a hypothesis
   (c) calculate which scores differ significantly from one another
   (d) make accurate diagnoses

Answers: 1. e; 2. False; 3. False; 4. True; 5. False; 6. True; 7. False; 8. b and d

Ten

ILLUSTRATIVE CASE REPORTS

T his chapter is the culmination of all of the information we have presented on how to write assessment reports. Our goal in this chapter is to bring together and exemplify all facets of writing good reports—from the technical aspects of writing to details of background, behavioral observations, tests results, diagnostic impressions, summary, and recommendations. The reports we include here present a variety of referral questions as well as diverse types of case reports (e.g., psychoeducational, forensic, clinical). In addition, in Chapter 7 of this book Dr. Rita McCleary presented the case of Elizabeth R that detailed a thorough personality assessment.

Each of these case reports exemplifies the cross-validating of hypotheses with behavioral observations, background information, and test data. The formats of the reports in this chapter vary, illustrating the varied approaches that clinicians take in report writing. Like all cases discussed in this book, the identifying client information has been altered to protect the confidentiality of clients.

ILLUSTRATIVE CASE REPORT 1: COGNITIVE AND EDUCATIONAL EVALUATION

Student: Martha Downing
Age: 11 years, 10 months
Grade: 5.7
School: Green Acres Country Day
Evaluator: Nancy Mather, PhD

Reason for Referral

Ms. Suzanne Dobson, a certified special education teacher, referred Martha for an evaluation. Ms. Dobson currently tutors Martha after school on a daily basis. She wished to obtain a better understanding of Martha's educational needs, any factors that were interfering with educational development, and her present performance levels in academic subjects. Questions were also raised about the need for Martha to attend a special school or a special program to address her unique learning needs. Ms. Dobson was also interested in programs and instructional techniques that would be the most effective for helping Martha to improve her basic skills.

Background Information

Martha is an 11-year-old girl who is currently being tutored daily by Ms. Suzanne Dobson, a certified teacher with a master's degree in learning disabilities. Instruction occurs each afternoon from 3:30 to 5:30 P.M. in Ms. Dobson's home. The primary purpose of the tutoring is to help Martha complete her nightly homework.

Martha was adopted as a baby, and all developmental milestones were reported by her mother as being within normal limits. She currently lives in Scottsdale, Arizona with her mother and an 8-year-old brother, Thomas, who is also adopted. Early history includes ear infections (ages 4 months to 2 years), asthma (ages 2 to 3), and extreme reactions to noise or sudden movement (preschool years).

Martha attended Desert Corner preschool from ages 4 to 5. In kindergarten, she attended Logan Academy, a local charter school. She remained in this educational setting until the end of Grade 4. At that time, a tutor recommended that Martha would benefit from a school that provided "more direction." She transferred to Green Acres Country Day, a private school known for its small class size, individualized attention, dedicated teachers, and accelerated and challenging pace. She repeated Grade 4. On her most recent report cards, Martha's teachers describe her as "polite, respectful, and cooperative." There are no indications of behavioral or social difficulties in the school setting or in the afternoon tutorials. Several teachers also commented upon how hard Martha has been working and noted that her schoolwork shows continued improvement. Her lowest grade was in math (C–). Her math teacher reported that Martha continues to work hard in math but "needs to keep working on mastery of her basic facts."

Prior Evaluations

Martha completed a comprehensive evaluation with Dr. Anne Fletcher three years ago. Martha was administered the Woodcock-Johnson-Revised Tests of Cognitive Ability and Tests of Achievement, the Wechsler Intelligence Scale for Children–Third Edition (WISC-III), the Developmental Test of Visual Motor

Integration (VMI-3), and a Screening Test of Auditory Processing Disorders (SCAN). Overall results indicated intellectual abilities in the Average range (WJ-R Broad Cognitive Ability SS = 98 and WISC-III Verbal SS = 93, Performance SS = 100, and Full Scale SS = 96); perceptual-motor skills in the Average range (VMI-3 SS = 103); and ability to understand information presented auditorially within the Average range (SCAN Composite SS = 107). On cognitive measures, Martha demonstrated significant strengths in reasoning and in her ability to hear speech sounds and significant weaknesses in her speed of processing symbols, as well as in short-term memory, the ability to recall and repeat information within a short period of time. Martha's academic areas, reading, writing, and math, were all below her predicted levels of performance, as well as significantly below grade level. Specific recommendations were made for improving reading, writing, and math performance, including individualized tutoring three times a week.

Last summer, Martha received individualized tutoring in reading through the SCORE program in California. On the California Achievement Test, Reading Program CAT level 13, her Total Reading Score was at the 5th percentile rank with a grade equivalency of 2.4. Her Vocabulary was at the 11th percentile, and her Reading Comprehension was at the 2nd percentile. At the end of last summer's tutoring, Dr. Pamela Reese, reading specialist, conducted an informal diagnostic session with Martha. She concluded that Martha was reading at about a third-grade level for instructional material and a mid-second-grade level for easy material.

Last fall, Dr. D. Owens, a neurologist, saw Martha for a Quantitative Neurological Examination that included blood work, an electroencephalogram, neurophysiological measures, parent rating scales, and academic testing. Results on the Parent Rating Scales and parent interview suggested mild evidence of inattentiveness, rage episodes, aggression, problems in socialization, and mild obsessiveness. Tests of attention showed unequivocal evidence of inattentiveness, and speed was below expectancy on a Rapid Automatized Naming test. In academic skills, minor problems were noted in decoding and fluency with adequate performance in reading comprehension, spelling, and handwriting. Math skills were described as weak. The dismissal diagnoses were as follows:

Inattention unassociated with hyperactivity, 304.0
Math calculation disorder, 315.1
Reading disorder, partially compensated, 315.0
Enuresis, 307.6
Parasomnia, 780.56
Oppositional defiant behavior, 313.82
Anxious obsessive personality, 300.02/300.3

A variety of possible medical therapies were discussed to address inattention, anxiety, low school performance, and depression. Dr. Owens wrote, however, that "None of the symptoms we have seen demand the use of a pharmaceutical agent."

Behavioral Observations

Martha was cooperative throughout all testing sessions, and she generally appeared at ease, comfortable, and attentive. She was willing to attempt all tasks and maintained a positive attitude even as the tasks increased in difficulty. On several occasions, she was briefly distracted by noises in the environment but was quickly redirected to the task by the evaluator. Martha commented that she liked school and her teachers and did not mind spending so much time each day on homework.

Tests Administered

Woodcock-Johnson III: Tests of Cognitive Ability (WJ III COG): #1–9, 11–18

Woodcock-Johnson III: Tests of Achievement (WJ III ACH): #1–11, 13–15, 18. 19

Diagnostic Supplement to the Tests of Cognitive Abilities (#21, 26)

Key-Math-Revised, Normative Update

Test Results

Because Martha has repeated fourth grade, the WJ III Tests of Cognitive Abilities and Tests of Achievement were scored by both grade and age norms. Results were similar for both sets of norms. Because these two batteries are conormed, direct comparisons can be made between Martha's cognitive and achievement scores. These comparisons help determine the presence and significance of any strengths and weaknesses among her abilities. A complete set of obtained scores is appended to this report. On the attached score summaries, Martha's abilities measured by the components of the WJ III are described as standard score (SS) and SS ranges created by 68% confidence bands (SS ± 1 SEM).

SS Range	<70	70–79	80–89	90–110	111–120	121–130	>131
	Very Low	Low	Low Average	Average	High Average	Superior	Very Superior

The percentile rank (PR) indicates where Martha's score would fall within the scores of 100 or 1,000 students of the same school grade and month. For example, a PR of 75 would indicate that her score was higher than 75 out of 100 grade-peers in the norm sample, whereas a percentile rank of 0.1 would indicate her score was higher than only 1 out of 1,000 grade-peers. The grade equivalent (GE) indicates the median raw score of students in that month and year of school. The Relative Proficiency Index (RPI) is a qualitative score indicating Martha's expected level of proficiency on similar tasks if her average grade-peers had 90% success. RPIs above 96/90 suggest that Martha will find the task to be easy, whereas RPIs below 75/90 suggest that she will find that type of task to be difficult. The following discussion of results is based upon the grade norms.

Cognitive Assessment Results

Based on the tests of the WJ III COG, Martha's General Intellectual Ability–Extended score fell in the Average range (SS 96, SS ± 1 SEM 93–98). This finding is consistent with previous testing on the WJ-R and the WISC-III, as are the findings of similar strengths and weaknesses noted in prior evaluations. Overall, a significant difference existed between Martha's Verbal and Thinking Abilities (Average) and her Cognitive Efficiency (Low). An overview of results is provided below.

Auditory and Phonological Processing. Martha demonstrated performance in the Very Superior range in her ability to hear and manipulate language sounds. Her score on both the Phonemic Awareness and Auditory Processing factors exceeds 99.9% of her grade-peers. This means that only 1 out of 1,000 people would obtain a higher score. In fact, Martha obtained a perfect score on the Sound Blending test, indicating very advanced facility to blend together speech sounds, an important ability for reading and spelling. Martha also obtained a score in the Superior range on a test requiring her to fill in missing speech sounds (Incomplete Words) and in the Average range on a test that required her to discriminate words with increasing background noise (Auditory Attention). These findings suggest that Martha will be able to use phonics skills with ease for reading and spelling.

Verbal Ability, Acquired Knowledge, and Oral Language. Martha demonstrated performance commensurate with her grade-peers in Oral Language, consisting of tests of vocabulary knowledge, ability to follow multiple-step directions, identification of the relationship between words, comprehension of spoken information, and retelling narrative information. Her score on the Verbal Ability–Extended cluster exceeded 61% of her grade-peers, as did her score on the WJ III ACH Oral Language cluster. Martha's general knowledge of information acquired through life experiences and school learning was in the Average range for her grade-peers (Knowledge cluster) and exceeded 52% of her grade-peers. These findings indicate that Martha will profit from all verbal instruction and will be able to understand verbal directions and communicate orally on a level commensurate with that of her grade-peers.

Visual-Spatial Thinking and Fluid Reasoning.   Results of the WJ III Visual-Spatial Thinking and Fluid Reasoning clusters were also in the Average range, indicating that Martha can think and reason with visual patterns, such as recalling pictures after a brief interval, perceiving part-whole relationships, and mentally manipulating pieces of a pattern to match a complete design. On the Visual-Spatial Thinking factor, her performance exceeded 53% of her grade-peers. On the Fluid Reasoning cluster, her performance exceeded 28% of her grade-peers. These findings suggest that Martha has adequate abilities to perceive visual patterns and to use reasoning for problem solving.

Memory.   Martha demonstrated mild to moderate weaknesses on several of the WJ III COG measures of memory, including long-term retrieval (the ability to store and retrieve associations) and working memory (the ability to hold information in immediate awareness while performing a mental operation on it). Significant differences existed, however, among the tests. On the Short-Term Memory factor, her performance exceeded 14% of her grade-peers. Her lowest score was on the Number Reversed test, where she was asked to recall a series of digits in reverse order. Her performance exceeded 9% of her grade-peers. On the Long-Term Retrieval factor, her performance exceeded 9% of her grade-peers. On the Working Memory cluster, her performance exceeded 12% of her grade-peers. In contrast, on the Associative Memory cluster, her performance was in the Average range and exceeded 52% of her peers. A significant difference existed, however, between her Low Average score on a miniature learning-to-read test designed to measure her ability to store and retrieve associations in context (Visual-Auditory Learning SS = 83) and her High Average score on a test involving retrieving the names of space creatures (Memory for Names SS = 114). In contrast, on tests that involved more language and meaningful memory, such as the WJ III ACH Understanding Directions and Story Recall tests, her scores were in the Average range. When viewed together, her performance on various memory tests suggests that tasks requiring memory of less meaningful material, such as memorizing multiplication facts, will be more difficult for her than tasks involving language and more meaningful memory.

Cognitive Efficiency, Perceptual Speed, and Rapid Picture Naming.   Martha's lowest scores were on timed measures. Cognitive Efficiency is the facility with which the cognitive system can process information automatically, without conscious thought, thus freeing it up for more complex thinking and reasoning tasks. This cluster involves measures of processing speed and working memory. Perceptual Speed measures the ability to perform simple or frequently practiced tasks quickly. Her test results indicated that her speed in processing simple tasks exceeded only 3% of her grade-peers. Martha's low score on the Cognitive Efficiency cluster was in large part due to her slow perceptual speed. Martha had the most difficulty on a Processing Speed test that involved scanning rows of numbers to find the two that matched (Visual Matching). Her score surpassed only 1% of her grade-peers. In addition, she had difficulty scanning rows of symbols to find the five symbols that matched (Cross Out) and naming simple pictures rapidly (Rapid Picture Naming). On the Rapid Picture Naming test, her score surpassed only 1% of her grade-peers. These findings suggest that Martha will work slowly on tasks that require rapid processing of information.

Academic Assessment Results

Present academic testing indicates that Martha has made considerable progress in both reading and writing. In contrast, she is still struggling with the mastery of basic math concepts and skills.

Reading and Written Language.   Martha's WJ III Broad Reading Score was in the Average range with a score higher than 31% of her grade-peers. In general, her word identification and word attack strategies were adequate, but her speed of recognizing words was slow. Her lowest score was on the Reading Fluency test, where she had to read simple sentences (e.g., A car rides on water) and decide whether the answer is true or false. Martha scored in the Low Average range on this test. Her score exceeded only 10% of her grade-peers. Although the accuracy of Martha's reading has improved greatly, her reading rate is still slow.

Martha obtained scores within the Average range on all writing tests with a Broad Written Language score better than 42% of her grade-peers. She seemed to enjoy writing, and she wrote sentences with ease and confidence. She was able to write short, simple questions quickly and easily (Writing Fluency) and to express her ideas in sentences (Writing Samples). Although her scores were within the Average range, when attempting to write more descriptive sentences she had difficulty organizing her thoughts and monitoring her spelling. She misspelled even simple words, such as writing *cum* for *come, were* for *where,* and *lookes* for *looks.*

Mathematics.   Martha's greatest difficulties are in the acquisition and mastery of basic math skills. Her score on the Math Calculation Skills cluster was better than only 4% of her grade-peers. Presently, she can add and subtract single-digit combinations, knows several multiplication facts, and can perform simple division (e.g., 10/2). She does not, however, have a firm foundation in fundamental math operations.

Martha did not attend to process signs consistently and has not memorized all of the multiplication facts. Because she did not attend to the process signs, she made mistakes on simple addition and subtraction problems (e.g., $3 + 3 = 0$). She was unable to solve simple computations because she does not understand place value or regrouping (e.g., $89 - 18 = 103, 17 - 8 = 20$). Martha does not understand how to multiply a double-digit number by a single-digit number, how to add and subtract fractions, or the steps involved in long division. Martha was unable to find a simple fraction of a number (e.g.,1/3 of 12), add or subtract simple fractions with common denominators (e.g., 1/4 + 2/4). In addition, Martha does not monitor her work to see if the answers make sense. Many of her answers had impossible results (e.g., 140/20 = 170).

Currently, Martha has minimal understanding of concepts regarding money. When shown pictures of various coins, she was unsure of which picture was a nickel and which one was a quarter. She was not able to add together simple combinations of coins. When shown real money, she identified the coins but did not understand their monetary value. She was not sure of how many pennies are in a nickel and could not count various groups of coins. When shown 36 cents, she said it equaled 65 cents. When shown 65 cents, she said it was equal to 11 cents.

Throughout all math tasks, Martha did not seem to have a clear understanding of number concepts and relationships. She could not discern the patterns in number sequences (e.g., 6, 8, _, 12) if the interval between numbers was more than one.

Because of her difficulties in mathematics on the WJ III ACH, Martha was administered the KeyMath–Revised, a diagnostic inventory of essential mathematics. The KeyMath-R has 13 subtests that measure three main areas: Basic Concepts, Operations, and Applications. The purpose of the evaluation was to determine appropriate instructional goals for Martha in mathematics. Martha obtained the following scores (10 is the mean subtest scaled score with a standard deviation of 3).

Subtest	Scaled Score
Operations	
Addition	7
Subtraction	4
Multiplication	5
Division	5
Mental Computation	5
Basic concepts	
Numeration	6
Rational Numbers	9
Geometry	11
Applications	
Measurement	8
Time and Money	7
Estimation	6
Interpreting Data	8
Problem Solving	8

Areas	Standard Score	Percentile Rank	Grade Equivalent
Basic concepts	92	30	4.8
Operations	73	4	2.7
Applications	84	14	3.8
Total test	81	10	3.6

Martha's score on Basic Concepts was significantly higher than her score on Operations. Her greatest difficulties were on tasks involving basic math operations (addition, subtraction, multiplication, and division) and concepts related to money. Many of her responses indicated limited knowledge of mathematical concepts. As examples, when asked the meaning of 3.7, she responded "3 to the 7th power." She could not answer questions such as "How many dimes are in a dollar?" When asked to write the number for one million, she wrote 1,000. Presently, she has minimal knowledge of how to perform all four operations. In contrast to her basic skills, she has grade-appropriate knowledge of concepts related to counting and geometry.

WJ III Discrepancies

On the WJ III, two types of discrepancies can be calculated to show the likelihood of a person obtaining a particular score: intra-ability (strengths and weaknesses among abilities) and ability/achievement (an ability is used to predict achievement). On the intra-ability discrepancies, the predicted score is based on the person's other cognitive and achievement cluster scores. Martha had significant intra-individual strengths in Auditory Processing and Phonemic Awareness. When these abilities are compared to the average of her other cognitive abilities, only 1 out of 1,000 people would obtain a score as high. This superior ability with sounds suggests that Martha has good aptitude for subjects such as phonics, linguistics, music, and foreign language learning. In contrast, when her Perceptual Speed is compared to her other cognitive abilities, only 3 out of 1,000 students with the same predicted score would obtain a score as low. This information, coupled with the slow rapid naming scores, suggests that Martha will have difficulty processing both verbal and visual information quickly. When her General Intellectual Ability–Extended score and her Oral Language–Extended score are compared to academic performance, Martha's Basic Math Calculation Skills are significantly below present predictions.

Summary and Conclusions

Martha is an 11-year-old girl with average general intellectual ability and oral language abilities. Her knowledge of general world information and school-related information are within the Average range for her grade-peers. Her abilities to reason and think with visual patterns are also in the Average range. In comparison to those of her grade-peers, her phonemic awareness skills are in the Very Superior range.

In contrast, Martha has relative weaknesses in Perceptual Speed, Working Memory, and Long-Term Retrieval, all abilities related to the learning of basic math skills and concepts. Her most significant weakness is in Perceptual Speed, a cognitive ability that provides a critical foundation for learning and automatizing procedural and conceptual information. This finding suggests that Martha will need more time for processing and practicing information. The effects of these cognitive weaknesses are evident in Martha's weak performance in basic math skills as well as her slow reading rate. In general, Martha obtained low scores on most tests that require rapid responses or facility with numbers.

When viewed in light of prior evaluations, Martha has made significant progress in all aspects of reading and writing. This is a tribute to the high quality of instruction from teachers and tutors as well as Martha's continued willingness to engage in hard work. In contrast, her basic math skills and understanding of mathematical concepts are still a significant weakness.

Educational Recommendations

General

1. Because Martha works hard and wants to succeed, provide frequent praise and reinforcement commending her for her hard work and effort.
2. Make sure that Martha continues in a supportive academic environment.
3. Encourage Martha to take increasing responsibility for completing her homework.
4. Help Martha to continue to gain confidence in her learning abilities. She is a capable learner and a hard worker, and she will continue to make steady progress.

Placement and Educational Therapy

1. Martha will continue to profit from instruction in a general education classroom as her intellectual abilities, and her levels of performance in reading and writing, are commensurate with those of her peers.
2. Martha will continue to profit from individualized instruction to address and resolve her difficulties in basic math skills, increase her reading rate, and improve her writing and editing skills.

3. Martha works hard, completes assignments, and gets along well with both teachers and peers. Her successful performance indicates that she will not require a more restrictive school setting and should continue to benefit from her present placement or a local public school, if the homework demands become too great.

4. If Martha is enrolled in a public school, it is likely that she would be eligible to receive learning disability services in the area of basic math skills.

Further Assessment

1. Use diagnostic teaching to continually evaluate Martha's mastery of basic math skills and concepts.

2. Before teaching math facts, give Martha a timed test to see what multiplication facts she can complete correctly within 2 minutes, or an oral test using flash cards to see which facts she can answer within 3 seconds. Use the results to develop a program for fact learning. Have Martha chart her progress as she masters new facts.

Accommodations

1. Because of her slowed reading rate and generally slow speed of processing information, Martha will require extended time on standardized tests as well as on some in-class assignments.

2. Because of her slowed reading rate, Martha will need adjustments in the amount of reading expected of her. It would be preferable to assign a certain amount of time for reading rather than a certain number of pages.

Reading Speed

Provide a program specifically designed to improve reading accuracy and fluency, such as Great Leaps Reading (*www.greatleaps.com*). This program increases reading speed and fluency while reinforcing phonics skills. One-minute timings are done that employ three stimuli: phonics, sight phrases, and short stories. Use the program designed for Grades 3–5. Chart performance on graphs so that Martha can see her progress. This activity will take approximately 10 minutes per day.

Writing

1. Martha needs increased practice revising and editing her writing. Encourage her to look for errors and then correct them, using a spelling checker if needed.

2. Help Martha to develop keyboarding skills so that she can write class assignments on a computer.

Mathematics

Accommodations

1. Because Martha has not developed automatic recall of math facts and algorithms, provide her with a calculator to use in all activities focused on mathematical reasoning. This will allow her to concentrate on the reasoning process without diverting attention to the more mechanical aspects of the task.
2. If possible, reduce Martha's homework assignments in mathematics so that she can concentrate upon mastering the basic skills and concepts that are critical to future learning. In lieu of homework, she could turn in daily lessons from her tutorial to document her work and progress. Martha needs to fill in the missing gaps before proceeding with additional skills and concepts.
3. Because she has not memorized her math facts, for computation problems provide Martha with pocket-sized charts with addition and multiplication facts. Teach her how to use the addition chart for subtraction and the multiplication chart for division. Visualizing the location of the answer may help Martha learn to retrieve it. When a fact has become truly automatic, have Martha block it out on the chart.

Resources

1. Have Martha work at least 10–20 minutes daily using the book *Math 4 Today* by Donna Pearson, published by Good Apple, an imprint of McGraw-Hill Children's Publishing Company. In this program, designed for a fourth- and fifth-grade math curriculum, 24 essential math skills and concepts are reviewed. The program is designed with a continuous spiral so that concepts are repeated weekly, and a 10-problem test is provided for the fifth day to ensure mastery of skills and concepts.
2. Provide Martha with additional practice using the book *5-Minute Math Problem of the Day* by Martin Lee and Marcia Miller, published by Scholastic Professional Books. This book provides seven broad categories in line with the National Council of Teachers of Mathematics (NCTM) standards: Whole numbers, decimals, fractions, measurement, geometry, percents, and algebra.
3. Martha would benefit from a program such as Great Leaps Math that will provide daily practice designed to make basic math skills automatic (*www.greatleaps.com*).

Basic Operations

1. Help Martha learn to pay attention to computational signs prior to solving a problem.
2. Martha needs practice reading and writing numbers that are greater than 1,000. Review the meaning of place value up to 1,000,000.
3. Using manipulatives, help Martha develop an understanding of place value. Help her understand the connection between the place of the digits comprising a number and the value of the digits.
4. Martha needs to become automatic with her math facts. Begin a systematic instructional program in which Martha graphs or charts the facts that she has mastered. Provide practice sessions with a few flash cards so that Martha can become automatic with her math facts. Use flash cards that have the answer recorded on the reverse side. Practice only a few facts for several minutes daily. Provide frequent review of the newly mastered facts. Computer software drill and practice games, such as MathBlaster, would also be helpful.
5. Reteach subtraction with two-digit, then three-digit, numbers without and then with regrouping.
6. Teach Martha how to multiply a two-digit number by a one-digit number. Have her use a facts chart until she has fully memorized her multiplication facts.
7. Teach Martha how to round numbers to the nearest 100 and then to the nearest 10.
8. Martha has difficulty performing mental computations. Encourage her to use paper and pencil when solving math problems.
9. Help Martha learn to determine the missing number in a sequence of numbers (e.g., 1, 3, _, 7).
10. Teach Martha how to divide a two-digit, then a three-digit number when regrouping is not required. As skill progresses, teach her how to divide when regrouping is required.

Fractions, Decimals, and Percents

1. Teach Martha the meaning of fractions, decimals, and percents. She does not understand the purpose or meaning of a decimal point in a number or understand how fractions, decimals, and percents are related.
2. Teach Martha how decimals relate to place value (e.g., $.1 = 1/10$).

3. Help Martha depict the meaning of a fraction with pictures (e.g., pie chart).
4. Teach Martha how fractions can be converted into decimals and percents.
5. Teach Martha how to add and subtract fractions with like and then unlike denominators.
6. Teach Martha how to add and subtract fractions and mixed numbers.
7. Teach Martha how to multiply and divide fractions with like and then unlike denominators.
8. Teach Martha how to multiply and divide fractions with mixed numbers.
9. Teach Martha how to perform the four basic operations with numbers that have decimals points.
10. When teaching Martha concepts of fractions and decimals, use tangible objects, such as money or food. For example, demonstrate cutting a pizza in pie-shaped pieces or use an empty egg carton to teach fractions with a denominator of 12.

Money

Martha is going to need a great deal of practice developing concepts and skills involving money. Presently, she does not identify coins consistently and does not know how to add together even small sets of change. Use real money to teach concepts.

1. Teach Martha the value of all coins and bills. Provide practice in counting various combinations of change. Begin with simple combinations (e.g., one nickel and two pennies) and gradually progress to more complex calculations (e.g., two quarters, one dime, a nickel, and four pennies). When she can add change accurately to one dollar, introduce bills, and practice counting and giving change for varied combinations.
2. Provide opportunities for Martha to practice making change. Discuss money in relationship to things that she wishes or needs to purchase. For example, if a soft drink costs .89 and she gave the cashier $1.00, how much change would she receive?
3. To increase the Martha's flexibility in making change, provide her with practice matching equal value of coins. For example, using real money, ask her to show you as many ways as she can think of to give someone

50 cents in change. Explain to her why the combination with the fewest coins is usually returned.

4. Teach Martha how to solve basic math operations (addition, subtraction, multiplication, and division) involving money.

ILLUSTRATIVE CASE REPORT 2: PSYCHOLOGICAL EVALUATION

Client: Edward K.
Age: 36
Examiner: Clark R. Clipson, PhD

Identification and Reason for Assessment

Mr. K is a 36-year-old divorced Caucasian male who has completed the eighth grade and is currently unemployed. He was arrested 9 years ago on one count of violation of Penal Code Section 187, murder. The essence of the offense is that he murdered his elderly homosexual lover by hitting and strangling him.

The patient was initially found incompetent to stand trial and was sent to the state hospital to be restored to competency twice. He was ultimately found guilty but not guilty by reason of insanity and committed to the state hospital two years after his initial arrest. He was granted outpatient status one month ago and is currently in residential placement to facilitate his transition to outpatient status. His maximum date of commitment is life.

Mr. K is the third of four siblings. His parents divorced when he was 10 years old. He lived for 2 years with his mother and then went to live with an elderly man, who, along with two other men, repeatedly molested the patient for the next 4 years. He then returned to live with his father. The patient described his father as physically abusive and stated, "I hate him." He reported that his mother was passive and unable to provide protection for him and his siblings. The family psychiatric history is notable for alcohol dependence (father).

Little is known regarding the patient's early developmental history. To his knowledge, there were no complications with his mother's pregnancy, labor, or delivery. He denied any history of developmental delays but described himself as a "slow learner" who was in special education classes. Behavioral problems included early drug use and running away from home because of his father's abuse. He was molested by a taxi driver at the age of 11. He reported that he dropped out of school following the eighth grade because of his drug use.

After leaving school, Mr. K worked several odd jobs, including being a painter, carpenter, landscaper, and tractor driver. He held this latter position for five years, his longest period of employment. At the age of 25, he married a woman but divorced after 2 years because of his arrest for the current offense. He stated, "We probably would have divorced anyway because we were both using drugs." Despite his involvement with a homosexual lover during this time, the patient describes himself as exclusively heterosexual.

Mr. K suffers from several medical problems, including hypertension, high cholesterol, and obesity. At the age of 21, he underwent surgery for a brain tumor located in the frontal lobe. He also reported a history of head injury from being hit with a baseball bat during a fight. There are no known allergies. At the time of assessment, he was receiving Lipitor and hydrochorthizide for his medical conditions.

The patient has an extensive history of substance abuse beginning at the age of 11, when he began smoking marijuana and drinking alcohol. He began using cocaine at the age of 16 and crank at age 25. In addition, he has tried PCP, inhaling gasoline, and heroin several times each. He reported that he experienced alcohol-related blackouts from an early age.

Mr. K had no psychiatric history prior to his arrest at age 27. At that time, he believed he was Jesus Christ and demonstrated paranoid ideation, depression, and pressured speech. He had made one prior suicide attempt. Psychological assessment while in the state hospital found him to be of low average intelligence with poor memory functioning and difficulty switching cognitive set. His score on the Psychopathy Checklist–Revised was noted to be low, contraindicating an impression of psychopathy. He is currently diagnosed with Bipolar Disorder, most recent episode mixed, Polysubstance Dependence, Cognitive Disorder NOS, Borderline Intelligence, and Personality Disorder NOS with borderline, paranoid, and dependent features. Present medications include Depakote, 750 mg. twice a day, and Zyprexa, 5 mg. at bedtime.

The patient has no known history of arrest as a juvenile. As an adult he was arrested once 12 years ago for hit and run and driving under the influence. No one was killed in this accident, for which he served 90 days.

At the present time, Mr. K resides in a residential treatment program. There he receives individual and group psychotherapy and medication monitoring. He also attends 12-step programs and undergoes random urine toxicology screenings, all of which have been negative to date. He is noted to have some mild difficulty interacting with peers in the program. Social supports are limited to his mother, sister, and brother-in-law. His current goals include "staying in treatment, having a support group through NA [Narcotics Anonymous] and AA [Alcoholics Anonymous], researching my child abuse issues, getting my GED [general equivalency diploma], and get a job, maybe as a painter."

After a review of the patient's records and consultation with his therapist, the following referral questions emerge:

1. Mr. K seems to be stable from a psychiatric perspective. What is the current status of his thought and mood disorder?
2. The patient stated that he would like to complete his GED, but he has a history of learning disabilities, head injury, and brain tumor. What is his current cognitive status, and what difficulties might he have in school?
3. The patient has difficulty getting along with others. What are his social abilities?
4. Mr. K has a long and extensive history of substance abuse. Under what circumstances is he likely to use drugs again?
5. What level of monitoring and supervision is indicated to minimize the likelihood of his again becoming violent? Under what circumstances might he be at increased risk for violence?

Means of Assessment

1. Review of records, including
   - Police department arrest report
   - Neuropsychological evaluation
   - Psychological evaluation
   - Letter regarding outpatient status
   - Face sheet
2. Consultation with therapist
3. Clinical interview, Mental Status Examination, and psychological testing that includes:
   - Wechsler Abbreviated Scale of Intelligence (WASI)
   - Neurobehavioral Cognitive Status Examination (NCSE)
   - Comprehensive Trail Making Test (CTMT)
   - Thematic Apperception Test (TAT)
   - Rorschach
   - Minnesota Multiphasic Personality Inventory, Second Edition (MMPI-2)
4. Violence risk assessment based on the HCR-20.

Committing Offense and Precursors

According to police records, at the age of 27 Mr. K murdered his 70-year-old male lover. He reports that he had known the victim for eight years. He stated that "while we were pretty close, he was verbally abusive to me. He gave me money to support my drug habit in exchange for sexual favors." During the months prior to the offense, the patient stated, "I was getting sicker and sicker. I tried to get help." For several weeks prior to the crime, Mr. K began using methamphetamine intravenously. He became more agitated: "I was pacing, had racing thoughts, thinking about my past history of abuse." At the time of the offense, he was delusional, believing that the victim was the devil and he was Christ. Asked why he thought this, he said, "My mother's name is Mary, my grandfather is named Matthew. I have a brother named Joseph. I thought my grandfather was God." He reported that he felt "a duty" to kill the victim "to free his soul." He believed the victim had raped his mother, his wife, and numerous children. Afterwards, he went to his pastor and confessed. At the time of his arrest, he was noted by police to be calm and passive.

Mental Status Examination

Mr. K is a tall, obese man, who was carelessly groomed but casually and appropriately dressed. He has scars from past surgeries but denies having any tattoos. Posture and gait are unremarkable. He was cooperative and friendly during interview, making good eye contact. Although his level of activity was unremarkable, there was a notable tremor in both hands.

During the administration of the various psychological tests, the patient demonstrated average frustration tolerance but tended to give up easily when faced with tasks he found difficult. He put forth adequate effort and worked at an average pace. He demonstrated good behavioral attention and did not engage in any form of self-talk.

The patient's speech was dysfluent and of normal rate and volume. He spoke in a monotone voice. He did not initiate conversation spontaneously but was responsive to questions. He had no apparent difficulty understanding questions or directions. Associations were logical and goal-directed.

When asked to describe his usual mood during the past month, Mr. K replied, "Getting used to the program here. Pretty good, I'm learning new things." He denied any recent symptoms of depression but admitted occasional bouts of anxiety, especially when asked to speak in front of a group. He appeared anxious with constricted affect during interview.

Thought content was negative for hallucinations, delusions, somatic complaints, obsessions, compulsions, phobias, and suicidal or homicidal ideation. He reported one prior suicide attempt from overdose, 2 years before his arrest: "I was fed up with the feelings I had. I was depressed." He stated that he is currently trying to lose weight.

Neuropsychological Screening

Mr. K scored in the Borderline range of intellectual ability on the Wechsler Abbreviated Scale of Intelligence (WASI) with a Full Scale IQ score of 75. This score places him at the 5th percentile relative to the standardization sample for his age group on this instrument. The 15-point difference between his mildly impaired score of 80 (9th percentile) on a measure of expressive vocabulary and his severely impaired score of 65 (1st percentile) on a measure of fluid reasoning is significant.

On the Neurobehavioral Cognitive Status Examination (NCSE), a global measure of neuropsychological functioning, the patient scored within the average range in several areas, including verbal and visual-spatial processing, verbal abstract thinking, and judgment. He demonstrated mild impairment on a measure of short-term memory while demonstrating severe impairment on measures of long-term memory and mental calculations. Examination of his responses to the memory task is suggestive of encoding difficulties.

The Trail Making Test (TMT) is a measure of visual attention, visual scanning, and speed of information processing that is sensitive to many types of cerebral dysfunction. Mr. K demonstrated mild impairment on Part A (48"), scoring at the 10th percentile using norms corrected for age, gender, and level of education. He also demonstrated mild impairment on the more difficult Part B (150"), placing him at the 7th percentile. This portion of the TMT also involves working memory and sequential processing.

Overall, his test results indicate that Mr. K is of limited intelligence and has problems with all aspects of attention and memory functioning. In addition, he is likely to demonstrate difficulties with fluid reasoning or executive functioning in situations where he must problem-solve, organize and plan his behavior, initiate or inhibit appropriate actions, use inductive or deductive reasoning, and so on.

Personality Functioning

Mr. K approached this portion of his evaluation in an open, self-disclosing manner. That is, he readily disclosed psychiatric symptoms and personal problems without minimizing or exaggerating his complaints. What follows is considered a valid and accurate assessment of his current level of functioning.

At the time of the assessment, the patient demonstrated symptoms of depression with low energy and a lack of general motivation. He is pessimistic and hopeless about his future, and he tends to be socially isolated. He has few interests and is prone to ruminate about his problems. He is overly sensitive to criticism from others and prefers to be alone.

Although Mr. K has a balanced ability to focus on himself and others, he does not have a very clear sense of himself and holds rather naive impressions of other people. He lacks self-awareness and has difficulty with self-examination and the ability to change his behavior. As a result, he has a vague, rather diffuse sense of identity that is based more on distorted fantasies than on realistic self-perceptions. He feels inadequate in relation to others and has low self-esteem. He is frustrated by his lack of accomplishment in life.

The patient is somewhat childlike in the level of his emotional maturity. That is, he tends to experience and express his feelings in overly dramatic and intense ways. His emotions tend to be shallow and superficial and are most likely to be expressed in impulsive episodes of dyscontrol during which he behaves in uncharacteristic ways he later regrets. Generally passive-dependent, he relies on others to take care of him, and he tends to believe he has little control over what happens to him. He harbors unacknowledged feelings of anger and resentment over his history of abuse. Whereas for the most part he will not respond to provocation appropriately most of the time, he will occasionally act out with an exaggerated aggressive response.

Mr. K lacks a consistent, well-defined coping style. He vacillates between responding emotionally and to what he knows he should do, often ineffectively and without a clear sense of purpose or direction. He has few internal resources for coping with stress, so situations that would normally be handled effectively for most people are likely to cause him acute distress and frustration and result in impulsive acting out. He avoids dealing with his feelings, relying on intellectualization as a way of limiting the impact of his emotions. Although much of the time he tends to internalize conflict, blaming himself, at other times he is likely to act out. His abuse of drugs and alcohol most likely served as a means of coping with stress.

Cognitively, the patient tends to think in a simplistic, all-or-nothing manner. His ability to perceive reality as most other people do is limited in all but the most obvious of situations. His thinking is vague, and he tends to disregard the more subtle nuances of social interactions. He has difficulty tolerating the anxiety that often accompanies making important decisions, so he is likely to make decisions quickly without giving much thought to the consequences. His tendency to distort his perceptions is most evident in social situations, as he is prone to misunderstand others' intentions and expectations. His thinking is also quite rigid and inflexible: Once he has formed an opinion, it is difficult to get him to look at things from any other perspective. He tends to perceive the world as threatening and life as unfair. His tendency to distort his perceptions is severe enough that he is very likely to exhibit behaviors that are inappropriate for a given situation and to have difficulty maintaining adequate adjustment for very long without sufficient support.

Interpersonally, Mr. K lacks even basic social skills, so he is often likely to be excluded from social groups because of his ineptitude. Most other people are likely to perceive him as immature, overly emotional, and impulsive. The patient is quite introverted and self-conscious. He feels alienated from others and tends to feel that others misunderstand him. Although he seems to anticipate positive interactions with others in an almost naive manner, he has little ability to establish or maintain a meaningful relationship. He tends to be quite submissive in a group and can be easily manipulated by others.

Treatment Planning Recommendations

1. At the present time, Mr. K appears free from any symptoms of psychosis, but he continues to demonstrate evidence of depression, social alienation, difficulty with anger, and identity problems. His capacity to distinguish fantasy from reality continues to be quite limited outside of the most obvious situations, and his self-control, while generally adequate, is occasionally tenuous.

It is recommended that treatment efforts focus on improving coping skills and developing self-esteem. Interventions need to be concrete and repetitive, as the patient's level of understanding and memory problems will make traditional therapeutic interventions unsuccessful. The therapeutic alliance will be most successful if it is consistent and supportive, with clear expectations and simple, brief cognitive-behavioral interventions. A day treatment setting, if available, might be appropriate for this patient. Mr. K is likely to be quite resistant to changing his opinions, and he will have to be encouraged to try new things in a safe, nurturing environment. Reevaluation of his medication may be indicated to see if another medication would be better at alleviating depressive symptoms.

2. Mr. K demonstrates significant cerebral dysfunction related to several factors, including a possible congenital condition (learning disabilities), head injury, surgical removal of a brain tumor, and his psychiatric condition. These impairments in attention, memory functioning, and executive functioning are likely to severely interfere with his ability to learn or hold a job. While having something to do, like painting houses, would be beneficial on many levels, the patient would need to be part of a work crew that is closely supervised and in which his idiosyncratic behaviors and poor so-

cial skills would be tolerated. He could benefit from further neuropsychological evaluation along with cognitive rehabilitation. It is unlikely that he would be able to pass a GED exam or succeed in classes that attempt to prepare him for this examination.

3. Socially, the patient lacks both basic social skills and the ability to relate to others in a meaningful manner. His deficits in this area are likely to result in repeated rejections by others. He could benefit from social skills training and from learning how his behavior affects others, perhaps through a supportive, highly structured group setting for low-functioning patients. Learning basic communication skills, such as "I" statements, active listening, and the like may be helpful.

4. At the present time, Mr. K most likely will require ongoing support and supervision in order to remain abstinent from drug abuse. His vulnerability to manipulation, his cognitive limitations, and his lack of internal coping resources leave him at significant risk to recidivate. He should continue to be required to attend 12-step meetings and undergo random urine toxicology screens. He is not likely to benefit from reading 12-step material, but the aphorisms common to AA may be quite helpful in providing simple organizing principles with which to guide his decisions and behaviors.

5. The HCR-20 is a structured risk assessment instrument that invites the examiner to systematically reflect on factors identified through the research literature that are related to violent reoffense. Given the patient's history, current situation, and plans for the near future, an appropriate risk management strategy should involve ongoing monitoring of Mr. K at a moderate level. Factors of concern include his substance abuse, the presence of a severe mental disorder, his limited coping skills, and his personality disorder, lack of insight, and impulsivity. Factors mitigating against future violence include the lack of any prior documented violence, absence of psychopathy or antisocial tendencies, the absence of undue stressors, his treatment supports, and his current compliance with therapy efforts. As long as the patient remains under supervision and abstinent from drug use, he is not likely to become assaultive. He should not require a level of supervision outside of that normally provided by the program, but he should receive the highest level of monitoring, structure, and support offered. He would be most likely to become assaultive should he become noncompliant with treatment and exhibit delusional thinking as he did during the current offense.

ILLUSTRATIVE CASE REPORT 3: PSYCHOLOGICAL ASSESSMENT

Name: Xander Young
Age: 5 years, 2 months
Grade: Junior Kindergarten
Examiner: Martha C. Hillyard, PhD

Reason for Referral

Xander Young was tested at the request of his parents due to concerns expressed by his school about behavioral and social issues.

Background Information

Xander lives with his mother, age 37, his father, age 38, and his sister, aged 7. Both parents are physicians.

Xander was born at 36 weeks gestation following an uncomplicated pregnancy and delivery. He was hospitalized at age 9 days with benign nocturnal myoclonus but was otherwise healthy during the newborn period. A CAT scan and EEG were subsequently found to be normal. Xander was breast fed until the age of 4 months with supplemental bottle feeding. Xander has a history of allergies and asthma, for which he takes Zyrtec and Singulair. Otherwise, he has been healthy.

Xander accomplished the early developmental milestones at an average to somewhat accelerated rate, with independent walking at age 12 months. However, he was late in his language development, and the parents had concerns about possible language delays from age 2. Xander began using some single words at this age but continued to have slow language development. His parents consulted a pediatrician who suggested waiting until age 3 to see if further intervention was needed. Xander was also slow in becoming toilet trained. When Xander was 3 1/2 years old (40 months), he had an evaluation with Dr. Chu, a developmental pediatrician, with the following age equivalencies on the Alpern-Boll reported: Physical, 40 months; Self-Help, 28; Social, 34; Academic, 44; Communication, 34. His PPVT III standard score was 69. Dr. Chu stated that Xander had language and fine-motor/self-help delays. There was some initial concern about a possible autism spectrum disorder, but Dr. Chu felt this was ruled out by play-related activities related by the father. Xander reportedly showed great improvements in his speech and language functioning after beginning speech therapy. At ages 3–7 he was also evaluated for Occupational Therapy services. This evaluation found "difficulties with auditory and multisensory processing," "slight delay in fine motor grasping and visual motor skills," and slight delay in "some areas of self-help skills." A sensory diet and OT services were recommended.

Xander has been cared for at home by his parents and a nanny since birth. He has had exposure to Spanish through his nanny and to a Pakistani language through his grandparents, although the main language of the home is English. Xander began preschool at age 2, attending 2 days a week for 3 hours for the first year and then 3 days a week for 4½ hours a day. He later transferred to Granite Elementary for Junior Kindergarten, and he has remained in this school.

Xander's mother's family immigrated from Pakistan. She reported that her in-laws, who followed traditional Pakistani ways, sent two teenage relatives to the United States to live with her parents and their family when she was young. They then all went to Pakistan for a visit. At this time, the grandmother took the children's passports away, forcing them to remain in Pakistan for about two years when Mrs. Young was 6 to 8 years of age. Mrs. Young's mother remained while her father returned here. This situation was very stressful and caused depression in Mrs. Young's mother. Mrs. Young's mother later got treatment from a psychiatrist after she returned to the United States. Mrs. Young has one nephew who was born prematurely and subsequently held back in school. She was aware of no other family history of learning difficulties or school problems. Apart from her mother's depression, Mrs. Young also reported no family history of developmental disabilities, mental illness, counseling, emotional problems, substance abuse, child abuse, sexual abuse, physical abuse, or family violence.

Mr. Young reported that his family members have all been high achievers in school and are generally quite energetic. However, three of eight nephews and nieces have had speech problems. Mr. Young reported being very shy as a young child. He indicated that a teacher sexually abused one of his brothers in fourth grade. This brother later had some problems with alcohol (now controlled) and engaged in some recreational drug use. Another brother also had a DUI incident. Mr. Young's parents reportedly had some marital counseling to help them deal with the stress posed by his grandfather's Alzheimer's disease. Mr. Young reported no other family history of developmental disabilities, mental illness, emotional problems, substance abuse, child abuse, physical abuse, or family violence.

Tests Administered

Wechsler Preschool and Primary Scale of Intelligence–Third Edition (WPPSI-III)

Wechsler Individual Achievement Test, Second Edition (WIAT-II): Word Reading subtest; Math Reasoning subtest; Written Expression subtest

Developmental Test of Visual-Motor Integration, Fourth Edition (VMI-4)

Kaufman Assessment Battery for Children–Second Edition (KABC-II) Hand Movements subtest; Number Recall subtest

Achenbach Child Behavior Checklist for Ages 1 1/2–5 (CBCL-1 1/2–5) completed by mother

Achenbach Teacher Report Form for Ages 1 1/2–5 (TRF)

Conners Parent Rating Scale–Revised:Long (CPRS-R:L) completed by mother

Conners Teacher Rating Scale–Revised:Long (CTRS-R:L)

Childhood Autism Rating Scale (CARS)

Gilliam Autism Rating Scale (GARS)

Play observation

Record review

School observation

School Observation

Xander was observed in his Junior Kindergarten classroom at Granite Elementary School. The class has 15 students and is held in a small cottage-like building with several connected rooms. The children were participating in circle time when I arrived, with Xander and one other boy seated in chairs at the back of the room while the other children sat on the rug just in front of them. Xander saw me when I arrived and waved at me. He then turned his attention back to the teacher, who was presenting a lesson on the calendar. Xander did not sing along with the group as they sang a song but did seem attentive. The teacher then led the class in an activity in which each child in turn made a statement in the form "My favorite special class is _____ because _____." Xander did not follow this at all and needed many prompts to produce a partial answer. Although a few of the other children needed a prompt to produce a complete answer, he was the only one who could not produce at least a partial answer on his own. The teacher then taught a lesson on geometric shapes using bean bags. Xander participated fully in this lesson and did as well as most of the children at both identifying the shapes and following the directions in an accompanying song. During the group activity, Xander seemed attentive, watched what the other children were doing, and laughed appropriately.

The class then broke into small groups and rotated to various activity centers. Xander managed the transitions easily. He worked diligently at the activities. At the first center, Xander persisted very well with a cutting and pasting task, even though he had to work very hard because of his extremely unusual and awkward style of using the scissors: When cutting, he held the scissors upside down and backward, cutting toward himself rather than away from his body. While working, the children conversed, and Xander joined in with the conversation, making appropriate comments. He also watched what the others did and showed a sense of humor. When he finished the cutting task, Xander went on to a letter-sorting task as previously instructed, sorting the letters accurately and persisting and concentrating well. His group then transitioned to a measuring task with the classroom aide. Xander did this as well as the others in his group. The group then went on to play an animal domino game. Again, Xander's participation was similar to the others in his group. The children then went to get snacks and then played with duplo blocks. Again, Xander worked on constructions and did respond when some comments were made to him by other children, although he did not initiate any contact.

The children were then asked to line up for music. Xander followed the instructions and held his partner's hand as they walked to music class. When the other class marched by, Xander waved a greeting at the other children, as did several of his classmates. In music, Xander participated in singing a song with hand gestures. While he only partially sang the song, probably because he does not yet know all the words, Xander followed closely with all the hand gestures.

Behavioral Observations

Xander is a tall, handsome boy with brown hair and eyes. He had a dry, occasional cough which his mother reported was due to the effect of the cold air on his asthma. He greeted me in a friendly way when I introduced myself to him and greeted his mother in the waiting room at the beginning of the first session. After a brief discussion with his mother, I suggested to Xander that he come with me, and he immediately started up the stairs. Mrs. Y then followed us to the testing room, and Xander separated easily from her when she said good-bye at the door. Once we were alone in the office, Xander was immediately compliant and did his best to respond to a brief interview about his home and school situations.

When the first cognitive assessment task was presented, Xander appeared interested in the materials but had a great deal of difficulty focusing on the task at hand, particularly when verbal directions or questions were given. Xander often turned away from me and would sit with a blank look on his face. He usually needed verbal prompts to refocus so that he could attend to successive items. With verbal tasks or instructions that seemed relatively difficult for him, judging by his hand motions and verbal comments, he often seemed to slip into fantasy rather than attending. For example, he pretended that the edges of the test booklet were a stair and made his hand into an animal that was walking up. At one point, he also began repeatedly scraping his chin along the table when faced with tasks that appeared to be beyond his comprehension. He stopped doing this immediately when told to stop. Xander was better focused and able to attend much more easily to the nonverbal tasks but did tend to be mildly impulsive in his response style and did need some prompts to attend appropriately. Xander's difficulties with maintaining an auditory focus as well as some comprehension problems tended to result in a markedly uneven performance on almost all of the verbal tasks in that he would miss some relatively easy items while getting more difficult ones correct. The apparent attention-related difficulties also produced some unevenness in Xander's performance on the visually based tests that required him to choose the correct alternative from several choices, but no unevenness was evident on the visual tasks in which he had to construct something (puzzles or block designs).

Xander tried hard to do well and enjoyed praise for his efforts. He was generally calm in mood and appeared comfortable in the situation. His range of affect was slightly restricted during formal test administration, but he did initiate conversation and communication with me.

After a period of structured testing, Xander was given a play break. During this break, he engaged in well-organized, flexible fantasy play with the toys in the adjacent playroom. His play themes were appropriate for a boy of this age, and he showed a good range of affect during this play. Xander also sometimes asked questions or initiated conversation with me during his play, showing me toys and animals and what he had done with them.

When Xander was asked to return to the small table and chair for administration of further formal tests. Xander came willingly when called and again seemed to make a good effort. However, it was necessary to provide prompts to secure his attention prior to the administration of each item.

At the beginning of the second session, Xander greeted me in a friendly way and easily separated from his mother. He was cooperative with testing, and his behavior was similar to that during the first session except that he seemed a little more relaxed and was more expressive. Xander also attended somewhat more easily during test administration, although he still needed frequent prompts, especially while instructions were being given.

The current results are thought to be reliable and to give a reasonably valid picture of Xander's present functioning. However, because of his young age, the current results cannot be considered to be predictive. Also, his attention-related difficulties may have lowered his scores to some extent.

Test Results and Interpretation

(95% confidence intervals used in reporting test scores where appropriate.) Xander was administered the Wechsler Preschool and Primary Scale of Intelligence–Third Edition (WPPSI-III), an individually administered test of a child's intellectual ability and cognitive strengths and weaknesses. The WPPSI-III comprises 14 subtests measuring verbal abilities and specific nonverbal abilities. On the WPPSI-III, he achieved a Verbal IQ of 81 (10th percentile; true score 76–88) and a Performance IQ of 98 (45th percentile; true score 91–105). His Verbal IQ falls within the Borderline to Low Average range of cognitive functioning while his Performance IQ falls within the Average range. The 17-point difference between his Verbal and Performance IQs is statistically significant and occurs in only about 13% of cases. Because of this discrepancy, his Full Scale IQ of 88 (true score 83–93; 21st percentile) is not a very meaningful representation of his overall abilities and must be interpreted very carefully. All of Xander's IQ scores must be interpreted with caution due to the uneven response pattern described and variability between subtests. The scores of the individual subtests were as follows:

Verbal Subtests	Scaled Score	Percentile Rank	Performance	Scaled Score	Percentile Rank
Information	7	16	Block Design	8	25
Vocabulary	7	16	Matrix Reasoning	12	75
Word Reasoning	6	9	Picture Concepts	9	37
Comprehension	5	5	Object Assembly	13	84
Processing Speed Subtests			**Global Language Subtests**		
Receptive Vocabulary	9	37	Symbol Search	8	25
Picture Naming	11	63	Coding	10	50

Xander shows a relative strength in his visually based reasoning and problem-solving skills. He performed particularly well on a task requiring him to understand the relationships between drawings in a matrix, performing at the 75th percentile compared to others in his age group. This relative strength in visually based reasoning was also evident in Xander's ability to complete puzzles (during which he concentrated better than on most tasks and performed at the 84th percentile). However, Xander performed at an Average level (37th percentile) on a picture similarities test, a task that can be verbally mediated and therefore may be affected by language difficulties.

In contrast to his relative strength in visual reasoning and problem solving, Xander has relative difficulties with integration. For example, on a nonverbal task requiring him to copy designs with blocks, he performed at the 26th percentile. When working on this task, Xander tended to have trouble integrating when attempting slightly complex designs. Mild difficulties with integration were also evident on the Developmental Test of Visual Motor Integration (VMI-4), a paper-and-pencil figure copying test, as was some possible slight immaturity with pencil control. Xander's observed use of scissors was also quite suggestive of possible fine-motor control and visual-motor issues. On the VMI-4, Xander earned a standard score of 82 (12th percentile), for an age equivalent of 4 years, 2 months.

On visual-motor tasks requiring speed but not complex visual-motor integration for success, Xander is able to perform in the Average range. For example, on the WPPSI-III Processing Speed Index, Xander achieved a standard score of 97 (42nd percentile; true score 89–106). This score indicates that Xander can visually scan and process information at an average rate when fine-motor demands are low.

Xander continues to have relative difficulty in the area of language development, although his performance is uneven in this area as well. Xander does perform at age level when naming and identifying pictures, which indicates that he knows as many words as most children his age. His WPPSI-III Global Language standard score of 100 (50th percentile; true score 92–108) reflects these basic vocabulary skills. On the other hand, Xander's verbal conceptual and verbal reasoning abilities and level of general information continue to be Below Average for his age and center at a 4- to 4 1/3–year level. He shows his most serious delays in the area of language comprehension: Xander often does not understand questions and lengthy verbal explanations. These issues can make it difficult for him to follow discussions and verbally presented lessons in school and lead him to make statements which seem irrelevant and off topic.

In spite of his difficulties, Xander does show good basic verbal and nonverbal sequential memory abilities. He was able to remember and imitate a series of hand movements and to remember and repeat a series of numbers as well as the average child his age. These abilities were demonstrated on both the KABC-II Hand Movement test and the KABC-II Number Recall test (on which he scored at the 50th percentile, Average level).

Xander was screened for his level of early academic achievement using several subtests of the Wechsler Individual Achievement Test–Second Edition (WIAT-II). He has clearly benefited from the program at school to learn many specific basic facts and skills. On the Word Reading subtest, which at this level requires the child to identify letters, sound-letter associations, and sound similarities, Xander achieved a standard score of 115 ± 4 (84th percentile). This score is equivalent to a 5:8 age level and a K:5 grade level. Xander is able to identify all lowercase letters of the alphabet, with a couple of rotation errors. He is aware of the sounds made by single letters and is beginning to differentiate some letter combination sounds. Probably because his comprehension difficulties interfered with his understanding of the directions, Xander had trouble when asked to identify words that begin or end with the same sound, performing inconsistently. He is able to blend some words when they are pronounced as separate sounds (e.g., identifying that "/k/ /at/" can be blended to "cat"), but he does not yet do this consistently. He is also able to write the alphabet and performed at a 5:8 age level (K:8 grade level) on the WIAT II Written Expression subtest.

Xander is able to count and recognizes geometric shapes and numerals. He can also solve simple problems using graphs and grids, but because of his comprehension difficulties he tends to get confused easily by verbal problems. On the WIAT-II Math Reasoning subtest, he earned a standard score of 99 ± 9 (47th percentile), indicating an age-appropriate overall math performance. This score is equivalent to a 5-year age level and a PK:2 grade level.

Behaviorally, Xander's ability to concentrate during the time he was observed in the classroom was within normal limits. In the testing situation, his attention was variable, with better attention to visual tasks than to verbally presented tasks. Mild impulsivity was evident during testing but not in the familiar routine of the classroom. Xander was not at all hyperactive in either setting. The parents' responses to the behavior questionnaires fell entirely within the normal range on the scales reflecting attention-related difficulties. The teacher's responses to the questionnaires fell in the clinically significant range on the scales reflecting inattention but not on the scales reflecting impulsivity and hyperactivity. Such differences in reports may reflect differences in the demands the various situations make on Xander's attentional and self-regulatory capabilities, differences in the perceptions of the adults involved, or a combination of factors. Weighing all of the evidence as carefully as possible, my impression is that Xander's inattention occurs primarily with auditory tasks, when he does not understand directions or lessons, or when he is faced with tasks that are relatively difficult for him. He also seems to turn to fantasy when overwhelmed and then may seem to be out of contact. Therefore, it may well be that his apparent inattention reflects these problems rather than a basic underlying Attention-Deficit Hyperactivity Disorder.

Socially, Xander is a sweet, well-behaved, even-tempered youngster who tries hard to please. He appears comfortable in the classroom situation and adapted easily to being alone with me for testing. No acting-out behaviors were reported in any setting. The behavior ratings provided by the parents fall entirely within average limits in all respects. In contrast, the behavior ratings provided by Xander's teacher do fall in the clinically significant range on scales reflecting social withdrawal. Interestingly, during my observation in the classroom, Xander did respond to and initiate interaction with other children. He also watched the other children for cues and responded to their emotions, laughing appropriately and once telling another boy that he did not like it when the other boy made an aggressive statement to him. When alone with me, Xander engaged in complex, age-appropriate fantasy play. In the classroom setting, Xander was less verbal than many of the other children, but this is thought to reflect his language delays and no deliberate social withdrawal or atypical behavior was observed. His mother was interviewed about specific atypical behaviors at home using the Childhood Autism Rating Scale (CARS) and Gilliam Autism Rating Scale (GARS). She reported some early stranger anxiety and issues relating to communication. For example, Xander will repeat what he has just heard when he does not understand something, and although he can start a conversation, he often has trouble maintaining a conversation. She also reported some difficulty with pronouns and frequent lack of comprehension. No self-stimulatory or repetitive behaviors were reported by his mother. I did observe the chin scraping during the evaluation, which seemed to be a response to boredom and confusion rather than true self-stimulation. As noted, the finger play, which can look like self-stimulation, is actually a form of fantasy play. His mother reported that Xander is able to verbally report his feelings and notices the feelings of others, and she described in detail specific incidents when Xander has shown empathy to other children. On the GARS, Xander registered a score of 62, indicating a very low probability of autism. On the CARS, Xander registered a score of 20.5, which falls in the nonautistic range.

Summary and Diagnostic Impression

Xander is a very nice, well-behaved, hard-working youngster who continues to struggle to overcome language delays and to attend to auditory presentations. His current cognitive pattern is quite uneven, with Above Average performance on certain types of visual reasoning and problem-solving tasks. However, there are some indications of mild problems with integration on some visual-motor tasks, and Xander also seems to have mild immaturity in his fine-motor development. In spite of this, he is able to perform at an average rate on routine visual-motor tasks with low fine-motor demands. Even more unevenness is evident in Xander's language development. While he has a good vocabulary, Xander has serious delays in comprehension, which impede his performance on verbal reasoning and verbal conceptual tasks and which often lead him to make statements that seem to be off topic. Also, he often does not understand verbal directions or explanations. Xander does demonstrate average rote, sequential memory skills, however, and is able to hold simple information in working memory as well as most children this age. Academically, Xander is clearly benefiting from his school experience and is making good progress in acquiring beginning basic prereading and number skills.

Behaviorally, Xander is a sweet, appealing youngster who wants to please. However, his language delays do impair his ability to follow what is going on at a verbal level in social situations and probably hinder his socialization with other children. There are no behavior problems, and my observations and specialized interviews with the parents using standardized questionnaires to assess possible autistic spectrum disorders do not indicate this type of disorder. My feeling is that the apparent withdrawal and communication issues observed by the teacher are therefore probably secondary to Xander's language issues.

There is more evidence that Xander may have trouble with auditory attention in many settings, and mild general impulsivity was noted during his first testing session but not at his second session or in the classroom. Hyperactivity is not reported in any setting. At this point, it is not possible with any certainty to separate the effects of his language issues from any possible additional underlying primary attentional disorder, but my feeling is that the language issues probably account for most of the observed attention-related difficulties. In any case, Xander does seem to benefit from environmental structure and clear expectations.

Recommendations

1. Xander's greatest need is for continued speech and language therapy, with an emphasis on comprehension and pragmatic language.
2. Xander is a visual learner and is likely to progress best with a school curriculum that relies heavily on visual presentations and hands-on learning activities. If oral explanations, demonstrations, or directions are given, Xander should be given an accompanying visual presentation such as a diagram, sequence of explanatory pictures, or demonstration. Whenever possible, concepts should be presented visually as well as orally.
3. Xander can also benefit from working with a trained learning disabilities expert to help him maintain his current good progress in acquiring academic skills. As he moves along and the curriculum becomes more conceptual and comprehension based, Xander will need extra support academically.

4. The speech therapists who have been working with Xander should be consulted about whether he might benefit from an auditory training program. If such a program is recommended, I would suggest that it be scheduled during the summer to avoid overloading Xander.

5. Continued OT consultation would be helpful to work on the fine-motor issues.

6. Xander's parents can be most helpful to him in facilitating social contacts with other children and in providing him with enjoyable recreational experiences. From an emotional point of view, it is usually best if parents do not become additional tutors in a child's life. Ordinary family experiences such as playing games together, cooking, building things, doing art projects, and visiting parks, historical sites, and museums are vital parts of a child's education and can help build a hands-on experiential base, which is vital to improving language comprehension and, later, reading comprehension.

7. A meeting with both parents has been scheduled to discuss the current evaluation and recommendations. At that time, they will be provided with a copy of this report and additional informational handouts.

ILLUSTRATIVE CASE REPORT 4: PSYCHOEDUCATIONAL REPORT

Name: Delia C. Fernandez
Age: 9 years, 11 months
School: Harper Elementary
Evaluator: Michael E. Gerner, PhD, NCSP

Reason for Referral

Mr. and Mrs. Fernandez referred their daughter, Delia, for a private evaluation because they have observed that she shows advanced verbal ability and problem-solving abilities. They requested this independent evaluation to gain a more comprehensive understanding of Delia's learning profile as well as to determine whether she would meet her school district's criteria for inclusion in the Gifted and Talented Program (GATE).

Background Information

Delia began school early, so she is approximately 1 year younger than most children in her grade. In first grade, she was screened for her school's Advanced

Learner Program. Results were not recorded in a report or in written form. Her parents were informed in a phone call that Delia earned a 90th percentile in verbal reasoning, a 75th percentile in mathematical reasoning, and a 77th percentile in spatial/pictorial reasoning. On the basis of these scores, Delia was not admitted into the school's Advanced Learner Program.

On the Stanford Achievement Test, Ninth Edition (SAT9), results from second grade showed that Delia scored beyond 73% of her peers nationally in Total Reading, 73% in Total Mathematics, and 76% in Total Language. In third grade, she scored beyond 73% of her peers nationally in Total Reading, 44% in Total Mathematics, and 44% in Total Language. In fourth grade, she performed beyond 67% of peers nationally in Total Reading, 87% in Total Mathematics, and 75% in Total Language.

William and Theresa Fernandez, Delia's parents, reported that her strengths include a perceptive wit, advanced conceptual understanding, and excellent, almost photographic memory. They noted that she sometimes gets bored in school and prefers the companionship of older children. At home, Delia challenges ideas that do not make sense to her. Her parents reported that Delia was outgoing when she was younger. In the last few years, however, they have observed that she has become quieter and less spontaneous.

Behavioral Observations

Throughout the evaluation, Delia was cooperative and attentive and put forth effort. She communicated her ideas clearly. On difficult problems, she only gave up after a concerted effort. For these reasons, the results appear to present an accurate picture of her current abilities.

Assessments Used

Stanford-Binet Intelligence Scale–Fifth Edition (SB5)
Interview

Interpretation

Understanding the Scores in This Report

In interpreting the scores discussed in this report, the Upper Extreme range are scores above 130, the Well Above Average range are scores from 120 to 129, the Above Average range are scores from 110 to 119, the Average range are scores from 90 to 109, the Below Average range are standard scores from 80 to 89, the Well Below Average range are standard scores from 70 to 79, and the Lower Extreme are scores below 70. The following table depicts the percent of individuals who score within each category as well as the percentile ranks associated with each range.

Standard Score	<70	70–79	80–89	90–109	110–119	120–129	>130
Range	Lower Extreme	Well Below Average	Below Average	Average	Above Average	Well Above Average	Upper Extreme
% people	2	7	16	50	16	7	2
Percentiles	2nd and below	3rd to 8th	9th to 24th	25th to 74th	75th to 90th	91st to 97th	98th and above

Assessment Design/Interpretive Considerations

The Stanford-Binet Intelligence Scale–Fifth Edition (SB5) was selected for this evaluation because speed of performance is not emphasized. It assesses cognitive functioning in five areas, both verbal and nonverbal: Fluid Intelligence, Verbal Intelligence/Knowledge, Nonverbal or Visual-Spatial Intelligence, Quantitative Intelligence, and Working Memory. Three of the five SB5 cognitive domains are typically evaluated by the school district's Gifted and Academically Talented Education (GATE) program (Verbal, Nonverbal/Visual-Spatial, and Quantitative). In addition, Fluid Intelligence can also be considered under the category of Nonverbal Intelligence.

Results

The Full Scale IQ (FSIQ) is derived from the sum of all the tasks in the SB5. It covers both the Verbal and Nonverbal domains of cognitive ability in a balanced design (10 subtests) and taps the five underlying factor index scales of the SB5 (each containing one verbal and nonverbal subtest). The FSIQ provides a global summary of the current general level of intellectual functioning. A global or unitary/single score is most meaningful if most of the factor indexes are within a comparable range. When there is wide divergence among the kinds of intelligence (verbal, nonverbal, fluid, quantitative, etc.) a composite or global score is less useful. In Delia's case, her overall verbal and nonverbal abilities were similar. On the SB5, Delia earned a Verbal Intelligence Score of 116 and a Nonverbal Intelligence Score of 115, resulting in a Full Scale Intelligence Score of 116. This Full Scale Score exceeds 86% of children Delia's age across the United States and falls in the Above Average Range. There is a 90% probability that Delia's true Full Scale IQ falls in the range of scores from 113 to 119.

The Nonverbal Intelligence Score measures the general ability to reason, solve problems, visualize, and recall information presented in pictorial, figural, and symbolic form. In this general cognitive area, Delia scored within the Above Average Range and exceeded 84% of her age-peers.

In contrast, the Verbal Intelligence Score measures general ability to reason, solve problems, visualize, and recall important information presented in words and sentences (printed or spoken). Additionally, it reflects the ability to explain verbal responses clearly, present rationales for response choices, create stories, and explain spatial directions. In this domain, Delia's performance fell in the Above Average Range, surpassing 86% of children her age.

To best understand Delia's learning profile, the individual factors of the SB5 are discussed separately. Delia exceeded 79% of children her age nationally on the Fluid Reasoning Factor, which measures inductive and deductive reasoning in either a verbal or nonverbal (less verbal) format. Inductive reasoning (as in Matrices or Verbal Analogies activities) is the ability to reason from the part to the whole, from the specific to the general, or from the individual instance to the universal principle. Deductive reasoning is the ability to infer a conclusion, implication, or specific example when given general information.

Delia surpassed 77% of her age-peers on the Knowledge Index, a measure of her vocabulary knowledge as well as her ability to correctly locate and explain pictorial absurdities. On the Quantitative Reasoning Factor, she exceeded 70% of her peers. This factor assesses an individual's facility with numbers and numerical problem solving, whether with word problems or with pictured relationships. The types of questions in the SB5 emphasize applied problem solving more than the specific mathematical knowledge that is acquired through school learning.

Delia's score on Visual-Spatial Processing, which measured her ability to see patterns, relationships, spatial orientations, or the gestalt whole among diverse pieces of a visual display, exceeded 91% of children her age across the United States. She was proficient at discerning how geometric shapes could be integrated into patterns as well as verbally using directional terms to find targets. Delia's score on the Working Memory Factor was equally advanced—she again surpassed 91% of her peers. Working memory is a type of memory in which diverse information stored in short-term memory is inspected, sorted, or transformed. The concept of working memory is not simply recalling details but mentally manipulating them or performing some type of operation without losing track of the information. Studies have documented the importance of working memory in school learning, vocational performance, and general problem-solving tasks.

Conclusions

Delia is a highly verbal child who has a keen sense of humor and takes an active social interest in people. Given her advanced verbal intelligence and visual-spatial reasoning, the more repetitive and predictable aspects of school will be the least motivating for Delia. She is, however, a kind and cooperative child who will probably comply rather than overtly indicating that she is bored or uninterested in activities. This evaluation suggests that her general intellectual development is advanced compared to the majority of children her age. When Delia's Above Average verbal intelligence, fluid reasoning, and quantitative analysis and Well Above Average visual-spatial intelligence and working memory are merged into a single intelligence score, her performance surpasses 86% of children her age. Both nonverbal intelligence and verbal intelligence fall in the Above Average range and surpass 84% to 86% of children her age, respectively.

In the classroom, the following suggestions will capitalize on Delia's intellectual strengths. First, because Delia performs in the upper quartile of her age and grade level overall, assignments designed to emphasize the application of ideas and concepts will be more beneficial than ones requiring the listing of details or categorizing of information. Second, a flexible academic program can provide her with unique opportunities for using different modalities and methods to investigate and explore areas of special interest. Third, her overall quantitative reasoning is strong and exceeds 70% of her peers; thus, continued progress in mathematics should be encouraged.

Delia is a bright and capable child who has many above-average abilities. She consistently performs in the Above Average to Well Above Average range in a number of key cognitive domains that are important to school performance. Not only is Delia capable of verbally comprehending and orally explaining higher-order concepts, but she also discerns complex visual relationships and has a good understanding of mathematical relationships. Moreover, she is able to inductively and deductively reason at a level above that of many of her classmates. Her well-developed working memory allows her to consider a number of details at once without becoming overwhelmed or confused.

Although Delia performs in the Above Average to Well Above Average range in a number of intellectual domains, her scores are somewhat below the level to be considered for inclusion in this school district's GATE Program. To be eligible for GATE, a student needs to score better than 97% or 98% of children that age nationally in one or more of the following areas: Verbal (Knowledge) Intelligence, Nonverbal (Visual-Spatial) Intelligence, or Quantitative Intelligence. Depending on the specific intellectual domain, Delia scores better than 79% in fluid reasoning, 86% in verbal intelligence, 91% in visual-spatial reasoning, and 91% in working memory. Nevertheless, these results do suggest well-developed scholastic aptitudes for academic success as well as a need for a challenging and enriched curriculum.

Stanford-Binet Intelligence Scales–Fifth Edition Score Summary
for Delia C. Fernandez

IQ and Factor Index Score Results

	Sum of Scaled Scores	Standard Score	Percentile	90% Confidence Interval Score Range	Percentile
IQ Scales					
Full Scale IQ (FSIQ)	125	116	86	113–119	81–90
Nonverbal IQ (NVIQ)	62	115	84	109–119	73–90
Verbal IQ (VIQ)	63	116	86	110–120	75–91
Factor Indexes					
Fluid Reasoning (FR)	24	112	79	104–118	61–88
Knowledge (KN)	24	111	77	104–116	61–86
Quantitative Reasoning (QR)	23	108	70	101–113	53–81
Visual-Spatial (VS)	27	120	91	112–124	79–95
Working Memory (WM)	27	120	91	111–125	77–95

Subtest Scores

Nonverbal	Scaled Score	Percentile	Verbal	Scaled Score	Percentile
Fluid Reasoning	11	63	Fluid Reasoning	13	84
Knowledge	11	63	Knowledge	13	84
Quantitative Reasoning	13	84	Quantitative Reasoning	10	50
Visual-Spatial	14	91	Visual-Spatial	13	84
Working Memory	13	84	Working Memory	14	91

Note. All scaled scores are normalized raw scores with mean of 10 and a standard deviation of 3.

ILLUSTRATIVE CASE REPORT 5: PSYCHOEDUCATIONAL EVALUATION

Name: Brianna Bailey
Age: 18 years, 9 months
Examiner: Nadeen L. Kaufman, EdD

Referral and Background Information

Dr. Ethan Sandalwood, her family physician, and Ms. Amy Moon, a learning specialist, referred Brianna for an evaluation of her cognitive abilities and emotional development. Dr. Sandalwood requested confirmation of his recent diagnosis of Attention-Deficit/Hyperactivity Disorder (ADHD). Brianna also participated in the referral and would like to know if she is capable of attending college with success. She is concerned because of her history of school difficulties and inability to complete many of her high school classes. Because she dropped courses before the end of the semester, she was required to attend summer school to make up the lost credits so that she could graduate on time.

Last summer she planned to begin full-time, permanent work in a retail business setting, but after starting and then quitting four different jobs, she decided to try to go back for further education. Brianna stated that her work problems stemmed from her inability to concentrate and attend to routines that she found boring. In addition to her troubles in both academic and work settings, Brianna indicated that she struggles to make and maintain friendships. Her inconsistent performances at school and work and her difficulties with relationships led Brianna to ask how she can become a more productive and happy person.

Brianna lives alone in her own apartment and is currently unemployed. She depends on her parents for financial support, which has caused some friction between her mother and father. She reported having problems with time management, following specific rules, and abiding by her work schedules; she also did not feel challenged by the work. She coped with these difficulties by quitting and looking for a new job as soon as she grew indifferent to the current one.

Brianna is the middle of three children from a two-parent family. She was raised in a small town in Iowa along with her two brothers, who are now 21 and 14 years old. She and her family moved to California 6 years ago. She indicated that presently she gets along well with her brothers; however, in the past, her relationship with her older brother was strained. Brianna and her mother (who participated in the intake interview at Brianna's request) stated that since childhood she has been impatient, easily frustrated, demanding, and moody. Brianna said that she tends to want results immediately and sometimes speaks without thinking.

Mrs. Bailey reported that Brianna was adopted at birth and little is known about her biological parents. Brianna reached all of her developmental milestones within a normal time frame. Both bronchitis and sleep disturbances troubled her throughout her childhood, but her medical history is otherwise unremarkable. Two months ago she was evaluated by Dr. Sandalwood, who found no structural evidence of any neurological disorder but suggested that she try Ritalin (15 mg. twice a day) to see if it helped her function better. Both Brianna and her mother stated that there has been a "big change" in Brianna and that she is doing well on Ritalin. Brianna noticed that she is able to remember dates and places and follow directions better. She and her mother also reported that when she is off the medication, she is distractible, has low frustration tolerance, and has difficulty staying focused.

Brianna attended a public school in Pine Tree, Iowa. She said that even as a young child she did not enjoy school and found it boring. She recalled having difficulty paying attention and staying in her seat. Her major problems were listening to and following her teachers' directions, especially in math, science, and French classes. In history, Brianna described the coursework as "blowing right over her." Whereas she stated that she has always been an avid reader, she has trouble recalling subject matter that she has just read. In second grade, the school's psychologist tested Brianna, but neither she nor her mother could recall the results from that assessment. Efforts to obtain those test results from Pine Tree Elementary School were unsuccessful because of the school's policy to destroy test records after the student has reached 18 years of age.

As a child, Brianna swam competitively from first to sixth grade, until the family moved. She still maintains a rigorous set of outdoor activities that she usually engages in alone. Even though she prefers being with only one friend at a time and does not enjoy being in groups, Brianna reported that she frequently experiences conflicts with friends, probably due to her outspoken and direct communication style: "I know I sometimes hurt other people's feelings, but I don't mean to."

Brianna's current plan is to study art in college. She believes that she can excel in interior design and graphics. When she took a 10th-grade course in this area, her difficulty concentrating and low frustration tolerance hindered her progress. During that time, the Baileys hired Ms. Moon to serve as a tutor and learning specialist for Brianna. According to Ms. Moon, Brianna had to make small models of her designs and move them around to be able to visualize the final products. Nevertheless, once she began a project, it often became the center of her attention to the exclusion of anything or anyone else. Brianna said that she becomes so involved with her art projects that she "forgets what is going on" around her: She stays up all night, or forgets to eat.

Appearance and Behavioral Characteristics

Brianna is an attractive Caucasian female, almost 19, with blond hair and a spontaneous and frequent smile. She was well groomed and casually dressed for each testing session, wearing her hair in a ponytail with occasional strands falling around her face and neck. She is of average height and weight, and she appears younger than her stated age. She was tested on three separate occasions; she arrived promptly and applied appropriate effort throughout each session.

For the first two sessions she was on her Ritalin medication. However, for the last testing session, in order to evaluate her performance on the computerized continuous performance test without medication, she did not take her morning dose of Ritalin. Her behavior during this last session was slightly different from the other two sessions. In general, Brianna was very serious about the evaluation, demonstrating motivation and active involvement throughout the process. Her off-Ritalin behavior was characterized by her good sense of humor and free and easy laughter. At one point in the middle of a task, she said with a laugh, "It's so quiet in here, it's driving me crazy!"

To enhance communication, Brianna gestured frequently and expressively with her hands. When she gave answers, she spoke in a strong and clear voice. She popped her gum while she thought through various tasks and laughed if she did not know an answer. For many of the oral vocabulary items, she responded with phrases and similes. When Brianna thought that she did not know an answer, she did not embellish or elaborate on her response, restricting herself to short and vague responses, or simply saying, "I don't know." If the examiner asked if she wanted to guess, she would say "nope!" and remained adamant that she did not know the answer. This behavior was most noticeable on math tests, on which she displayed a defeatist attitude. On the KTEA-II tests of math achievement, she made much use of pencil and paper, writing out numerous computations, even simple ones like "4 + 2." She seemed to write down information to compensate for her attentional difficulties. But even after writing down many numbers and equations, she still occasionally refused to guess if she was unsure. During a test of oral arithmetic that did not allow the use of paper and pencil, her behavior was even more extreme. On more advanced questions, she refused to guess, saying quickly, "I can't do it in my head. I need a piece of paper."

Off her medication, Brianna had more difficulty making eye contact, was fidgety in her seat, and spoke with clipped speech. When she felt frustrated or irritable, she demonstrated these feelings through physical movement. For example, during the tedious but attention-demanding continuous performance test, she kept swinging her legs under the testing table and moving around in her seat. The excess motor activity occurred on medication as well. While giving the word that best solved a verbal riddle, she repeatedly pulled off her hairclip and redid her ponytail. Toward the end of this session (the second of three), Brianna grew more restless and irritable. She refused to answer a question on an achievement test of listening comprehension, sighed frequently, frowned, and cracked her gum loudly.

Brianna was quick to process information and maintained a rapid pace throughout all testing sessions. She performed quickly and efficiently when she used a simultaneous approach (integrating information holistically) to problem solving. This style was evident on two tasks that required her to manipulate visual stimuli. On a task in which she had to put blocks together to match a design, she worked from a specific reference point and built upon it. During a task that required Brianna to move a toy dog across a grid to reach his bone in as few moves as possible, she studied the checkerboard grid carefully—sometimes closing her eyes in deep concentration to visualize the best path—and then moved the toy dog quickly and accurately to the goal.

She sometimes, however, applied this simultaneous approach inefficiently to problem-solving tasks that are better suited to systematic planning than to visualization. For example, when trying to complete a story told with pictures by inserting missing pictures into the sequence, she studied the whole set but did not handle the picture stimuli at all. Then she suddenly picked up two or three pictures at once and inserted them into the sequence. Her simultaneous problem-solving technique was not effective for this storytelling task, and it was not effective with some other tasks that required a slower and more cautious approach. For example, on a test in which she had to select from an array of stimuli the missing design to complete a complex logical sequence, Brianna often scanned the pictures to obtain an overview of the stimuli, and responded too quickly, even impulsively. Her wrong responses tended to be *perceptually* similar to other stimuli in the array, whereas the correct response had to fit in *conceptually* with the sequence. Interestingly, when she was prompted to take her time on this conceptual task, after two blatant impulsive responses, she complied and was able to improve her performance notably.

Overall, Brianna followed each task to completion. Although she appeared anxious at times and did not seem comfortable taking risks, she still persevered and did the required work, asking for clarification and structure when needed.

Tests Administered

Clinical interview with Mrs. Bailey

Telephone interview with principal of Pine Tree Elementary School

Kaufman Assessment Battery for Children–Second Edition (KABC-II)

Wechsler Abbreviated Scale of Intelligence (WASI)

Arithmetic subtest from Wechsler Adult Intelligence Scale–Third Edition (WAIS-III)

Kaufman Test of Educational Achievement Comprehensive Form–Second Edition (KTEA-II), Form A

Intermediate Visual and Auditory Continuous Performance Test (IVA)

Behavior Assessment System for Children (BASC): Parent Rating Scale–Adolescent Form (PRS-A) and Self-Report of Personality–Adolescent Form (SRP-A)

Minnesota Multiphasic Personality Inventory–Second Edition (MMPI-2)

Rorschach Inkblot Test

Thematic Apperception Test (TAT)

Kinetic family drawing

Strong Interest Inventory (SII)

Test Results and Interpretation

Cognitive Assessment

Brianna was administered both a brief measure of intelligence (Wechsler Abbreviated Scale of Intelligence [WASI]) and a comprehensive test of general cognitive abilities (Kaufman Assessment Battery for Children–Second Edition [KABC-II]) to understand her overall level of functioning as well as her profile of intellectual abilities. The four-subtest WASI was the first test administered to her to obtain a quick, reliable measure of her intellectual functioning in case she was unable to maintain her attention and concentration during the more comprehensive KABC-II. In fact, scores on both measures are believed to accurately portray her ability spectrum. She earned a WASI Full Scale IQ of 99 ± 3, which classifies her overall intellectual functioning as Average and ranks her at the 47th percentile relative to other 18-year-olds. She earned a significantly higher Performance IQ of 108 (70th percentile) than Verbal IQ of 89 (23rd percentile) on the WASI, a discrepancy that is unusually large, occurring less than 10% of the time among normal adults. This discrepancy suggests that she has substantially better nonverbal than verbal ability, but that finding is tentative because the WASI is a brief measure of intelligence and because she displayed notable variability on the subtests that constitute both the Verbal and Performance Scales.

The KABC-II permits the examiner to select one of two models of cognitive and processing abilities that best fits the reasons for referral. The Cattell-Horn-Carroll (CHC) model includes tests of acquired knowledge (crystallized ability), whereas the Luria model excludes such measures. Brianna was administered the Luria model of the KABC-II for clinical reasons. Because of Brianna's attentional problems, the examiner selected the shorter 4-scale Luria model instead of the 5-scale CHC model. Crystallized ability is an important aspect of Brianna's ability spectrum, but the WASI Verbal Scale had already adequately assessed it. She earned a KABC-II Mental Processing Index (MPI) of 105, ranking her at the 63rd percentile and classifying her overall mental processing ability in the Average range. The chances are 90% that her true MPI is within the 102 to 108 range.

Her WASI Full Scale IQ of 99 and KABC-II MPI of 105 are consistent with each other, but neither global score meaningfully represents her cognitive abilities because of the high degree of variability in her scores on both instruments. Her profile fluctuations were consistent on both the WASI and KABC-II, revealing the same pattern of cognitive strengths and weaknesses. On the four KABC-II scales, her standard scores ranged from a high of 128 (97th percentile, Above Average) on the Simultaneous/Gv scale to a low of 88 on the Planning/Gf scale (21st percentile, Average range). Both of her high and low standard scores not only deviated significantly from her own mean standard score on the KABC-II but were also unusually large in magnitude, occurring less than 10% of the time in normal individuals.

Brianna's significant area of strength is in her simultaneous, visual processing of information—the ability to synthesize input simultaneously (holistically) such that the separate stimuli are integrated into a group or conceptualized as a whole. This strong ability was demonstrated during her performance on a KABC-II subtest that required her to visualize the quickest path to get Rover, a toy dog, to his bone (99th percentile). She also performed quite well (93rd percentile) on two other visual-spatial tasks: a KABC-II subtest requiring her to count groups of blocks when several of the blocks are hidden from view and a WASI subtest in which she constructed abstract designs with blocks. On the latter task, she was goal-directed and efficient and earned numerous bonus points for solving items quickly. Brianna seemed highly engaged in this subtest, persisting even when constructing the most difficult designs. She acknowledged that she "enjoyed" the task when she was finished. Brianna used her intrinsic interest to keep herself working productively. Overall, she performed well on tasks of nonverbal and visual-spatial reasoning, especially when the tasks provided bonus points for speed.

In contrast to her strong visual processing abilities, Brianna demonstrated significant weaknesses in planning ability (decision making) and fluid reasoning: that is, in her ability to generate hypotheses, revise her plan of action, and evaluate the best hypothesis to solve a given abstract reasoning problem. She had a significant weakness (9th percentile) on the KABC-II Planning/Gf subtest that required her to complete a sequence of pictures to tell a story. Her difficulties in reasoning were also evident on two WASI tasks, one on the Verbal Scale (5th percentile when figuring out how two verbal concepts are alike) and one on the Performance Scale (34th percentile when solving abstract matrices). When her results are viewed together, Brianna performed exceptionally well when solving problems that depend on visualization and simultaneous processing for success, but relatively poorly when solving problems that are facilitated by the verbal mediation that is needed to generate hypotheses and make decisions. These results are entirely consistent with the simultaneous, visual approach to problem solving that she applied on most tasks even when it was not the optimal approach.

Interestingly, Brianna was able to use her visualization skills as an aid to her performance on a WASI measure of word knowledge, on which she performed much better (63rd percentile) than she did on the WASI verbal reasoning subtest (5th percentile). As mentioned earlier, Brianna is quite expressive when she speaks, giving examples and visual images. Although vocabulary is a test of language and acquired knowledge, it is less subject to those influences that would affect her general learning. Also, her avid reading may have improved her vocabulary.

In contrast to the notable disparity between her strong visual processing abilities and her weak reasoning and planning abilities, Brianna's scores on the remaining two KABC-II scales both reflected performance in the Average range that were consistent with her overall level of functioning. She earned a standard score of 103 (58th percentile) on the Learning/Glr scale, which measures her ability to learn, store, and retrieve newly learned information, and a standard score of 98 (45th percentile) on the Sequential/Gsm, which measures her sequential, step-by-step processing of information and her short-term memory.

Assessment of Achievement

On the Kaufman Test of Educational Achievement–Second Edition (KTEA-II) Comprehensive Form, Brianna demonstrated relative strengths in her ability to read words and understand what she reads, earning a Reading Composite of 110, which classifies her at the upper end of the Average range (75th percentile). In contrast, she had relative weaknesses in auditory comprehension and in mathematics, earning a Listening Comprehension standard score of 86 (18th percentile) and a Mathematics Composite of 85 (16th percentile), both classifying her achievement at the lower end of the Average range.

Brianna's score on Listening Comprehension is best understood by comparing it to her standard score of 109 on Reading Comprehension, because both subtests measure understanding of passages using different methods of presentation (oral versus printed). Her 23-point difference in favor of Reading Comprehension is significant and unusually large, indicating that she understands written material much better than orally presented material. Brianna seemed to have subtle difficulties in simultaneously listening to and processing complex linguistic material, and, once again, her test performance was facilitated by visual stimuli. Also, her attentional problems were most noticeable when auditory stimuli were unaccompanied by visual stimuli and when she considered information to be irrelevant or uninteresting. Based on the KTEA-II Error Analysis (presented at the end of this report), Brianna displayed weakness on the Listening Comprehension items that measure *inferential* comprehension, a finding that is entirely consistent with her relatively weak reasoning ability as demonstrated on the KABC-II and WASI.

Brianna had broad-based difficulties in mathematics, including her computational skill, knowledge of concepts, and application of mathematics principles. During the WAIS-III Arithmetic subtest, which presents problems orally and does not permit paper and pencil, she was resistant, displayed a negativistic and defeatist attitude toward math, and complained that she needed paper and pencil to succeed. However, her score on WAIS-III Arithmetic (9th percentile) was roughly comparable to her performance on the KTEA-II Mathematics Computation (13th percentile) and Mathematics Concepts & Applications (19th percentile) subtests, both of which provide paper and pencil. Although she made extensive use of the paper and pencil during the KTEA-II, as noted earlier, the visual stimuli did not substantially enhance her success. Her negative attitude about math and resistance may have contributed to the mistakes she made on math tests during the evaluation, but she also has real difficulties in math. Brianna's specific areas of weakness are presented in the results of the KTEA-II Error Analysis at the end of this report, following the Psychometric Summary.

Overall, Brianna's achievement is commensurate with her ability. She displayed wide variability in both domains, but, when her performance is viewed as a whole, she is achieving at the level that would be expected based on her cognitive abilities. All standard scores on the KABC-II and WASI scales and on the KTEA-II composites and subtests fall within the Average Range (85–115), with two exceptions: Brianna demonstrated High Average functioning on the KABC-II Simultaneous/Gv scale (128) and scored marginally below the Average Range on KTEA-II Math Computation (83).

Assessment of Attention

To objectively assess Brianna's ability to attend and concentrate, she was given the computerized Intermediate Visual and Auditory Continuous Performance Test (IVA), which is designed to help in the identification and diagnosis of ADHD. It is a relatively short task developed to create conditions that require sustained attention to a repetitive, mildly boring task and demand inhibition of responses after a response set has been established. Brianna was required to watch and listen for a target stimulus (the number 1) and to click a mouse whenever she heard or saw this stimulus. Additionally, she was required *not* to click the mouse whenever she saw or heard the nontarget stimulus (the number 2). Brianna was administered this test both on and off Ritalin. On both of these test administrations, her scores were within the acceptable domain. However, some significant differences existed between her performance on and off medication. When on her medication (relative to her performance when off medication), she demonstrated (1) mildly better ability to focus on auditory stimuli, (2) moderately better ability to remain alert and respond as quickly as possible, and (3) moderately better ability *not* to overreact and jump the gun. When she was not on medication, relative to the norms, she had moderately impaired attentional energy and difficulties maintaining the speed of mental processing.

Behavioral Assessment

Adolescent forms of the Self-Report of Personality (SRP-A) and Parent Rating Scale (PRS-A) of the Behavior Assessment System for Children (BASC) were administered to obtain information on the presence of a wide array of potentially problematic behaviors. Mrs. Bailey's responses on the PRS-A indicated mild to moderate concerns about Brianna on both the Hyperactivity scale (76th percentile) and Attention Problems scale (90th percentile). Not surprisingly, impulsivity, overactivity, inattention, and distractibility were all reported. On the SRP-A, Brianna indicated moderate problem levels on the Social Skills scale (94th percentile) and Hyperactivity scale (89th percentile) relative to other females her age. These BASC results help corroborate and validate much of the other data collected that point to an ADHD diagnosis.

Personality Assessment

Several personality measures were administered to provide insight into Brianna's personality structure and overall emotional and behavioral style. She approached these tests in a guarded manner, admitting to moderate stress during the evaluation. Although Brianna seems normally to have appropriate coping skills, when faced with more than the usual stressors in her life she may become disorganized, anxious, and confused. This response can result in difficulty communicating her needs to others and understanding how she is feeling as well. For example, when she is upset, Brianna may have difficulty telling someone else what is wrong because she cannot identify clearly what is wrong. In addition, her emotions do not consistently influence her thinking and problem solving. In one instance, her feelings may strongly influence her thinking, whereas in different circumstances, emotions may play only a minimal role.

Brianna appears to feel somewhat defeated and frustrated with life. These feelings are very common for adults with ADHD. Although she is not clinically depressed, her long-standing difficulties with this disorder have created a pattern of negative expectations about herself and the world. She needs to feel in control of her environment because unpredictable events create anxiety for her. These negative expectations about trying new things and interacting with others may result in her isolating herself, which perpetuates the negative feelings.

Because she seems unsure of herself and her interactions with others, Brianna tends to avoid emotional situations. She works hard to control her feelings and is hesitant to express them openly, fearing that she may "put off" others. This self-doubt leads her to question her self-worth, and it appears to be reinforced by her pattern of beginning projects and then losing motivation to finish. The result is expectation of continued failure and hesitancy to try new things.

Brianna has difficulty hearing criticism about herself, as she often feels that the criticism is unfair and her motives were misunderstood. While she may outwardly appear opinionated and stubborn at times, she still has difficulty asserting independence and may rely heavily on others, such as her parents, to make important decisions for her.

When Brianna is on her medication, she appears to be more in control and less depressed. Off medication, she becomes more oppositional, especially with authority figures, when she experiences frustration and boredom. For example, during the off-medication session, she reacted to several questions that she did not want to answer by saying "I won't do this" and then proceeded to the next problem.

Because Brianna has difficulty defining what she wants in life, she also has difficulty setting goals. While she may have a long-term goal in mind, such as getting a degree in art design, the steps she must take to attain this goal may prove to be frustrating, putting her at risk of losing her motivation. This issue is exemplified in her response to a picture of a boy sitting at a table with a violin. When asked to tell a story about the picture, she stated, "A child who takes violin lessons. Dreading practicing. Probably feels a sense of dread. Rather be out playing but wants to be a violin player too. He has to stay in and practice. That's probably what I would have to do."

A final area explored was vocational interest to see how Brianna's abilities and personality interact with available career opportunities. Brianna was administered the Strong Interest Inventory (SII), a measure of interests (not aptitudes) that provides general prediction of occupations in which she may find satisfaction.

The results of the SII suggest that Brianna may be happiest when she works independently or in a position of authority over others. She is most comfortable in jobs that produce tangible results in an active, but structured, environment. Brianna's response inventory revealed that she is more interested in action than thought and prefers concrete problems to ambiguous, abstract problems. She values aesthetics, independence, and self-expression. The areas she endorsed as most interesting are adventure, art, and photography. The occupations she may enjoy most include artist (both fine arts and commercial arts), photographer, advertising executive, musician, and florist. Her vocational pattern on the SII reflected a willingness to be involved in adventuresome undertakings. In her case, this may be expressed as readiness to make a change, wanderlust, and love of travel. Her goal of becoming an art designer or interior decorator seems to fit her interests very well. Because she does not possess a strong interest in intellectual activities or feel particularly comfortable in an academic environment, she should consider some alternative ways of managing college so that she may reach her educational goals.

Summary and Diagnostic Impression

Brianna is an attractive young woman who was referred for a neuropsychological and personality assessment, vocational information, and confirmation of a diagnosis of ADHD recently made by Dr. Sandalwood, who prescribed 15 mg. of Ritalin twice daily. If the diagnosis was confirmed, recommendations for dealing with this neurologically based disorder were requested.

Brianna would like to gain an understanding of her lack of productivity and difficulties with learning, work, and personal relationships. This evaluation was performed to give her input on how to enhance her learning strategies to become a successful student. Cognitive, achievement, personality, and vocational tests were administered over the course of three afternoons. One of the three sessions was conducted after Brianna omitted her morning dose of Ritalin in order to observe her behaviors clinically. Detailed behavioral observations of the testing, as well as information provided by Brianna and Mrs. Bailey during a clinical interview, provided further insight into Brianna's strengths and weaknesses.

On the KABC-II Brianna earned an MPI of 105, similar to her WASI Full Scale IQ of 99. Although both global scores indicate cognitive functioning in the Average range, neither one meaningfully represents her overall abilities because of substantial variability among her cognitive abilities. On the KABC-II, she had a relative strength in simultaneous and visual processing (97th percentile) and a relative weakness (21st percentile) in planning and fluid reasoning. The results from profile analysis of the WASI were in agreement with the KABC-II results.

Brianna was a hard worker who often possessed strong concentration skills in this brief, controlled setting and persisted in tasks she felt comfortable solving and that were interesting to her. Occasionally her attention and motivation waned, although the results of this evaluation are deemed valid nonetheless. Brianna's inattentiveness, motor activity, and tendency to become off-task were exacerbated when she was off medication. These behaviors were most evident in her performance on the IVA Continuous Performance Test. Her attention and mental processing speed were moderately impaired when she was off her medication.

On the KTEA-II Comprehensive Form, Brianna demonstrated relative strengths in her ability to read (75th percentile) and relative weaknesses in auditory comprehension (18th percentile) and in mathematics (16th percentile). Despite great variability within both the cognitive and achievement domains, she is achieving commensurately with her abilities. Despite her lack of confidence with school and academics, according to these results, she possesses the skills to succeed in college. Her strongest area of cognitive ability, simultaneous and visual processing, is especially pertinent to her chosen area of study, art and graphic design. According to Ms. Moon, Mrs. Bailey, and Brianna herself, however, and as verified by the Strong Interest Inventory, her temperament style is more action oriented, impulsive, physical, and concrete. Brianna is more receptive to practical or applied problems than theoretical or research problems, which probably relates to her relative weakness on tasks that were most dependent on abstract reasoning. She is not highly motivated by or interested in academic pursuits. Consequently, she will need to work on gaining better coping mechanisms to help her reach her educational goals.

Emotionally, Brianna is a capable young woman who has adequate coping skills. She is certainly able to attain the goals she sets for herself, but she has difficulty maintaining motivation, a problem many adults with ADHD experience. As Brianna continues to learn about herself and how this disorder affects her, she will probably feel more in control, with decreasing anxiety and frustration.

Brianna was diagnosed with ADHD by her pediatrician, Dr. Sandalwood, who prescribed Ritalin and is managing her medication. Whereas Brianna's scores on the IVA Continuous Performance Test are not indicative of a person with an attentional deficit, her performance was noted to be significantly better in several areas when Brianna was on medication, compared to when she was not. Additionally, the results of BASC rating scale inventories filled out independently by Brianna and her mother indicated mild to moderate concerns with Brianna's hyperactivity, attention, and social skills. When these findings are taken together, a *DSM-IV* diagnosis of (314.01) Attention-Deficit/Hyperactivity Disorder, Combined Type, is warranted.

Recommendations

The following recommendations have been made to assist Brianna with her attentional, learning, and relationship difficulties:

1. The overall findings from this evaluation indicate that Brianna is able to focus and attend (and therefore perform) mildly to moderately better when she is on her prescribed dose of Ritalin. It is recommended that Brianna continue taking Ritalin as prescribed by her doctor but also see a psychologist who can serve as therapist and monitor her medication dosage needs.

2. Brianna can address several topics with her therapist; perhaps the most complex one is how to gain more independence and take more responsibility for her life decisions, including learning successful methods of communicating and negotiating with her parents.

3. Brianna repeatedly stated how valuable her work with Ms. Moon has been for her. She has been able to develop better study techniques, raise her self-esteem and confidence, and learn new ways to process and retain information. Continuing with Ms. Moon until Brianna has demonstrated success in college will be beneficial.

4. Brianna's relative cognitive strengths in simultaneous and visual processing, coupled with her relative weaknesses in planning and fluid reasoning, need to be understood by Brianna and Ms. Moon to help her succeed in her college coursework. She is already able to apply a simultaneous, integrative, visual approach to problems that require it, such as putting blocks together to match a design and finding the shortest route for a dog to get to a bone on a checkerboard-type grid. Her visualization also seemed to facilitate her verbal skills when she defined words. However, she used a simultaneous strategy for planning and reasoning tasks that would have been better served by verbal mediation and reflective strategies. Brianna will benefit from guidance on how to plan more effectively, including making use of verbal mediation strategies to reason more effectively. Process-based instruction will be helpful for her, not only to improve her planning abilities but also to improve her listening comprehension. She was

able to improve her performance on one reasoning subtest simply by being encouraged to take her time, which suggests that she should be amenable to process-based guidance. Even though the remedial suggestions were intended primarily for elementary and high school students, the suggestions will, nonetheless, be valuable for Brianna when she takes college-level courses that require reasoning abilities and logical thinking. Recommended source: J. A. Naglieri, *Essentials of CAS Assessment* (New York: Wiley, 1999).

5. In addition to receiving support from her learning specialist, Brianna might want to consider an ADHD coach. Trained ADHD coaches have a thorough understanding of the complex dynamics of this disorder. Referrals for adults are available from the National Coaching Network.

6. ADHD is a disorder of performance, not one of skills. Brianna's evaluation revealed that her achievement is commensurate with her ability. The impairment results in not doing what she knows rather than not knowing what to do. Following a positive approach, Brianna's college work can thrive if she takes advantage of all the support available to her, which should provide her with frequent feedback, structure, emphasis on her abilities, and new coping mechanisms to deal with the challenges ahead.

7. Many excellent books are available on behavior modification that have been specifically designed for adults. These books can help Brianna create her own strategies to help master various situations that cause her difficulty. A list will be given to Brianna at the feedback conference.

8. For Brianna to succeed in college, she must take care to select the appropriate learning environment. Whereas she may do well in a small school with limited class size, less structured lectures, and more hands-on experience to complement the required coursework, the most important variable will probably rest on the services for students with ADHD available to her. Brianna's decision-making process will require the specific information on the types of support programs offered at each school contemplated. A brief list of the components of a postsecondary student services program designed to support and assist students with ADHD will be made available to Brianna at the feedback conference.

9. Brianna's unrewarding school experiences, relationship difficulties, and her sense of being different need to be addressed. In approach-

ing these issues, she also needs to understand how ADHD complicates the picture. Educating herself about ADHD is perhaps the single most important treatment for ADHD. She has had this burden, unnamed and not understood, through all of her growing up experience. Now is the time to talk to other teens and adults who have ADHD. A list of contacts for support groups and local and national organizations (like Children and Adults with Attention Deficit Disorder [CHADD]) will be made available to Brianna at the feedback conference. A new government-funded information clearinghouse at *www.help4adhd.org* also provides helpful information.

10. The National Resource Center on ADHD (NRC) also offers extensive information on educational rights and provides tips to help teenagers transition smoothly to college.

Psychometric Summary for Brianna Bailey

Wechsler Abbreviated Scale of Intelligence (WASI)

Scale	IQ	Percentile Rank
Verbal	89	23
Performance	108	70
Full Scale	99	47

Kaufman Assessment Battery for Children–Second Edition (KABC-II): Luria Model

Scale	Index	Percentile Rank
Learning/Glr	103	58
Sequential/Gsm	98	45
Simultaneous/Gv	128	97
Planning/Gf	88	21
Mental Processing (Global Scale)	105	61

Note: Each of the KABC-II indexes has a mean of 100 and a standard deviation of 15.

**Kaufman Test of Educational Achievement–Second Edition (KTEA-II):
Comprehensive Form**

Scale	Standard Score	Percentile Rank
Reading composite	**110**	**75**
Letter & Word Recognition	113	81
Reading Comprehension	109	73
(Nonsense Word Decoding)	(110)	(75)
Mathematics composite	**85**	**16**
Mathematics Concepts & Applications	87	19
Mathematics Computation	83	13
Oral language composite	**97**	**42**
Listening Comprehension	86	18
Oral Expression	108	70
Written language composite	**100**	**50**
Written Expression	105	63
Spelling	94	34

KTEA-II Error Analysis

Brianna's responses on several subtests were further examined to identify possible specific strengths and weaknesses. First, her errors on each subtest were totaled according to skill categories. Then the number of errors Brianna made in each skill category was compared to the average number of errors made by the standardization sample students, similar in age, who attempted the same items. As a result, Brianna's performance in each skill category could be rated as strong, average, or weak. The diagnostic information obtained from Brianna's error analysis is summarized in the table.

KTEA-II Area	Skill Category	Definition	Example
Strengths			
Letter/Word Recognition	Prefixes and Word Beginnings	Common prefixes such as in-, un-, pre-; Greek and Latin morphemes used as word beginnings such as micro-, hyper-, penta-	progressive, hemisphere
Letter/Word Recognition	Vowel Digraphs	The first letter in a vowel pair occurring within a syllable corresponds to the first vowel's predicted long vowel sound, while the second vowel is not sounded	reach, oat, say
Nonsense Word Decoding	Final-e Conditional Rule	The vowel of the final-e pattern corresponds to the predicted long vowel sound, while the final e is not sounded	telephone, before, lane
Reading Comprehension	Literal comprehension items	Questions that require a response containing explicitly stated information from a story	Who is the story about? What is the animal doing? Where are the kids going?
Weaknesses			
Math Concepts & Applications	Fractions and Decimals	Problems involving converting fractions and percents; ordering fractions and percents according to value	Convert .75 into a fraction equivalent. Which of these decimals is least in value? .6, .623, .5984, .74, .02

Category	Subcategory	Description	Example
Math Concepts & Applications	Geometry, Shape, and Space	Problems involving geometric formulas, shapes, or computing the space contained within them	Find the value for the side of a right triangle. Determine the length of the diameter of a circle given the radius.
Math Concepts & Applications	Higher Math Concepts	Concepts involving derivatives, calculus functions, probability, and algebra	Find the value of a variable in an equation. Write an equation to help solve an algebraic problem.
Math Computation	Algebra—Order of Operations	The correct order of operations was violated when solving an equation	The student violated the order of parenthesis/exponents, radicals, multiply/divide, add/subtract.
Math Computation	Algebra—Combining Unlike Terms	Terms are incorrectly combined when solving an equation	$3x + 4 = 7x$ $x^2 + 4x = 4x^2$
Math Computation	Algebra—Performing Different Operations on Each Side of an Equation	Operations performed on either side of an equation are not identical	Student subtracts 4 from one side of an algebraic equation and adds 4 to the other side $(3x + 4 - 4 = 10 + 4)$.
Listening Comprehension	Inferential comprehension	Questions that require a student to use reasoning to respond correctly (e.g., deduce the central thought of a passage, make an inference about the content of the passage, or recognize the tone and mood of the passage).	These questions can require prediction, taking the point of view of the writer or a character, or integration by the reader of implicit information contained in the text.

Appendix

Information About Tests Cited in the Text

Achenbach Child Behavior Checklist (CBCL)
T. Achenbach (1981)
ASEBA (Achenbach System of
    Empirically Based Assessment)
1 South Prospect Street, Room 6436
Burlington, VT 05401-3456
(802) 656-8313 or (802) 656-2608
Fax: (802) 656-2602
http://www.aseba.org

Bayley Scales of Infant Development, Second Edition (BSID-II)
N. Bayley (1993)
The Psychological Corporation
555 Academic Court
San Antonio, TX 58204-2498
(800) 211-8378
Fax: (800) 232-1223
http://www.PsychCorp.com

Beck Anxiety Inventory
A. T. Beck and R. A. Steer (1990)
The Psychological Corporation
555 Academic Court
San Antonio, TX 58204-2498
(800) 211-8378
Fax: (800) 232-1223
http://www.PsychCorp.com

Beck Depression Inventory-II
A. T. Beck, R. A. Steer, and G. K.
    Brown (1996)
The Psychological Corporation
555 Academic Court
San Antonio, TX 58204-2498
(800) 211-8378
Fax: (800) 232-1223
http://www.PsychCorp.com

Beery-Buktenica Developmental Test of Visual-Motor Integration, Fourth Edition (VMI)
K. E. Berry and N. A. Buktenica
    (1997)
Modern Curriculum Press
299 Jefferson Road
Parsippany, NJ 07054
(800) 321-3106
http://www.ehhs.cmich.edu

Behavior Assessment System for Children (BASC)
C. R. Reynolds and R. W. Kamphaus
    (1992)
AGS—American Guidance Service
4201 Woodland Road
Circle Pines, MN 55014-1796
(800) 328-2560
Fax: (800) 471-8457
http://www.agsnet.com

Behavior Assessment System for Children—Student Observation System (BASC SOS)
C. R. Reynolds and R. W. Kamphaus (1992)
AGS—American Guidance Service
4201 Woodland Road
Circle Pines, MN 55014-1796
(800) 328-2560
Fax: (800) 471-8457
http://www.agsnet.com

Behavior Assessment System for Adolescents: Parent Rating Scale
C. R. Reynolds and R. W. Kamphaus (1992)
AGS—American Guidance Service
4201 Woodland Road
Circle Pines, MN 55014-1796
(800) 328-2560
Fax: (800) 471-8457
http://www.agsnet.com

Behavior Assessment System for Adolescents: Teacher Rating
C. R. Reynolds and R. W. Kamphaus (1992)
AGS—American Guidance Service
4201 Woodland Road
Circle Pines, MN 55014-1796
(800) 328-2560
Fax: (800) 471-8457
http://www.agsnet.com

Bell Object Relations and Reality Testing Inventory (BORRTI)
M. D. Bell (1995)
Western Psychological Services
12031 Wilshire Boulevard
Los Angeles, CA 90025-1251
(800) 648-8857
http://www.wpspublish.com

Bender Visual Motor Gestalt Test
L. Bender (1946)
American Orthopsychiatric Association Inc.
19 W. 44th Street
Suite 1616
New York, NY 10036
(212) 564-5930
Fax: (212) 564-6180
http://www.amerortho.org

Childhood Autism Rating Scale (CARS)
E. Schopler, R. J. Reichler, and B. R. Renner (1986)
AGS—American Guidance Service
4201 Woodland Road
Circle Pines, MN 55014-1796
(800) 328-2560
Fax: (800) 471-8457
http://www.agsnet.com

Comprehensive Trail-Making Test (CTMT)
C. R. Reynolds (2003)
PRO-ED
8700 Shoal Creek Blvd.
Austin, TX 78757-6897
(512) 451-3246 or (800) 897-3202
Fax: (800) FXPROED
www.proedinc.com

Conners' Continuous Performance Test II

K. C. Conners (1990)
MHS (Multi-Health Systems)
908 Niagara Falls Blvd.
North Tonawanda, NY 14120-2060
(800) 456-3003
Fax: (888) 540-4484
www.mhs.com

Conners' Parent and Teacher Rating Scales—Revised

K. C. Conners (1990)
Multi-Health Systems Incorporated
908 Niagara Falls Boulevard
North Tonawanda, NY 14120-2060
(800) 456-3003;
Fax: (888) 540-4484
www.mhs.com

Das•Naglieri Cognitive Assessment System (CAS)

J. A. Naglieri and J. P. Das (1997)
Riverside Publishing Company
425 Spring Lake Drive
Itasca, IL 60143-2079
(800) 323-9540
http://www.riverpub.com

Gilliam Autism Rating Scale (GARS)

J. Gilliam (1995)
AGS—American Guidance Service
4201 Woodland Road
Circle Pines, MN 55014-1796
(800) 328-2560
Fax: (800) 471-8457
http://www.agsnet.com

HCR-20: Assessing Risk of Violence (Version 2)

C. D. Webster, K. S. Douglas,
    D. Eaves, and S. Hart (1997)
Psychological Assessment Resources,
    Inc.
16204 N. Florida Ave.
Lutz, FL 33549
(813) 968-3003
http://www.parinc.com

Illinois Test of Psycholinguistic Abilities-3 (ITPA-3)

D. Hammill, N. Mather, and R.
    Roberts (2001)
PRO-ED
8700 Shoal Creek Blvd.
Austin, TX 78757-6897
(512) 451-3246 or (800) 897-3202
Fax: (800) FXPROED
http://www.proedinc.com

Intermediate Visual and Auditory Continuous Performance Test (IVA)

J. A. Sandford and A. Turner (1993)
Psychological Assessment Resources,
    Inc.
16204 N. Florida Ave.,
Lutz, FL 33549
(813) 968-3003
http://www.parinc.com

Kaufman Assessment Battery for Children—Second Edition (KABC-II)
A. S. Kaufman and N. L. Kaufman (2004)
American Guidance Service
4201 Woodland Road
Circle Pines, MN 55014-1796
Ordering phone #: (800) 328-2560
http://www.agsnet.com

Kaufman Test of Educational Achievement—Second Edition (KTEA-II)
A. S. Kaufman and N. L. Kaufman (2004)
American Guidance Service
4201 Woodland Road
Circle Pines, MN 55014-1796
Ordering phone #: (800) 328-2560
http://www.agsnet.com

Key Math Diagnostic Arithmetic Tests—Revised—Normative Update (NU)
J. A. Connolly (1997)
American Guidance Service
4201 Woodland Rd.
Circle Pines, MN 55014-1796
(612) 786-4343 or (800) 328-2560
Fax: (612) 786-9077
http://www.agsnet.com

Leiter International Performance Scale, Revised (Leiter-R)
G. Roid and L. J. Miller (1997)
C. H. Stoelting Co.
620 Wheat Lane
Wood Dale, IL 60191
(630) 860-9700
Fax: (630) 860-9775
http://www.ehhs.cmich.edu

Millon Clinical Multiaxial Inventory-III (MCMI-III)
T. Millon, C. Millon, and R. Davis (1994)
Pearson Assessments
P.O. Box 1416
Minneapolis, MN 55440
(800) 627-7271, ext. 3225
http://www.pearsonassessments.com

Minnesota Multiphasic Personality Inventory-2™ (MMPI-2)
S. R. Hathaway and J. C. McKinley (1989)
Pearson Assessments
P.O. Box 1416
Minneapolis, MN 55440
(800) 627-7271, ext. 3225
http://www.pearsonassessments.com

Neurobehavioral Cognitive Status Examination: Cognistat
R. J. Kiernan, J. Mueller, and
    J. W. Langston (1995)
Psychological Assessment Resources, Inc.
16204 N. Florida Ave.,
Lutz, FL 33549
(813) 968-3003
http://www.parinc.com

Peabody Picture Vocabulary Test, Third Edition (PPVT-III)
L. Dunn and L. Dunn (1987)
American Guidance Service
4201 Woodland Road
Circle Pines, Minnesota 55014-1796
Ordering phone #: (800) 328-2560
http://www.agsnet.com

Rey Complex Figure Test and Recognition Trial (RCFT)
J. E. Meyers and K. R. Meyers (1995)
Psychological Assessment Resources, Inc.
16204 N. Florida Ave.,
Lutz, FL 33549
(813) 968-3003
http://www.parinc.com

Rorshach Test
H. Rorschach (1920)
Hogrefe & Huber Publishers, Inc.
Customer Service Department
30 Amberwood Parkway
Ashland, OH 44805
Fax: (419) 281-6883
Phone (800) 228-3749
http://www.hhpub.com

Sentence Completion Test
F. S. Irvin (1972)
Psychologists and Educators
P.O. Box 513
Chesterfield, MO 63006

Stanford-Binet Intelligence Scales, Fourth Edition (Binet 4)
R. L. Thorndike, E. P. Hagen, and
    J. M. Sattler (1986)
Riverside Publishing Company
425 Spring Lake Drive
Itasca, IL 60143-2079
(800) 323-9540
http://www.riversidepublishing.com

Stanford-Binet Intelligence Scales, Fifth Edition (SB5)
G. Roid (2003)
Riverside Publishing Company
425 Spring Lake Drive
Itasca, IL 60143-2079
(800) 323-9540
http://www.riversidepublishing.com

Strong-Campbell Interest Inventory (SCII)
D. B. Campbell and J. Hansen (1981)
Consulting Psychologists Press
577 College Avenue
Palo Alto, CA 94306
(650) 969-8901
http://www.cpp-db.com

Thematic Apperception Test (TAT)
H. A. Murray and L. Bellak (1973)
The Psychological Corporation
555 Academic Court
San Antonio, TX 58204-2498
(800) 211-8378
Fax: (800) 232-1223
http://www.PsychCorp.com

Vineland Adaptive Behavior Scales: Interview Edition
S. S. Sparrow, D. A. Balla, and D. V. Cicchetti (1984)
American Guidance Service
4201 Woodland Rd.
Circle Pines, MN 55014-1796
(612) 786-4343 or (800) 328-2560
Fax: (612) 786-9077
http://www.agsnet.com

Wechsler Abbreviated Scale of Intelligence™ (WASI)
The Psychological Corporation (1999)
555 Academic Court
San Antonio, TX 58204-2498
(800) 211-8378
Fax: (800) 232-1223
http://www.PsychCorp.com

Wechsler Adult Intelligence Scale-Third Edition™ (WAIS-III)
D. Wechsler (1997)
The Psychological Corporation
555 Academic Court
San Antonio, TX 58204-2498
(800) 211-8378
Fax: (800) 232-1223
http://www.PsychCorp.com

Wechsler Individual Achievement Test—Second Edition (WIAT-II)
The Psychological Corporation (1992)
555 Academic Court
San Antonio, TX 58204-2498
(800) 211-8378
Fax: (800) 232-1223
http://www.PsychCorp.com

Wechsler Intelligence Scale for Children-Third Edition™ (WISC-III)
D. Wechsler (1991)
The Psychological Corporation
555 Academic Court
San Antonio, TX 58204-2498
(800) 211-8378
Fax: (800) 232-1223
http://www.PsychCorp.com

Wechsler Intelligence Scale for Children-Fourth Edition™ (WISC-IV)
D. Wechsler (2003)
The Psychological Corporation
555 Academic Court
San Antonio, TX 58204-2498
(800) 211-8378
Fax: (800) 232-1223
http://www.PsychCorp.com

Wechsler Memory Scale-Third Edition™ (WMS-III)
D. Wechsler (1997)
The Psychological Corporation
555 Academic Court
San Antonio, TX 58204-2498
(800) 211-8378
Fax: (800) 232-1223
http://www.PsychCorp.com

Wechsler Preschool and Primary Scale of Intelligence-Third Edition™ (WPPSI-III)
D. Wechsler (2002)
The Psychological Corporation
555 Academic Court
San Antonio, TX 58204-2498
(800) 211-8378
Fax: (800) 232-1223
http://www.PsychCorp.com

Wide Range Achievement Test-3 (WRAT-3)
G. S. Wilkinson (1993)
Jastak Associates/Wide Range, Inc.
P.O. Box 3410
Wilmington, DE 19804-0250
(800) 221-9728
Fax: (302) 652-1644
http://www.widerange.com

Woodcock-Johnson III™, Tests of Achievement (WJ III ACH)
R. S. Woodcock, K. S. McGrew, N. Mather (2001)
Riverside Publishing Company
425 Spring Lake Drive
Itasca, IL 60143-2079
(800) 323-9540
http://www.riversidepublishing.com

Woodcock-Johnson III™, Tests of Cognitive Abilities (WJ III COG)
R. S. Woodcock, K. S. McGrew, N. Mather (2001)
Riverside Publishing Company
425 Spring Lake Drive
Itasca, IL 60143-2079
(800) 323-9540
http://www.riversidepublishing.com

References

Achenbach, T. M. (1982). Assessment and taxonomy of children's behavior disorders. In B. B. Lahey & A. E. Kazdin (Eds.), *Advances in clinical child psychology* (Vol. 5, pp. 1–38). New York: Plenum.

Achenbach, T. M. (1986). *Child Behavior Checklist—direct observation form* (Rev. ed.). Burlington: University of Vermont.

Ackerman, M. J. (1995). *Clinician's guide to child custody evaluations.* New York: Wiley.

Allen, J. G. (1981). The clinical psychologist as a diagnostic consultant. *Bulletin of the Menninger Clinic, 45*(3), 247–258.

American Psychiatric Association. (1994). *Diagnostic and statistical manual of mental disorders* (4th ed.). Washington, DC: Author.

American Psychiatric Association. (2000). *Diagnostic and statistical manual of mental disorders* (4th ed., text revision). Washington, DC: Author.

American Psychological Association. (1991). *Specialty guidelines for forensic psychologists.* Washington, DC: Author.

American Psychological Association. (1994). *Guidelines for child custody evaluations in divorce proceedings.* Washington, DC: Author.

American Psychological Association. (1999). *Standards for educational and psychological testing.* Washington, DC: Author.

American Psychological Association. (2001). *Publication manual of the American Psychological Association* (5th ed.). Washington, DC: Author.

American Psychological Association. (2002). Ethical principles of psychologists and code of conduct. *American Psychologist, 57*(12), 1060–1073.

Barkley, R. A. (1998). *Attention Deficit Hyperactivity Disorder* (3rd ed.). New York: Guilford Press.

Bates, J. D. (2000). *Writing with precision: How to write so that you cannot possibly be misunderstood.* New York: Penguin Books.

Bird, H. R., Gould, M. S., & Stagheeza, B. (1992). Aggregating data from multiple informants in child psychiatry epidemiological research. *Journal of the American Academy of Child and Adolescent Psychiatry, 31,* 78–85.

Bradley-Johnson, S., & Johnson, C. M. (1998). *A handbook for writing effective psychoeducational reports.* Austin, TX: PRO-ED.

Brooks, R., & Goldstein, S. (2001). *Raising resilient children: Fostering strength, hope, and optimism in your child.* Lincolnwood, IL: Contemporary Books.

Chess, S., & Thomas, A. (1996). *Know your child.* New York: Basic Books.

Connolly, A. J. (1988). *KeyMath–Revised normative update manual: A diagnostic inventory of essential mathematics.* Circle Pines, MN: American Guidance Service.

Cruickshank, W. M. (1977). Least-restrictive placement: Administrative wishful thinking. *Journal of Learning Disabilities, 10,* 193–194.

Cunningham, P. M. (1979). Teaching vocabulary in the content areas. *NASP Bulletin, 613*(424), 112–116.

Exner, J. (1974). *The Rorschach: A comprehensive system, vol. 1* (1st ed.). New York: Wiley.

Gardner, J. (1983). *The art of fiction: Notes on craft for young writers.* New York: Alfred A. Knopf.

Glutting, J. J., & Oakland, T. (1993). *Guide to the assessment of test session behavior for the WISC-III and the WIAT*. San Antonio, TX: Psychological Corporation.

Goldstein, S., & Goldstein, M. (1998). *Understanding and managing Attention-Deficit/Hyperactivity Disorder in children: A guide for practitioners* (2nd ed.). New York: Wiley.

Gregory, R. J. (1999). *Foundations of intellectual assessment: The WAIS-III and other tests in clinical practice*. Needham Heights, MA: Allyn and Bacon.

Joint Committee on Testing Practices. (1988). *Code of fair testing practices in education*. Washington, DC: American Psychological Association.

Kamphaus, R. W. (1993). *Clinical assessment of children's intelligence*. Needham Heights, MA: Allyn and Bacon.

Kamphaus, R. W., & Frick, P. J. (1996). *Clinical assessment of child and adolescent personality and behavior*. Needham Heights, MA: Allyn and Bacon.

Kashani, J. H., Orvaschel, H., Burk, J. P., & Reid, J. C. (1985). Informant variance: The issue of parent-child disagreement. *Journal of the American Academy of Child and Adolescent Psychiatry, 24,* 437–441.

Kaufman, A. S. (1994). *Intelligent testing with the WISC-III*. New York: Wiley.

Kaufman, A. S., Kaufman, N. L., Dougherty, E. H., & Tuttle, K. S. C. (1994). *Kaufman WISC-III Integrated Interpretive System Checklist for behaviors observed during administration of WISC-III subtests*. Odessa, FL: Psychological Assessment Resources.

Kaufman, A. S., & Lichtenberger, E. O. (2002). *Assessing adolescent and adult intelligence* (2nd ed.). Needham Heights, MA: Allyn and Bacon.

Keller, H. R. (1986). Behavioral observation approaches to personality assessment. In H. M. Knoff (Ed.), *The assessment of child and adolescent personality* (pp. 353–390). New York: Guilford Press.

Kirk, S. A., Kirk, W. D., & Minskoff, E. H. (1985). *Phonic remedial reading lessons*. Novato, CA: Academic Therapy.

Loeber, R., Green, S. M., & Lahey, B. B. (1990). Mental health professionals' perception of the utility of children, mothers, and teachers as informants on childhood psychopathology. *Journal of Clinical Child Psychology, 19,* 136–143.

Lovinger, P. W. (2000). *The Penguin dictionary of American English usage and style: A readable reference book, illuminating thousands of traps that snare writers and speakers*. New York: Viking Press.

Markwardt, F. C. (1991). *Peabody Individual Achievement Test–Revised*. Circle Pines, MN: American Guidance Service.

Mastropieri, M. A., Scruggs, T. E., & Shiah, S. (1991). Mathematics instruction for learning disabled students: A review of the research. *Learning Disabilities Research & Practice, 6,* 89–98.

Mather, N., & Jaffe, L. E. (2002). *Woodcock-Johnson III: Reports, recommendations, and strategies*. New York: Wiley.

McCarney, S. B., & Bauer, A. M. (1995). *The learning disability intervention manual*. Columbia, MO: Hawthorne Educational Services.

McCarney, S. B., Wanderlich, K. C., &, Bauer, A. M. (1993). *The pre-referral intervention manual: The most common learning and behavior problems encountered in the educational environment*. Columbia, MO: Hawthorne Educational Services.

McCleary, R. W. (1992). *Conversing with uncertainty: Practicing psychotherapy in a hospital setting*. NJ: The Analytic Press.

McConaughy, S. H. Achenbach, T. M., & Gent, C. L. (1988). Multiaxial empirically based assessment: Parent, teacher, observational, cognitive and personality correlates of child behavior profile types for 6- to 11-year old boys. *Journal of Abnormal Child Psychology, 16,* 485–509.

National Association of School Psychologists (NASP). (2000). *Professional conduct manual: Principles for professional ethics*. Bethesda, MD: Author.

O'Neill, A. M. (1995). *Clinical inference: How to draw meaningful conclusions from psychological tests.* Brandon, VT: Clinical Psychology Publishing.

Ownby, R. L. (1997). *Psychological reports: A guide to report writing in professional psychology* (3rd ed.). New York: Wiley.

Rappaport, D., Gill, M., & Schafer, R. (1945–1946). *Diagnostic psychological testing, 2 vols.* Chicago: Year Book Publishers.

Reed, M. L., & Edelbrock, C. (1983). Reliability and validity of the direct observational form of the Child Behavior Checklist. *Journal of Abnormal Child Psychology, 11,* 521–530.

Reynolds, C. R., & Kamphaus, R. W. (1992). *BASC: Behavioral Assessment System for Children manual.* Circle Pines, MN: American Guidance Service.

Rider, R., & Goldstein, S. (2002). Case report. Unpublished manuscript, Neurology, Learning, and Behavior Center, Salt Lake City, UT.

Sabin, W. A. (2001). *The Gregg reference manual* (9th ed.). New York: Glencoe/McGraw-Hill.

Salend, S. R., & Salend, S. J. (1985). Writing and evaluating educational assessment reports. *Academic Therapy, 20,* 277–288.

Sattler, J. M. (2001). *Assessment of children: Cognitive applications* (4th ed.). San Diego, CA: Author.

Schafer, R. (1954). *Psychoanalytic interpretation in Rorschach testing.* New York: Grune & Stratton.

Schrank, F. A., & Woodcock, R. W. (2002). Report writer for the WJ III [Computer software]. Itasca, IL: Riverside Publishing.

Shapiro, D. (1965). *Neurotic styles.* New York: Basic Books.

Shapiro, E. S. (1987). *Behavioral assessment in school psychology.* Hillsdale, NJ: Lawrence Erlbaum.

Stern, W. (1938). *General psychology from the personalistic standpoint.* New York: Macmillan Company.

Tallent, N. (1993). *Psychological report writing* (4th ed.). Upper Saddle River, NJ: Prentice-Hall.

Thomas, A., Chess, S., & Birch, H. G. (1968). *Temperament and behavior disorders in children.* New York: New York University Press.

Thurlow, M. L., House, A. L., Scott, D. L., & Ysseldyke, J. F. (2000). Students with disabilities in large scale assessments: State participation and accommodation policies. *Journal of Special Education, 34,* 154–163.

Williams, M. A., & Boll, T. J. (2000). Report writing in clinical neuropsychology. In G. Groth-Marnat (Ed.), *Neuropsychological assessment in clinical practice: A guide to test interpretation and integration* (pp. 575–602). New York: Wiley.

Wolber, G. J., & Carne, W. F. (2002). *Writing psychological reports: A guide for clinicians* (2nd ed.). Sarasota, FL: Professional Resource Press.

World Health Organization. (1992). *International statistical classification of diseases and related health problems* (10th rev.). Geneva, Switzerland: Author.

Zuckerman, E. L. (2000). *Clinician's thesaurus, fifth edition: The guidebook for writing psychological reports.* New York: Guilford Press.

Annotated Bibliography

Bates, J. D. (2000). *Writing with precision: How to write so that you cannot possibly be misunderstood.* New York: Penguin Books.

This handbook offers 10 principles and seven axioms that professional writers use to express their thoughts clearly and effectively. The book includes an extensive glossary of American idiomatic expressions, developed to assist users from other backgrounds and cultures. Also included are tips on little-known facts of usage, such as compound words, hyphenation, numeration, and capitalization, and explanations of technical problems encountered in writing and editing, with tips and exercises to help solve them.

Bradley-Johnson, S., & Johnson, C. M. (1998). *A handbook for writing effective psychoeducational reports.* Austin, TX: PRO-ED.

This handbook is devoted to helping practitioners write effective psychoeducational reports and improve report-writing skills. It includes procedures for improving drafts of reports, suggestions for organizing information, a detailed description of a successful format for each section of a report, a discussion of common style problems, and a checklist for evaluating reports. It also provides numerous examples (both positive and negative) that will help clarify report-writing issues.

Ownby, R. L. (1997). *Psychological reports: A guide to report writing in professional psychology* (3rd ed.). New York: Wiley.

This book provides a systematic approach to writing psychological reports for optimal clarity, thoroughness, and impact. The book begins with a theory-based analysis of report-writing problems, which is then used to construct a framework for identifying and correcting them. It includes practice exercises that help readers build report-writing skills and features sample reports representing a wide range of applications.

Tallent, N. (1993). *Psychological report writing* (4th ed.). Upper Saddle River, NJ: Prentice Hall.

This book orients the reader to the concepts and practices of psychological report writing. Topics include the rationale of the psychological report, the distinctions between testing reports and assessment reports, pitfalls in reporting, the content of psychological reports, an examination of the characteristics of the consumers of psychological reports, and a discussion of how to meet their needs.

Wolber, G. J., & Carne, W. F. (2002). *Writing psychological reports: A guide for clinicians* (2nd ed.). Sarasota, FL: Professional Resource Press.

This guide for students, interns, and clinicians describes how to write a general psychological report. A single report format is presented with an explanation of the content for each section of the format. A sample confidential psychological evaluation is included in the appendix. The text does not describe test administration, scoring, or interpretation.

Zuckerman, E. L. (2000). *Clinician's thesaurus, fifth edition: The guidebook for writing psychological reports.* New York: Guilford Press.

This guidebook provides easy access to the language of the mental health professions. It offers practical guidelines for how to shape raw data into a cogent report. Useful words, phrases, and interview questions are provided to help practitioners collect the client information they need and accurately describe the clinical situation.

Index